WITHDRAWN

Carnegie Mellon

The Renegotiation of the Just War Tradition and the Right to War in the Twenty-First Century

The Renegotiation of the Just War Tradition and the Right to War in the Twenty-First Century

Cian O'Driscoll

THE RENEGOTIATION OF THE JUST WAR TRADITION AND THE RIGHT TO WAR IN
THE TWENTY-FIRST CENTURY
Copyright © Cian O'Driscoll, 2008.

First published in 2008 by
PALGRAVE MACMILLAN™
175 Fifth Avenue, New York, N.Y. 10010 and
Houndmills, Basingstoke, Hampshire, England RG21 6XS.
Companies and representatives throughout the world.

PALGRAVE MACMILLAN is the global academic imprint of the Palgrave
Macmillan division of St. Martin's Press, LLC and of Palgrave Macmillan Ltd.
Macmillan® is a registered trademark in the United States, United Kingdom
and other countries. Palgrave is a registered trademark in the European
Union and other countries.

ISBN-13: 978-0-230-60583-1
ISBN-10: 0-230-60583-4

Library of Congress Cataloging-in-Publication Data

O'Driscoll, Cian.
   The renegotiation of the just war tradition and the right to war in
the twenty-first century / Cian O'Driscoll.
      p. cm.
   Includes bibliographical references and index.
   ISBN 0-230-60583-4
   1. Just war doctrine. 2. Bush, George W. (George Walker),
1946—Military leadership. 3. Blair, Tony, 1953—Military leadership.
4. Iraq War, 2003—Moral and ethical aspects—United States. 5. Iraq
War, 2003—Moral and ethical aspects—Great Britain. I. Title.

U21.2.O285 2008
172'.42—dc22   2007039540

A catalogue record of the book is available from the British Library.

Design by Scribe Inc.

First edition: April 2008

10 9 8 7 6 5 4 3 2 1

Printed in the United States of America.

For Sheila

Contents

Preface

The invasion of Iraq, and the manner in which it was justified by President Bush and Prime Minister Blair, its main backers, has aroused a great degree of controversy within the community of scholars interested in the just war tradition. Bush and Blair proffered three main justifications for the invasion. They variously presented the use of force against Iraq as an anticipatory war designed to forestall any potential threat that Iraq might pose to international peace and security, a humanitarian war to liberate the Iraqi people from Saddam Hussein's cruel misrule, and a punitive war to ensure that Iraq's Ba'athist regime was held to account for its violation of international law. These justifications were also occasionally supplemented by Manichean references to the cosmic struggle between good and evil. Intriguingly, these justifications were phrased in the terms of the just war tradition, being presented as valid *just causes* for war. This book examines exactly how Bush and Blair's arguments correspond to the just war tradition, paying special attention to commonalities they share with some of the more seminal articulations of the right to war, as well as the deviations that differentiate them. It contends that these justifications, and the debate they provoked, appear to mark both a resurgence of classical tropes within the *jus ad bellum* and a shift away from the legalist paradigm, the dominant just war discourse since the conclusion of the First World War. In doing so, it draws our attention to the stories of change, continuity, and contestation that animate the historical development of the tradition, and examines what they might tell us about the modalities of the tradition, and the direction in which it is moving today.

Acknowledgments

This book started life as my PhD thesis, and so I have acquired numerous debts of gratitude (as well as numerous financial debts) over the course of writing it. In particular, I owe a very big thank you to my doctoral supervisors at Aberystwyth. Toni Erskine and Ian Clark were a wonderful supervision team, the best that anyone could hope for. They were unstintingly generous with their time and encouraging in their words, and I am very grateful. Both Toni and Ian contributed to making my time in Wales a very positive one. It was both a pleasure and a privilege to work with them. I hope I will have more opportunities to do so in the future.

Mention should also be made of Richard Wynn Jones and Will Bain, who stepped in when Toni and Ian were on sabbatical. Both Richard and Will were a huge help during these times. Other members of the Department of International Politics at Aberystwyth were also very generous toward me: Alastair Finlan, Hidemi Suganami, Nick Wheeler, and Mike Williams. I am especially thankful to Mike for helping me out in the summer of 2006 as I prepared to meet the job market. Beyond Aberystwyth, Alex Bellamy and Tony Lang have both read my work and offered their insights. Alex in particular has been a real source of inspiration and his interest in my work was a great boon at a time when I was beginning to tire of it myself. My thanks go to him. James Turner Johnson has also been extremely kind and helpful to me. I have long admired his work, and his engagement with my research has been a real thrill. Serena Sharma (1979) has read the entire draft of this manuscript and her thoughtful criticism has forced me to sharpen my argument at numerous points. She has helped me to think through many of the issues I try to tackle in this book, and I have learned a lot from her. I really appreciate her input, but more so her friendship over the past year, and am looking forward to more discussions about the just war tradition in the years to come. Chris Brown and Howard Williams have also offered very valuable feedback on an earlier draft of this work.

Within the "Interpol" graduate community at Aberystwyth, there are many people to thank: Alex Behnisch, Sarah Bennett, Patrick Carlin, Phil

Cunliffe, Darren Brunk (for all those breakfasts, and then some), Frazer Egerton, Ed Frettingham, Jana Fritzsche, Lora Gibson, Jay Hwang, Seb Kaempf, Adam Kamradt-Scott, Suzanna Karllson, Costas Laoutides, Tom Lundborg, and Dan McCarthy. I would also like to thank Nick Vaughan-Williams for joining me in promenade-based activities, and for the engaging (if mostly poststructuralist) conversation. All contributed in many ways to making my time at Aberystwyth a very enjoyable experience.

I must also make special mention of Lisa Denney and Columba Peoples. Lisa read most of these chapters at some point or other, and offered sound advice at various stages in the process. More than this though, Lisa made what might otherwise have been a very difficult year one of the best I've known. She is a dear friend and someone who I value greatly. I should also take this opportunity to wish Lisa good luck with her PhD, which she began last September. Columba has been a close friend and colleague since I moved to Wales in 2003. We have collaborated on a number of small projects since, and this has been immensely enjoyable (for me at least). Occasionally, we even get some work done. I have learned a lot from Columba, and look forward to working on more projects with her in the future.

Since April 2007, I have been based at the Department of Politics at the University of Glasgow, where I am fortunate enough to work in a very friendly and vibrant department. My colleagues, Chris Berry, Maurizio Carboni, Kevin Francis, Brian Girvan, Paul Graham, Kelly Kollman, Ana Langer, Andrew Lockyer, Tom Lundberg, Kurt Mills, Sarah Oates, Barry O'Toole, Chris Thornhill, and Alasdair Young, have all been very welcoming to me. On top of this, a special word of thanks goes to Mo Hume and Dave Featherstone. Mo and Dave have been very kind to me since I moved to Glasgow, supplying me with cooking utensils and a taxi service to Ikea when most needed.

There are, of course, a number of friends beyond both Aberystwyth and Glasgow whose support I must also mention: Darren Gilligan, Dee Mangaoang, Kieran McGourty, Eimear O'Leary, Andrew O'Malley, and Susan Thomson. Ever modest, Bernadette Sexton has requested that I acknowledge her help: thanks Bernadette! Finally, I would like to thank my brother and sister, Cormac and Aoife, my brother-in-law Eamon, and my parents, Peter and Jacinta. Without their support, none of this would have been possible for me. I am very grateful for your help and support.

Introduction

From 9/11 to Iraq

The invasion of Iraq, and the period immediately preceding and following it, has been characterized as a period of great "uncertainty" and "disequilibrium."[1] It marks a time when a whole series of truths, conventions, and practices that had been previously taken for granted have been called into question. This is nowhere more evident than with respect to the just war tradition. The right of states to wage war in certain circumstances has been subject to concerted scrutiny as theorists and interested observers have examined whether the received *jus ad bellum* should be retained unaltered, scrapped, or modified to fit today's security environment. This intense period of questioning and reappraisal is a direct consequence of the terrorist attacks of September 11, 2001, the shockwaves of which are still rippling through international society.

Jean Bethke Elshtain has famously compared the impact of 9/11 upon the present-day international system to the shock wrought upon the medieval world by the sack of Rome in AD410.[2] Both events, she argues, shook the moral foundations of their age and led to periods of pronounced instability and anxiety. The pertinence of this comparison is borne out by the revival of the rhetoric of good and evil—always an indicator of moral upheaval—that followed the terrorist attacks on the United States. The first reaction of both President Bush and Prime Minister Blair to the terrorist attacks of 9/11 was to identify the presence of a "new evil in our world."[3] We might recall here Bush's statement, issued just nine months later, to the effect that the events of September 11, 2001, marked the first contact in a renewed "conflict between good and evil."[4] The recourse of state leaders to such language is an indicator of the enormous jolt that 9/11 administered to international society. It reflects a surrender of conventional moral discourse to the sense of dislocation imparted by such an epoch-defining event. Evil is a term that crops up only when everyday moral reasoning is questioned and found wanting.[5]

One area of conventional reasoning that has explicitly been called into question in the aftermath of 9/11 concerns the right to use force in international society. Blair was one of the first to remark upon the fact that the traditional way of thinking about force and statecraft had been upset by 9/11. He put forward the idea in a number of keynote addresses that the rules governing the use of force in international society need to be revised in light of the advent of the threat of global terrorism. It no longer makes sense, he urged, to restrict the justification of military action to defense against aggression. It is time to question the conventional arrangements of international society, and to look beyond them by rethinking how we speak and think about the right to war today. "This is a moment to seize. The kaleidoscope has been shaken. The pieces are in flux. Soon they will settle again. Before they do, let us re-order this world around us."[6] What Blair recognized, of course, was that the events of 9/11 had created a window of opportunity where the rules governing the right to force in international affairs might be recast. It was against this backdrop that the invasion of Iraq (led by United States–United Kingdom forces) took place in March 2003.

The invasion of Iraq was highly contentious at the time it was undertaken. Millions of people turned out on the streets of capital cities across the world to protest against what was widely portrayed as an unnecessary and precipitate war. Against this general unease, Bush and Blair, the main proponents of the invasion, proffered three core justifications for the invasion. They variously presented the use of force against Iraq as an anticipatory war designed to eliminate the menace posed by Iraq to international peace and security, a humanitarian war to rescue the Iraqi people from the tyranny of Saddam Hussein, and a punitive war to ensure that the Ba'athist regime in power in Baghdad was brought to book for its failure to comply with international law. Quite often, these justifications were bolstered by recourse to the rhetoric of good and evil. Intriguingly, these justifications were explicitly couched in the idiom of the just war tradition, being presented as valid *just causes* for war.

This book attempts to identify and track these justifications, locating them within the just war tradition, as they invoke it. To this end, it examines exactly how Bush and Blair's arguments correspond to the tradition, paying special attention to points of convergence and divergence they share with some of the seminal articulations of the right to war. It contends that these justifications, and the debate they precipitated, appear to mark both a resurgence of classical tropes within the jus ad bellum and a turn away from the legalist paradigm, the dominant just war discourse since the conclusion of the First World War (and the one with which contemporary just war theorists are likely most familiar). It is this intriguing possibility that provides the point of departure for this work.

From the Legalist Paradigm to a Broader Jus ad Bellum

The legalist paradigm reflects a very narrow and restricted jus ad bellum. It reserves defense against aggression as the only just cause for war. There is no scope here for punitive war or any far-reaching right to humanitarian or anticipatory war: "Nothing but aggression can justify war."[7] Michael Walzer coined the term "legalist paradigm" in 1977 to describe the consensus position regarding the right to war evident in the practices of international society. It was not intended as a prescriptive statement proposing a set of rules that ought to govern the use of force in international affairs; instead, it was presented as a summary statement of those rules *already embedded* in the conventions of international society. It achieved a great degree of accuracy in this respect: numerous scholars have remarked that the discussion of war in the twentieth century was framed almost entirely in terms of aggression and defense against aggression. While this account of the right to war was challenged by the advent of humanitarian war in the 1990s, its authority survived more or less intact until the invasion of Iraq.

The various justifications offered by Bush and Blair, and their respective governments, for the invasion of Iraq, and subsequently considered by contemporary just war theorists and political commentators, appear to break the legalist paradigm mold. Put bluntly, they disregard the legalist paradigm almost entirely, suggesting a much broader, more expansive account of the jus ad bellum in its place. This book submits that Bush and Blair's rather unorthodox justifications for the invasion of Iraq must be understood as an innovative engagement with the just war tradition. These justifications represent a clear challenge to the extant jus ad bellum and suggest a shift away from the legalist paradigm and toward a broader right to war.

If Bush and Blair's justifications for the invasion of Iraq do turn out to be indicative (or even precipitative) of some broader loosening of the jus ad bellum, this would be a very significant development where the just war tradition is concerned. The modern history of the just war tradition—that is, the history of the tradition since the nineteenth century—tells a tale of the progressive restriction and narrowing of the right to war. Where in medieval times three just causes were generally accepted for war—punishment, the righting of a wrong received, and self-defense—the last two hundred years has seen this list whittled down to the extent that only self-defense survived as a casus belli. Bush and Blair's arguments (and the debate they gave rise to) suggest a very real possibility that this process may have been checked, and perhaps even reversed.

This book constitutes a response to, and an exploration of, this possibility. In this regard it has a straightforward remit. Primarily, it aims to identify and track the justifications offered by Bush and Blair for the invasion of Iraq, and locate them within the just war tradition. In doing so, it seeks to draw our attention to the stories of innovation and contestation that animate the historical development of the just war tradition, and to question what they might tell us about, on the one hand, the currents of change and continuity that provide for the ebb and flow of the tradition, and, on the other, the direction in which the tradition is moving today.

Outline

The outline of this book proceeds in two steps. First, it assesses the justifications for the invasion of Iraq put forward by Bush and Blair qua proposals for enacting change upon the jus ad bellum. It emphasizes the challenges the various themes of anticipation, punishment, and humanitarianism pose to the legalist paradigm. Following this, it examines whether these proposals for change are reflected in the recent development of the just war tradition. That is, are they indicative of broader trends and developments in the tradition? In particular, it focuses upon the response that Bush and Blair's justifications for the invasion have provoked from contemporary just war scholars. It inquires whether Bush and Blair's arguments have been contested, accepted, rejected, or renegotiated by today's just war scholars. The aims underlying this book are as follows: first, to identify and locate Bush and Blair's arguments within the just war tradition; second, to ascertain whether there is any substance to the claim that we are currently witnessing a loosening of the jus ad bellum in the aftermath of the terrorist attacks of 9/11 and the subsequent invasion of Iraq; and third, to inquire as to the modalities of this process, if this claim does indeed have some substance.

Chapter 1 opens proceedings by setting the possible loosening of the jus ad bellum against a wider historical perspective that takes in the development of the just war tradition over the past two centuries. It submits that the legalist paradigm crystallized during the first half of the twentieth century as international law and popular sentiment contributed to the denunciation of force as an instrument of foreign policy, leaving defense against aggression as the only possible just cause for war. The resulting state of affairs was captured nicely by Robert Tucker in 1960: "The just war is war fought either in self-defense or in collective defense against an armed attack. Conversely, the unjust war . . . is the war initiated in circumstances other than those of self- or collective defense against armed aggression."[8] Chapter 1 contends that it was only with the rise of humanitarian war in the 1990s that the first fractures started to appear in the legalist paradigm. These fractures would become more evident circa the invasion of Iraq.

Chapters 2, 3, and 4 are dedicated to the invasion of Iraq. More specifically, these chapters look to provide an account of the justifications for the invasion offered by Bush and Blair. Chapter 2 focuses on the justification for anticipation, while 3 and 4 deal respectively with the punitive and humanitarian justifications for the recourse to force. These chapters stress how these various justifications all seemingly look beyond the legalist paradigm and suggest a broader conception of the jus ad bellum that trades in moralistic rather than strictly legal language. Additionally, Chapters 2 through 4 demonstrate that these various justifications resonate with a number of tropes, themes, and commitments usually associated with more classical articulations of just war. These arguments call to mind some of the more prominent medieval and early-modern statements of the right to war—we might mention the writings of Augustine, Aquinas, Vitoria, Suarez, Grotius, and Vattel as examples here—even as they signal their disregard for the legalist paradigm. In sum, these chapters are concerned to locate Bush and Blair's justifications for the invasion of Iraq within the context of the just war tradition that they invoke. These chapters proceed by tracing Bush and Blair's justifications against the writings of some of the more influential contemporary just war theorists—for example, Michael Walzer, Jean Bethke Elshtain, and James Turner Johnson—as well as against both the classic just war tradition and the legalist paradigm. Viewed collectively, these chapters comprise an extended analysis of the innovative and potentially consequential manner in which the just war tradition was engaged by Bush and Blair as they sought to legitimate a war that many deemed to be dubious at best.

Chapter 5 expands on one aspect of the previous chapters just noted. It analyzes the manner by which Walzer, Elshtain, and Johnson have engaged with Bush and Blair's arguments pertaining to Iraq. In particular, it pays detailed attention to the platforms of understanding that conditioned their exchanges. The general purpose of this undertaking is to examine the terms of their engagement with Bush and Blair's arguments and also with the just war tradition more generally. The result is a form of second-order analysis focused on how the idiom of the just war was taken up and engaged by the scholars just mentioned in the context of the invasion of Iraq. This analysis contributes to our understanding of how the tradition is referred to, and deployed in the course of moral debate, while also indicating how the tradition might be reconstituted through this process.

Chapter 6 examines how the tradition's capacity for reconstitution has manifested itself in the context of the war on terror and, more specifically, the Iraq debate. In this respect, it is concerned to treat the just war tradition as a site of contestation and explore the response to Bush and Blair's arguments from today's just war scholars. How have Bush and Blair's proposals for a reformed jus ad bellum been received and negotiated by contemporary just war theorists and commentators? Does their response indicate some level of support for the idea of an expanded right to humanitarian war and a more permissive articulation of anticipatory war, as well as the notion of punitive war as a twenty-first century practice? More to the point, does it suggest a general shift toward a broader conception of the jus ad bellum? By examining these questions, the present work seeks to provide a theoretical account of the stories of innovation and contestation that animate the historical development of the just war tradition, and reflect upon the modalities of change and continuity as they provide for the ebb and flow of the tradition.

Three caveats must be kept in mind before going any further. First, this book is not concerned to pronounce upon the justice (or lack thereof) of the invasion of Iraq. Emphatically, it is not *testing* the Iraq war against any so-called "just war checklist." Rather, it takes as its point of departure the manner by which Bush and Blair (and other actors) engaged with the idiom of the just war. In this respect, it entails a study of the language of justification—as it centered upon the just war tradition—that attended the invasion of Iraq. As such, it is more concerned with *what* was said rather than the sincerity with which it was said. My concern is not to examine whether Bush and Blair were truthful with their respective publics in their speeches, but to scrutinize the way these speeches often drew upon the just war tradition. Of course, skeptics may take the hardheaded view that we ought to pay little attention to the vaunted moral principles politicians and other public figures invoke in order to justify their decisions. Such talk, they suggest, comprises little more than a moral cloak in which to shroud otherwise dubious activities. This seems too cynical to me. Moreover, it represents a failure to appreciate the close connection between language and the constitution of political life. As Michael Hunt writes, "Public rhetoric is not merely a screen, tool, or ornament."[9] Rather, it reflects the structures of meaning that govern the conduct of politics and public life at any given time. Public discourse is not an "epiphenomenon" of the international realm, but lies at its very core.[10] In the same light, how we talk about war must go someway toward determining how we conceive of it and, thus, how and when we resort to it. The point is that rhetoric is never merely rhetoric: it establishes the conditions of possibility that circumscribe international politics.

The second issue follows from the first, but is presentational in character. Due to the nature of this work, with its emphasis upon political rhetoric, I have tried to present the thoughts of the actors and theorists that appear in this book in their own words. Some readers may find my extensive use of direct quotations excessive, but it allows me to engage with these characters on their own terms, while also providing something of a flavor of the style of presentation. Among those quoted extensively are President Bush and Prime Minister Blair. Critics may point out that I have overstated both the affinity between these two leaders and their autonomy vis-à-vis their respective governmental apparatuses.[11] Both of these charges hit their mark, but they do not unduly hinder the argument I wish to present. Where Bush and Blair are concerned, my purpose is merely to examine the manner by which they, as leaders of their respective governments, took up the idiom of the just war tradition in the context of the Iraq debate. As such, my insensitivity to the divergences between these two leaders, and my decision to focus almost exclusively on them at the expense of other influential figures within their governments, is regrettable but not of great significance for the argument I wish to make.

Finally, the third caveat is that I do not intend to argue that the idiom of the just war tradition was the sole discourse attending the invasion of Iraq. Indeed, there were a number of very powerful discourses in play during the Iraq debate, the discourse pertaining to imperialism/anti-imperialism being the most obvious in this instance, though there were also others. The focus of this study is upon understanding how the idiom of the just war tradition was engaged during this debate, rather than accounting for the totality of discourses that figured in the debate over Iraq.

Negotiation

Revealed in this book is, I hope, a glimpse of the processes of change, continuity, and contestation that comprise the ongoing development of the just war tradition. As Terry Nardin writes, the story of a tradition such as the just war is a story of development and revision. Traditions are "resilient but not immutable practices that are constantly modified in use." To engage with a tradition is to "move back and forth between the general and the particular—to draw upon general principles in reaching particular judgments and decisions and, at the same time, to revise those principles in light of the particular circumstances in which they are used."[12] Accordingly, every time we draw on a tradition, we are participating in an "ongoing debate about where to draw the lines of that tradition, and how it might properly be interpreted and applied given changing circumstances."[13] Such a process is probably best characterized as a negotiation, as it entails a process of treaty, a mode of engagement, and a contest of wills. This book should, I hope, provide some insights as to how this dynamic unfolds within the just war tradition. Additionally, it should also afford us some indication of whether we are currently witnessing an expansion of the jus ad bellum beyond the strictures of the legalist paradigm.

CHAPTER 1

The Just War Tradition and the Invasion of Iraq: A Historical Perspective

Introduction

The end of the cold war, brought about by the collapse of the Soviet Union, signaled a sea change in the conduct of world politics. One of the more significant changes to take place was the "loosening" of the just war tradition, which has occurred in the wake of the Soviet Union's disintegration.[1] This loosening amounts to a more favorable disposition toward interventionist politics and represents a reversal of the narrowing and tightening of the jus ad bellum that took place over the previous two hundred years. The reality of such a shift was made most visible by the unorthodox just cause arguments that accompanied the invasion of Iraq in March 2003. The invasion of Iraq was variously justified by President Bush and Prime Minister Blair in terms of anticipatory war, humanitarian war, and punitive war. These arguments appear alien to the modern jus ad bellum, focused on aggression and self-defense as it is, with which most contemporary just war theorists will be familiar.[2] Yet these unorthodox arguments were represented time and again by Bush and Blair as providing a bona fide just cause for war.

This chapter examines the loosening of the just war tradition set against a wider historical perspective that takes in the development of the tradition over the past two hundred years or so. In undertaking this approach, a number of claims are advanced. First, the just war tradition is undergoing a period of upheaval since the end of the cold war. Second, the historical development of the just war tradition cannot be understood without reference to wider developments in the social, military, and political world. That is, the just war tradition is not a purely intellectual construct that exists in isolation from the material historical world. As James Turner Johnson writes, "The just war tradition represents above all a fund of practical moral wisdom, based not in abstract speculation or theorization but in reflection on actual problems encountered in war as these have presented themselves in different historical circumstances."[3] Third, and finally, it will be shown that the historical development of the just war tradition betrays a marked lack of linear development. There is no metaphysical *geist* or teleology unfurling itself here, only the contingent interplay between the ever-changing nature of warfare and man's efforts to limit, regulate, and justify it. While the second and third claims might not be particularly novel, they must be factored in to any discussion pertaining to the historical development of the just war tradition.

This chapter is structured quite simply. The discussion commences with a description of the modern just war tradition, as it was understood for the most part of the twentieth century. To this end, the first section of this chapter will focus on the "legalist paradigm," Michael Walzer's account of the orthodox reading of the jus ad bellum in the twentieth century.[4] The principle aim of this discussion is to show how this reading of the just war tradition must be understood in the context of the cold war, built as it was upon superpower rivalry and the ever-present fear of nuclear war. Moving on from here, the second section details the disturbance of the modern just war tradition in the wake of the cold war's abrupt conclusion. This disturbance initially took the form of the expansion of the jus ad bellum to allow for humanitarian intervention, as occurred in the 1990s. The third section carries this discussion through to the present day. It does so by outlining how Bush and Blair's arguments in reference to the invasion of Iraq suggest the further expansion of the jus ad bellum to include punitive war and a wider reading of anticipatory war. The fourth section locates these developments within the historical evolution of the just war tradition over the past two centuries. It contends that they represent a fairly radical change of direction for the tradition: the expansion of the jus ad bellum seems to fly in the face of the development of the tradition since the eighteenth century. In the conclusion, I suggest that these post–cold war developments, although reflecting a degree of discontinuity with just war thinking since the early nineteenth century, resonate with the more classical expressions of the just war tradition from the Middle Ages and early modern period.

Twentieth Century Just War Thought and the Legalist Paradigm

Between the end of the Second World War and the collapse of the Soviet Union, one issue dominated all others in international affairs—the cold war.

The cold war involved an intense, confrontational rivalry between the world's two superpowers, the United States and the Soviet Union. This rivalry assumed the form of adversarial alliances (NATO versus the Warsaw Pact), arms racing and spheres of influence, as well as the occasional proxy war (e.g., Vietnam and Korea). This antagonistic relationship was underwritten by the fact that both the United States and the Soviet Union possessed nuclear weapons. These strategic realities gave rise to a bipolar world order that determined, to a large degree, how international politics was conducted in these years. For instance, the United Nations (UN) provisions for collective security mechanisms were sidelined (as was, to some extent, the organization as a whole) by the United States–Soviet Union rivalry and their willingness to extend this rivalry into the voting chambers of the UN. The fear of a third world war loomed large in this era. After all, the devastation wrought by the "mechanized slaughter" of the First and Second World Wars was still a fresh memory in the 1940s and 1950s.[5] The possibility that any future war could take the form of a cataclysmic nuclear exchange only aggravated these fears. Given the possibility that even a limited engagement could trigger a wholesale nuclear exchange, it stood to reason that the right to use force in international affairs should be highly circumscribed.

Not surprisingly, the restrictiveness of this bipolar world order weighed upon the just war tradition in the twentieth century. Johnson argues in *Morality and Contemporary Warfare* that the just war tradition was bound, almost hand and foot, to this cold war order.[6] Its acquiescence is evident, according to Johnson, in the attention paid by just war theorists at this time to issues such as nuclear deterrence, proxy wars, and militarization, and in the general aversion to nondefensive war in all circumstances. Johnson refers to the 1983 pastoral letter on war and peace, *The Challenge of Peace*, issued by the National Conference of Catholic Bishops (NCCB), to illustrate his case.[7] He argues that the bishops' reading of the just war tradition, with its prohibition of all recourse to war bar that in self-defense, reflects the paradigmatic expression of just war thought during the cold war.[8] While Johnson's discussion of the NCCB pastoral letter is both interesting and informative, Michael Walzer's legalist paradigm provides a more accessible example of twentieth century orthodoxy.[9]

According to Walzer, there was a clearly discernible consensus on the fundamental moral issues pertinent to the practice of waging war in twentieth century international society. As Walzer describes it, this orthodoxy consisted of two tiers of moral judgment. He writes, "War is always judged twice, first with reference to the reasons states have for fighting, secondly with reference to the means they adopt. The first kind of judgment is adjectival in character:

we say that a particular war is just or unjust. The second is adverbial: we say that the war is being fought justly or unjustly."[10] This moral categorization is analogous to William V. O'Brien's insistence that the just war tradition comprises two logically independent bodies of reasoning; "war-decision law" and "war-conduct law."[11] For both O'Brien and Walzer, these tiers of moral judgment relate, respectively, to the jus ad bellum and *jus in bello*, although Walzer does not always refer to them in these terms. Walzer refers to the jus ad bellum, in its twentieth century variant, as the "legalist paradigm," and the twentieth century jus in bello as the "war convention." These terms provide the vocabulary for Walzer to describe the twentieth century just war orthodoxy, which is constructed upon two major commitments.

The first commitment is to a narrow reading of the jus ad bellum, one that is centered upon the recognition of aggression as the "crime of war."[12] Walzer defines aggression as an intrusive act that challenges the rights and autonomy of a political community through the threat of violence. It is a crime because it is coercive and tyrannical: it "forces men and women to risk their lives for the sake of their rights. It is to confront them with the choice: your rights or (some of) your lives."[13] It follows from this that states have a right to resist aggression with the use of force, where necessary. Such resistance might have two sanctioned purposes. Firstly, a state may resist aggression with force so as to defend the local object of the aggression—i.e., the victim state and its people. Secondly, on a more abstract level, states have a right to resist aggression because aggression stands as an affront to those foundational values of the society of states. On this level, the act of resistance is directed toward reaffirming and reasserting the norms of political sovereignty and territorial integrity, which all members of the society of states have a stake in. Resistance, then, may take two forms: "a war of self-defense by the victim and a war of law enforcement by the victim and any other member of international society."[14] One must be careful, however, not to overstate the distinction between these two forms of resistance. Both are, to a greater or lesser extent, justified as a means of upholding the rules of international society and vindicating the prohibition on aggression.[15]

Aggression appears to be the sole concern of the legalist paradigm. The right to war is phrased entirely in terms of resistance to aggression: "Nothing but aggression can justify war."[16] The resistance of aggression is, apparently, the "single and only *just cause*" for waging war.[17] Walzer writes, "The legalist paradigm rules out every other sort of war. Preventive wars, commercial wars, wars of expansion and conquest, religious crusades, revolutionary wars, military interventions—all these are barred and barred absolutely . . . all these constitute aggressive acts on the part of whoever begins them and justify forceful resistance."[18] As this last line demonstrates, even the constraints upon the ends for which war may be fought are expressed in terms of aggression. War can be fought to reverse and restrain aggression, but cannot be fought for any purpose which extends beyond this: "To press the war further than that is to re-commit the crime of aggression."[19]

It is possible from this to see how central the concept of aggression was to the jus ad bellum of the twentieth century. This overriding concern with aggression is also reflected in international law, which stipulates that the only right of war that remains in the hands of states is the inherent right of self-defense (Articles 2[4] and 51 of the UN Charter), though provisions exist for the multilateral use of force where the UN Security Council recognizes a threat to international peace and security (Chapter VII of the UN Charter).[20] It also mirrors the position adopted by NCCB[21] and the Vatican[22], as well as a number of prominent just war commentators of the day.[23] Yet, even in international law, the concept of aggression has remained highly problematic, as the tortuous definition of aggression proposed by UNGA resolution 3314 suggests.

The second commitment is to what Walzer calls the "moral equality of soldiers."[24] That is, the strictures of the war convention—the jus in bello—apply "equally and indifferently" to all soldiers, regardless of whether they are fighting for a just cause or not.[25] Though a soldier may be fighting in the service of an unjust cause, we afford that soldier the same rights and privileges as we would a soldier fighting in the service of a just cause. This is because we do not judge (or treat) a soldier on the basis of the cause he or she is fighting for, but on the basis of how he or she conducts him or herself in battle. In this sense, all soldiers are clean slates when they enter battle and must not be considered criminals by dint of the cause for which they fight.[26] This commitment constitutes a refusal to hold the rights of soldiers conditional upon the cause for which he or she fights. All soldiers, irrespective of their cause, are endowed with equal rights once fighting commences. This commitment is the foundational premise upon which the war convention rests. It rests upon the understanding that the jus in bello is always "logically independent" of the jus ad bellum.[27] "In our judgment of the fighting," Walzer writes, "we abstract from all considerations of the justice of the cause."[28] We judge soldiers only on the basis of how they fight their battles, without any regard for the ends for which those battles are fought. The jus in bello and the jus ad bellum are thus treated as very separate categories, which do not inform one another. "We draw a line between the war itself, for which soldiers are not responsible, and the conduct of war, for which they are responsible, at least within their own sphere of activity."[29] No special rights or liabilities accrue to soldiers as a consequence of the cause for which they fight; whatever rights and liabilities soldiers accrue on the battlefield are purely a matter of the war convention. This arrangement permits us to treat even aggressive war, when it occurs, as a rule-governed activity.

The two commitments at the heart of Walzer's presentation of twentieth century just war tradition more generally reflect the experience of two world wars and the ensuing cold war order. The enshrinement of *defense against aggression* as the only just cause for war may have amounted to a ban on the first use of force in any conflict, but it appeared a responsible move in an era when the cost of warfare was deemed prohibitive, a calculation informed by the destruction wrought between 1914 and 1918 and again between 1939 and 1945.[30] This was the logic contained in Pope John Paul II's Coventry Cathedral homily: "Today the scale and horror of modern warfare—whether nuclear or not—makes it totally unacceptable as a means of settling differences between nations."[31] Arguments such as this draw upon certain considerations born of the twentieth century experience and germane to the cold war order. These considerations pertain to the awesome destructive potential of modern nuclear arsenals, the total nature of twentieth century warfare, and the fear that any war between the Soviet Union and the United States would be an ideological war fought without restraint.[32] Underpinning all of this is the Clausewitzian fear that modern war must always tend toward extremity, in this case all-out nuclear exchange.[33]

The second commitment of twentieth century just war thought also reflects a concern with issues specific to the cold war. The desire to establish the independence of the war convention from the theory of aggression was, in part, a response to the fear that any war between the Soviet Union and the United States would be an ideological war which would tend toward unlimited warfare. The only means of ensuring restraint in cases of ideological warfare is to insist on a rigid separation of the jus in bello from the jus ad bellum. Such an arrangement ensures that the justice of one's cause does not become an excuse for the erosion of restraint in one's conduct of war: hence the independence of the war convention from the theory of aggression. To summarize briefly, I have argued that both the commitments Walzer depicts as lying at the heart of twentieth century just war thought reflect their historical circumstances—the cold war order and the sustained shock imparted by two cataclysmic world wars. It follows from this that the legalist paradigm is best understood as a consensus reading of the just war tradition developed in the historical context provided by two world wars and the ensuing cold war era.

The Post–Cold War New World Order

The twentieth century just war orthodoxy outlined by Walzer appears to have been disrupted in the years following the end of the cold war. The most obvious form this disruption took was the expansion of the jus ad bellum to allow for humanitarian war or intervention. This development overturned the position, central to the legalist paradigm, that only defense against aggression provides a just cause for war. State practice in the 1990s strongly indicated that such a development was indeed taking place. This was a decade defined by President Clinton's "new American interventionism" [34] and Boutros-Boutros Ghali's *Agenda for Peace*, and marked by numerous cases of humanitarian intervention. Interventions took place in Northern Iraq, Somalia, Rwanda (though on a meager scale), Bosnia, Kosovo, and East Timor.[35] The intervention in Kosovo is perhaps the most interesting case. It has been labeled the first truly humanitarian *war*, owing to NATO's use of force against the Yugoslavian state in order to end the abuse of Kosovo's Albanian community at the hands of forces loyal to Slobodan Milosevic. Add to this the fact that the 1990s saw the UN, acting under the rubric of Article 2(4) of the Charter, delegating peace-keeping and peace-enforcement work to regional (and even state) actors, and one is presented with a "de facto redistribution [through the UN] of the right to resort to force for reasons other than national defense against armed attack."[36] The narrow jus ad bellum, which allows for only one just cause for war—defense against aggression—had seemingly been disregarded, and states displayed a new willingness to use force for humanitarian purposes, circumstances allowing.[37]

It is worth focusing on the Kosovo case, because it, in particular, was justified by its supporters in the language of the just war tradition; more specifically, they appealed to an extended jus ad bellum that allows for war for human rights. For example, the British secretary of defense, George Robertson, published an article on the war in Kosovo entitled "This is a Just War" in a Sunday newspaper while military action was still ongoing in the Former Republic of Yugoslavia. He argued that "the Kosovo action was a just war based on human rights."[38] A number of journalists and foreign policy experts made similar arguments for the Kosovo intervention in terms of a just war for human rights. Melanie McDonagh, for example, argues that "the Kosovo conflict was a war . . . and it was just. Fighting against organized ethnic violence is a just cause."[39] This idea—that war for human rights could in some cases be a just war—has subsequently filtered through to the mainstream literature of the just war tradition.

Walzer's feelings toward humanitarian intervention have always aroused controversy.[40] The legalist paradigm that he set out as representative of the just war consensus in the twentieth century had no place for humanitarian war, and even his own revisions of this paradigm only allowed for it as an exception to the rule. Yet, Walzer's aversion to humanitarian war softened in the 1990s, and he declared his support for a number of high profile interventions, including that in Kosovo. In *Arguing about War*, Walzer announces a slight revision of his just war theory to allow more easily for humanitarian intervention. He writes, "Faced with the sheer numbers of recent horrors—with massacre and ethnic cleansing in Bosnia and Kosovo; in Rwanda, the Sudan, Sierra Leone, the Congo, and Liberia; in East Timor (and earlier, in Cambodia and Bangladesh)—I have slowly become more willing to call for military intervention. I haven't dropped the presumption against intervention that I defended in my book, but I have found it easier and easier to override the presumption."[41]

The NCCB also revised their opinion on the place of humanitarian intervention in the just war tradition in the 1990s. As previously noted, the bishops formulated a very restrictive reading of the jus ad bellum, allowing that only self-defense provides a just cause for war, in their 1983 pastoral letter. Ten years later, in 1993, they issued a new letter on war and peace, *The Harvest of Justice is Sown in Peace*.[42] While following the same format as the 1983 pastoral letter, the 1993 epistle does introduce one significant change: the bishops signal their approval of humanitarian intervention. The bishops explicitly state that military intervention may be justified "to ensure that starving children can be fed or that whole populations will not be slaughtered."[43] Seyom Brown comments that the bishops' belated conversion to armed humanitarianism is reflective of a larger development: the "enlargement of the just cause principle to embrace human rights and humanitarian concerns."[44] Brown's argument appears to be supported by the rash of just war tradition literature in the 1990s that treats humanitarian intervention as a valid just cause argument.[45]

Although much of the literature on humanitarian intervention treats its emergence in the 1990s as a purely normative process, divorced from the material facts of international affairs, it is probably more accurate to locate this development within the context of the end of the cold war.[46] The end of the cold war gave rise to three developments relevant to this discussion. In the first place, the human rights discourse acquired great momentum following the collapse of the East-West rivalry. This created a climate favorable to humanitarian intervention.

Second, the end of the cold war unmasked the phenomena of failed states, ethnic conflict, and brutal civil wars, which had been kept under control by the bipolar cold war order. In the years immediately following the fall of the Berlin Wall, the international community was faced with the collapse of both the Soviet and Yugoslav empires, resulting in a profusion of bloody conflict in such far-flung countries as Somalia, the Sudan, Sierra Leone, Angola, Liberia, Rwanda, Indonesia and East Timor, Sri Lanka, Russia and Chechnya, and the

Federal Republic of Yugoslavia.[47] This led to an increase in demand in the 1990s for humanitarian intervention or war.

This leads us to the third development, which is that this increased demand for humanitarian war met with an amenable political climate: the end of the cold war arguably created a world order favorable to the practice of intervention. If the end of the cold war had given rise to an international order more in need of management than ever before, it also made the management of such an order appear a real possibility. A conjunction of political and technological factors contributed to this development. While new challenges have emerged that need tending to, sometimes by military means, the old fear of bipolar war has receded, leaving the United States (the sole remaining superpower) with a free hand to maintain international order as it sees fit.[48] Furthermore, the UN Security Council is no longer always gridlocked by bloc voting and extensive use of veto powers on the part of both the United States and the Soviet Union, and is subsequently better able to authorize humanitarian intervention where it deems it appropriate. As such, the end of the cold war rivalry has "created a space for third party states and the international community to intervene in local conflicts" with a view to mitigating their destructiveness and preserving international peace and security.[49] Of course, the easing of the Security Council gridlock would count for little if states did not possess the capabilities to take on the more robust role that has become possible. Recent developments in military technology have seemingly increased the capacity of the United States to perform the "order-maintenance" or "managerial" role that it must play as the sole remaining superpower.[50] The so-called Revolution in Military Affairs (RMA) places in the hands of the United States a formidable array of new weapons technology. This new weapons technology holds out the promise that the use of force might now be "controlled" and humane" in its application.[51] This suggests that force can be applied in clearly defined increments and accurately delivered. The state that possesses the capacity to wage warfare in this manner is in a better position to use force, and might be more inclined to undertake humanitarian interventions than in the past. The logic behind this is simple: where a state can so easily and cleanly resort to force, there is little to dissuade it from doing so.[52] In addition, then, to having a free hand in the maintenance of international order, the United States now possesses the means, through the RMA, to manage the post–cold war order and intervene where necessary.

These historical factors—the maturation of the human rights regime, the end of bipolarity and the new opportunities this created for United States–led order maintenance, the RMA and the advent of controllable and humane force—provide some context for the expansion of the jus ad bellum to include humanitarian intervention as a just cause for war. However, these same circumstances also introduce the possibility that the use of force could be resorted to for a wider range of reasons than just defense against aggression and humanitarian intervention. This possibility is worth bearing in mind as we turn to the war in Iraq of March 2003.

The War in Iraq of March 2003

The United States and Great Britain initiated a military invasion of Iraq on March 19, 2003. President Bush and Prime Minister Blair proffered three primary justifications for this invasion. The war was variously justified as an anticipatory war, designed to forestall the threat posed by Saddam Hussein's Iraq, and a humanitarian war to depose Iraq's cruel Ba'athist regime. It was also sometimes justified by its proponents as a punitive war, that is, a war of punishment. On occasion, Bush and Blair bolstered this argument for punitive war by fitting it out in the rhetoric of good and evil. Rather than appealing to Article 51 of the UN Charter and every nation's inherent right to self-defense, Bush and Blair appeared to spend the best part of the build-up to the outbreak of hostilities in the Gulf addressing the UN Security Council on the need to wage a humanitarian war against Iraq and make Saddam Hussein pay for his disregard of UN resolutions.[53] Significantly, both Bush and Blair consistently represented these arguments as valid *just cause* arguments for war. President Bush's State of the Union address was typical in this regard. He declared, "If war is forced upon us, we will fight in a just cause and with just means."[54]

There was, of course, a certain pragmatism attached to Bush and Blair's arguments; they were, after all, attempting to justify what would prove to be a very controversial military endeavor. On this perspective, the justifications proffered by Bush and Blair reflected little more than what they and their advisers thought would prove most palatable to the international community.[55] Jutta Brunnee and Stephen J. Toope suggest, however, that there was more to it than this. They argue that Bush and Blair's unorthodox justifications for the war in Iraq represent part of an attempt, on their part, to move toward a more "expansive doctrine of just war, one rooted in broad moral, rather than restrictive legal, assessments of threats and punishments."[56] This raises the interesting question of whether we might read Bush and Blair's arguments as a deliberate attempt to extend the boundaries of the jus ad bellum. Whether or not this is the case, they still challenge our understanding of what constitutes a just cause for waging war today.

Putting Post–Cold War Developments in Context

To this point, this chapter has concentrated on describing the trends evident in the just war tradition since the end of the cold war. These trends encompass the opening up of the legalist paradigm to allow for a wider range of just causes for war and a more expansive, moralistic articulation of the jus ad bellum. Conversely, the jus in bello has seen little development during this period. Yet these trends actually represent a fairly radical change in direction in the just war tradition when viewed through a wide historical lens. This wider perspective involves the periodization of the history of the modern just war tradition into two distinct eras: the period from the late eighteenth century up until the First World War, which I will refer to as the long nineteenth century, and the period from the end of that war right up until the fall of the Berlin Wall. Each of these periods marks a change of direction in the just war tradition. The long nineteenth century witnessed the de-emphasis of the jus ad bellum, while the seventy years following World War I saw a step back from this, as the jus ad bellum, albeit in much formalized and revised form, resumed its central place in the normative discourse on war.

The Long Nineteenth Century: Focus on the Jus in Bello

The first thing to mention is that the whole weight of the just war tradition between the late eighteenth century and the outbreak of World War I was on the development of the jus in bello rather than the jus ad bellum. To quote Geoffrey Best, the eighteenth and nineteenth centuries comprised a time when "the jus ad bellum withered on the bough [while] the jus in bello flourished like the green bay-tree."[57] This emphasis stands in stark contrast to the emphasis on the jus ad bellum, which is evident since the end of the cold war. The emphasis on the jus in bello between the late eighteenth and early twentieth century is perfectly understandable, however, in terms of the history of the era. The late eighteenth century saw the relatively controlled and limited "cabinet wars" of the post-Westphalian era give way to revolutionary warfare and the new idea of the nation in arms, *la nation armee*, following the French Revolution and the Napoleonic Wars.[58] This new turn brought with it the democratization of warfare, as the working classes were drafted en masse to serve in the new conscript armies sprouting up all over Europe. This raised fears that the chivalric code would be lost as warfare became less and less a place for knights and gentlemen, and more a place for the common man. It was General Halleck, commander of the Union Army during the American Civil War (1861–64), who first recognized that an army such as his own, primarily made up of members of the working class and unschooled in the code of chivalry, would require a new disciplinary code. This code would take the form of a manual laying out the rules of conduct in war, for the benefit of the Union's more uneducated soldiers. This manual was known as U.S. General Army Orders No. 100 (1863) or Lieber's Code (after Francis Lieber, the jurist who compiled the manual).[59]

Lieber's Code initiated a series of attempts to codify the law of war. Directly inspired by Lieber's Code, a number of European jurists sought to create a similar military handbook for European warfare. To this end they convened the 1874 Brussels Conference on the Proposed Rules for Military Warfare.[60] These developments contributed to a movement across Europe to codify the laws of war. This movement was helped off the ground by Henri Dunant who was instrumental in convening the first Geneva Convention of 1864. This convention succeeded in legislating for the protection of the victims of war—i.e., those injured on the field of battle and those tending to them. It is properly recognized as the first multilateral humanitarian treaty to deal with what would later become known as the law of armed conflict.[61] A number of similar endeavors followed over the next century: the Saint Petersburg Declaration of 1868, the two Hague Conferences of 1899 and 1907, and a further two Geneva Conventions in 1929 and 1949. These conventions and conferences were all concerned to stipulate the means and methods of warfare, as well as the protection of those innocently caught in the crossfire of war. That is, they dealt, by and large, with the jus in bello. These laws of war developed during the nineteenth and early twentieth centuries, Nicholas Rengger affirms, "concerned themselves primarily with what it was permissible to do in war rather than under what circumstances war should be waged. In other words . . . they concentrated on jus in bello questions rather than those of jus ad bellum."[62]

This sudden drive to codify the laws of war must be understood in the context of new military developments taking place in the nineteenth century. I have already mentioned the novel phenomenon of the nation at arms in this regard. No less important, however, were the great leaps being taken in the field of military technology.[63] It was around the 1860s that a host of new inventions, techniques, and materials began to make their mark on how war was waged. The metal-hulled, screw-propelled ship first came into service around this time, as did national railroad services across Europe. These inventions revolutionized strategy by increasing the mobility and reach of armies. On the battlefield, the needle-gun, the chassepot, and the machine gun also first appeared around this time. The result of these developments is easy to surmise: "both the means and the measure of destruction and killing became far greater than they ever had been before."[64] For Best, this explains the sudden drive to codify the laws of war. Because the destructive capacity of warfare had increased, "the need for more precise ideas about restraint and limitation became, for some, acute."[65]

This still leaves the question of why it was the jus in bello rather than the jus ad bellum that became the main target of the jurists' efforts in the long nineteenth century. There were two reasons for this focus. First, this was a period when thinkers in the West perceived development of the jus in bello rules of war as the best way to limit the destructiveness of war.[66] This was simply because they thought "the jus ad bellum limits [to] have diminished usefulness" in the nineteenth century context.[67] There was little prospect they submitted, of states reaching "agreement about the moral principles to be observed in limiting the occasions of war" in our pluralistic international system.[68] In such a pluralistic system, they argued, it is easier to agree to limit the destructiveness of war when it arrives than it is to forge a consensus on what would constitute a just cause for the resort to war. Focusing on extant disagreements regarding what might constitute a just cause for war would not contribute toward the successful restraint of war, but would only serve to aggravate longstanding antagonisms. In this sense, a focus on jus ad bellum issues could actually lead to less restraint, not more, in the conduct of war.[69] In such circumstances, it made sense to focus on the more functional issues such as arms limitation treaties and measures to protect noncombatants in times of war.

The second reason for the greater focus on jus in bello follows from the first. If the prioritization of the jus in bello held out more potential for the restraint of war, then this must be the direction jurists should look when seeking to codify the laws of war. Such a direction, however, enjoins a refusal to take into account jus ad bellum considerations for pragmatic reasons. There is a pragmatic reason for this: the existence and viability of international law was understood to "depend upon the un-stated assumption that each party is neither more right than wrong in having gone to war in the first place; all laws of war must assume that both parties are equally in the right."[70] In other words, in order for the laws of war to be effective, they must be understood to apply to all parties regardless of the justice of their war in ad bellum terms. Hedley Bull provides a good summary of this development. He states, "International legal theory in the eighteenth and nineteenth centuries came to play down the distinction between the just and unjust causes of war, and ultimately to exclude it from positive international law altogether. The doctrine was proclaimed that international law sought only to regulate the conduct of war, regulating the controversy about the reasons for resorting to war to the sphere of morals or politics. The view was firmly stated that the law of war applied equally to both sides."[71] This position was earlier endorsed by the testimony of W. E. Hall, a leading British jurist in the late nineteenth century. He declared, "International law has consequently no alternative but to accept war, independently of the justice of its origin, as a relation, which the parties to it may set up if they choose, and to busy itself only in regulating the effects of the relation."[72] In this manner, the distinction that might be drawn between just and unjust wars was disregarded and, irrespective of whether one or both sides lack just cause, war was treated as a legal relationship between two equal sovereign parties.[73] This is indeed what occurred. International law focused primarily on issues of jus in bello divorced from any considerations of jus ad bellum for the best part of the long nineteenth century.

After World War I: Return to the Jus ad Bellum

The prevalent idea in the long nineteenth century with regards to the restraint of war was, as we have seen, best achieved by means of the jus in bello, rather than the jus ad bellum. This led to the codification of the jus in bello, as detailed earlier. However, the very process of codifying the jus in bello in international law required that the jus ad bellum be de-emphasized. Subsequently, Best argues, from about the time of Emmerich de Vattel until the years immediately following the First World War, there was hardly any meaningful talk about jus ad bellum. Indeed, the language of the jus ad bellum was virtually anathema to international law during this period. In this regard, it is perhaps significant that the terms "just" and "unjust" fail to appear even once in the Geneva Conventions and Hague Regulations.[74] Neither international lawyers nor the international community, it seems, were very interested at this time in discovering which side in any particular war was "right" or "wrong."[75] States were simply assumed to possess a right to war by virtue of their sovereign status. As Rengger writes, "States were presumed from roughly the eighteenth century onwards to have a *right* of war in defense of their interests, which therefore made the traditional questions of the jus ad bellum irrelevant."[76] This was the doctrine of *competence de guerre*: so long as states openly declared war and submitted to the proper legal processes, they were held to possess an unconditional right to war.[77]

The shock supplied by the ghastly death toll of the First World War upset these arrangements. As Nicholas Politis comments, "The conflagration of 1914 forced upon the attention of all the absurdity of the system of the absolute right of war . . . It showed that for the civilized world, war is too great a calamity to be permitted."[78] The doctrine of *competence de guerre* was deemed bankrupt in an era defined by the Gatling gun and the trenches of the Somme. There was now good reason to doubt that the jus in bello alone could prevent another "Great War" from occurring, and cause to rethink the notion that states possess an unconditional right to war by virtue of their sovereign status. Best sums up the effects of the First World War as they relate to this discussion:

> So profound and unsettling . . . was the impression made upon that generation of survivors by, as they called it, the Great War, that their consequent responses went far beyond such patching of the jus in bello. It was no doubt desirable that war should never again be fought in ways as beastly as those in which the Great War had specialized. But how much more desirable that great wars should never happen again, and that the use of force among states, so far as it could not be absolutely prevented, should be controlled to serve the common good![79]

Instead, then, of looking to the jus in bello as the most promising means of limiting warfare, state leaders and international lawyers began to seek more radical solutions in the jus ad bellum. There followed a wholesale revision of the jus ad bellum such that the distinction between the lawful and unlawful resort to war was declared of central importance, and a ban on aggressive war enacted.[80] Such revisions instituted a formalization of the jus ad bellum, which recast it almost entirely in legal terms; this in turn enjoined a general lockdown on the right to war in international law (excepting wars of self-defense).

Arising from this, the first issue to discuss is the formalization of the jus ad bellum. The nineteenth century aversion to speaking of wars as either just or unjust, right or wrong, was given a new twist in the direct aftermath of World War I when jurists commenced speaking about war in terms of lawfulness or the lack thereof. The Covenant of the League of Nations, for example, concentrated on legislating for the lawful resort to war rather than on stipulating what might qualify as a right or just reason for waging war. Superficially, at least, considerations of justice were bracketed. The postwar jurists saw their task as the formulation of legal categories and rules that were clear and objective, and, crucially, did not encourage debate about the moral rights of states. This goes some way toward accounting for the heavy emphasis placed on categories such as aggression and the first use of force. These categories were, of course, intended to establish clear-cut rules of conduct that state leaders would be in doubt about.[81] All of this contributed to the narrowing of the jus ad bellum, in that it filtered out any normative considerations or conceptions of justice that did not accord with the emergent postwar legal system (which was coming increasingly to resemble the legalist paradigm).

The second issue to discuss is the lockdown on the right to war. It took the form of a ban on the first use of force, and the criminalization of such actions. In the years immediately following World War I, wars of aggression were defined as ipso facto illegal, and self-defense was enshrined as the only legitimate cause for lawful resort to war.[82] This set of provisions was stipulated in a number of international agreements running right through the twentieth century. It was given first expression in the Covenant of the League of Nations, Article 10 of which included a total prohibition on war except in self-defense.[83] This prohibition was reaffirmed in the first lines of the preamble to the Covenant, which declared that the League had been established "in order to promote international cooperation and to achieve international peace and security by the acceptance of the obligation not to resort to war."[84] This message was repeated by the Locarno Agreement of 1925, primarily a nonaggression pact between a number of European states. However, the best expression of the prohibition on the use of force, except for self-defense, prior to the Second World War, was the Kellogg-Briand Pact of 1928. This was formally known as the General Treaty for the Renunciation of War 1928, and attracted sixty-four signatories.[85] The pact announced that the High Contracting Parties (HCPs) were "persuaded that the time has come when a frank renunciation of war as an instrument of national policy should be made to the end that the peaceful and friendly relations now existing between their peoples may be perpetuated."[86] More to the point perhaps, it declares in Article 1, "The HCPs solemnly declare in the names of their respective peoples that they condemn recourse to war for the solution of international controversies and renounce it as an instrument of national policies in their relations with one another."[87] According to international law in the first half of the twentieth century, there was now only one legally recognized cause for resorting to war—self-defense.

This position did not change very much in the aftermath of the Second World War. In fact, it was given a further push by the advent of nuclear weapons, which, once again, upped the stakes vis-à-vis the resort to war. As Henry Stimson wrote of the destruction of Hiroshima and Nagasaki by the use of atomic bombs, "In this last great decision of the Second World War we were given final proof that war is death. War in the twentieth century has grown steadily more barbarous, more destructive, more debased in all its aspects. Now, with the release of atomic energy, man's ability to destroy himself is nearly complete. The bombs dropped on Hiroshima and Nagasaki ended a war. They also made it wholly clear that we must never have another war."[88]

The drafters of the UN Charter understood this, and they confirmed, in the Charter, the ban on all aggressive war and the acceptance of self-defense as the only legal grounds for the resort to war. Thus, as William V. O'Brien notes, by further curtailing the right of states to use force as an instrument of foreign policy, the UN Charter confirmed a trend started by the League of Nations Covenant: "The only form of legally permissible war now available to a state is a war of individual or collective self-defense, reiterated in Article 51 as a right to be exercised pending Security Council action under Chapter VII."[89] Chapter VII provisions for collective action aside, the drafting of the Charter copper-fastened the idea that there was only one legal basis for war, that being self-defense, and that all other recourse to war would be equated with aggression. This position was further buttressed during the course of the Nuremberg and Tokyo Criminal Tribunals as the surviving leaders of Germany and Japan were tried for their roles in planning, preparing, and waging an aggressive war.[90]

Toward the Legalist Paradigm

Summing up this section, we might want to consider how the just war tradition appeared in light of the developments in the two periods we have concentrated on. We might start by noting that the distinction between just and unjust wars, de-emphasized by nineteenth century jurists, was reestablished over the course of the twentieth century, only this time it was stated in legal terms.[91] In the legalistic parlance of the twentieth century, just wars became equated with wars of national defense while wars of aggression became synonymous with unjust wars.[92] However, underlying this shift in emphasis was a development of perhaps even greater significance: the narrowing of the jus ad bellum. This means two things. In the first place, it refers to the constriction and tightening of the jus ad bellum such that fewer just causes would be recognized for going to war. The proof of this is in the restrictive doctrine that emerged following World War I that self-defense constituted the only legitimate grounds for war. Secondly, it refers to the *formalization* of the jus ad bellum such that the right to war was restated in legalistic terms. The proof of this is in the excision of the language (and consideration) of justice and morality from the jus ad bellum, and in the fact that it now dealt only in legal categories. In this way, any normative considerations or conceptions of justice that did not accord with the emergent postwar legal system were filtered out and bracketed. This did much to contribute to the framing of a very narrow jus ad bellum.

In conclusion, it is clear that the jus ad bellum, and particularly the category of just cause, has been radically circumscribed in the period between the early eighteenth century and the mid-twentieth century. It is at this point that we reencounter the legalist paradigm as depicted by Walzer, and treated in the first section of this chapter. Now, however, it is possible to see the narrow and restrictive right to war as the product of a historical trend within the just war tradition that dates back to the eighteenth century. It is only with this context in mind that we can understand how radical a departure the post–cold war loosening of the jus ad bellum truly is.

Conclusion

The story I have just told about the narrowing of the jus ad bellum is well known to students of the modern just war tradition. Indeed, Douglas Lackey suggests that it is *the story* of the modern just war tradition. "The history of the subject," he writes, "is the history of how this repertoire of just causes was originally cut down to the modern standard, which accepts only the single cause of self-defense."[93] The possibility, then, that subsequent to the end of the cold war there has been a certain loosening or opening up of the jus ad bellum is intriguing.

This chapter has suggested jus ad bellum that such a loosening is indeed evident in contemporary international society. It has argued that the first indications of this loosening became apparent in the early 1990s, with an increased willingness to condone humanitarian war within international society. Viewed against a wider historical perspective, such as this chapter has presented, this loosening appears as a radical change in direction for the just war tradition. It constitutes a reversal of the narrowing of the jus ad bellum that had taken place over the previous two hundred years. In light of this, it is very interesting that President Bush and Prime Minister Blair put forward some rather unorthodox arguments for the war in Iraq, relating to anticipatory war, humanitarian intervention, and punitive war. These arguments were framed in terms of the just war tradition, being presented as "just causes," but promote a broader right to war than many just war theorists might be expected to be comfortable with. Chapters 2 through 4 will examine Bush and Blair's justifications for the invasion of Iraq with a view to ascertaining whether or not they signal a loosening of the jus ad bellum. Chapters 3 and 4 analyze, respectively, the justifications submitted by Bush and Blair for punitive war and humanitarian war, while Chapter 2 focuses on their case for anticipatory war.

CHAPTER 2

Anticipatory War: Sufficient Threats, Just Fears, and Unknown Unknowns

Introduction

Anticipatory war, as it relates to both preemptive defense and preventive strikes, is a contentious subject that has attracted much attention from political theorists over many years. Thucydides, for instance, framed the struggle between the Athenians and Lacedaemonians in terms of anticipation, while Machiavelli praised the prince who showed enough prudence and fortitude to act early and wage war in order to forestall threats from materializing.[1] In the nineteenth century, Otto von Bismark took the opposite position and suggested that anticipatory war is very often a rash and foolish endeavor.[2] Prompted by the March 2003 U.S.-UK invasion of Iraq, the debate regarding anticipatory war has recently been rekindled. In light of President Bush and Prime Minister Blair's efforts to justify what many perceived as a dubious war on the basis of "preemption," or "anticipation," a fresh round of enquiry into the moral dilemmas raised by the anticipatory use of force has been initiated.

Following the events of September 11, 2001, both Bush and Blair expressed concern that the nexus between transnational terrorism, rogue states, and nuclear proliferation poses a novel threat that requires "new thinking" on how best to respond. In particular, our understanding of the limits of self-defense needs to be reexamined. A right to self-defense that takes into account only conventional threats will no longer suffice, they argued, when the world is threatened by shadowy terrorist networks who can strike without warning. It was against this background that Bush and Blair spoke the language of anticipation when making the case for war against Iraq. This was not the only justification they offered for the war—they also offered arguments relating to the enforcement of international law and humanitarian concerns—but it was the most prominent. In Bush's case, it was even enshrined in *The National Security Strategy of the USA* (NSS), published in September 2002.[3]

In putting forward such a position, Bush and Blair knowingly invoked a discourse regarding the right to anticipatory war, which is usually the preserve of international lawyers and just war theorists. This chapter examines exactly how Bush and Blair's arguments correspond to this discourse, paying special attention to points of convergence and divergence they share with some of the more seminal articulations of the right to anticipatory war. It is contended that Bush and Blair's arguments suggest a more permissive approach to anticipatory war than is generally accepted within the just war tradition. They urge that a threat may give rise to a right of self-defense even *before that threat has fully materialized*, where previously such a right only arose in the face of a clear and present danger or an *imminent* threat. More specifically, it will be shown that Bush and Blair's case for anticipatory war against Iraq occupies the middle ground between the standard account of preemption suggested by Daniel Webster and found in the legalist paradigm and the classical case for preventive war as represented by the writings of Francis Bacon among others. The primary objective, then, is to achieve some critical purchase on the Washington-London consensus regarding threats and the right of response they give rise to, and to locate this thinking within the framework of the just war tradition.

The first section lays the ground for this discussion by providing an overview of Michael Walzer's seminal treatment of anticipatory war in *Just and Unjust Wars*. It presents the argument that Walzer draws on the writings of Francis Bacon and Thomas Hobbes in revising the legalist paradigm position on anticipation. The end result of this move sees Walzer adopt a standpoint very close to that assumed by the Swiss jurist Emmerich de Vattel in the eighteenth century. The second section outlines Bush and Blair's arguments for anticipatory war against Iraq, and is historical descriptive in form. The third section is more analytical. Its principle concern is Bush and Blair's treatment of the question of how extant or proximate a threat must be before it justifies defensive action. Specifically, it looks to identify what this position has in common with, and where it deviates from, more orthodox or classical just war positions such as those provided by Walzer and the thinkers he draws upon.

Michael Walzer and Anticipatory War

Michael Walzer devotes an entire chapter in *Just and Unjust Wars* to the matter of anticipatory war.[4] The starting point for this discussion is the legalist paradigm, which Walzer presents as a reflection of the consensus view in international society regarding the rights of war and peace. The right to anticipatory war is tightly circumscribed within this framework.

Imminent Threats

According to Walzer, the legalist paradigm defines the right to anticipatory war along the lines of the criteria for national self-defense, as enunciated by the U.S. Secretary of State, Daniel Webster, during the course of the Caroline Affair from 1837 to 1842.[5] This affair began in 1837, when the Caroline, an American ship moored in U.S. waters, was boarded and sunk by British soldiers operating from Canada on the grounds that they suspected the vessel was set to partake in a cross-border raid somewhere along the Niagara River. Lord Ashburton of the British government subsequently defended this action as an instance of legitimate self-defense. Webster famously retorted that this action did not qualify as an act of national self-defense, on the grounds that defensive action must always be a response to "a necessity of self-defense, instant, overwhelming, leaving no choice of means, and no moment for deliberation."[6] Walzer argues that these criteria—necessity and imminence, along with proportionality—circumscribe the right to national defense as it is conventionally understood in international society. These criteria clearly allow some scope for anticipatory action, though only of a very limited preemptive nature. They provide for the possibility that "states can rightfully defend themselves against violence that is imminent but not actual; they can fire the first shots if they know themselves about to be attacked."[7]

Walzer is keen to emphasize the limited nature of this right to anticipatory war. Anticipatory war of a preemptive nature, he writes, "is like a reflex action, a throwing up of one's arms at the very last minute."[8] It would permit us to do little more than respond to an attack once we see it coming but before we feel its impact. In order to illustrate the limited nature of the right to preemptive defense, Walzer locates it on what he calls a spectrum of anticipation. This spectrum provides a powerful conceptual aid for understanding the point at which a threat may be considered to have reached a level of gravity where it justifies defensive action. As Walzer presents the spectrum, it is book-ended by the Caroline standard for preemption at one pole and the classic argument for preventive war at the other.[9] Both of these positions mark different understandings of when a threat may be deemed sufficiently serious to warrant defensive action. Webster's Caroline standard supposes that a right of defense only arises when a threat is truly imminent, and so lies on one end of the spectrum. The argument for preventive war occupies the opposite pole: it assumes that even a threat that is still far off may generate a right to defense on the grounds that one has a *just fear* of attack.

Walzer is not wholly satisfied with the legalist paradigm position, and deems the Caroline standard a defective logic. In particular, he has issues with the notion that a threat must be truly imminent before we may react to it.

Such a formulation is too "restrictive" according to Walzer.[10] It does not equip the threatened state with a proper fighting chance to defend itself. This dissatisfaction prompts Walzer to suggest a revision of the legalist paradigm. He proposes that the point at which a threat is adjudicated to justify defensive action ought to be repositioned on the spectrum of anticipation so as to allow for earlier defensive action. That is, he wishes to recalibrate the right to anticipatory war so that it is more permissive than Webster's tightly circumscribed conception of preemption. In sketching out this position, he sets the legalist paradigm doctrine of preemption against what he terms the classic argument for preventive war, which he associates with the writings of Francis Bacon and Thomas Hobbes and the idea of just fear that they propose. In essence, Walzer draws upon the writings of Bacon and Hobbes in order to highlight the deficiencies in the legalist paradigm position.

Just Fears

The notion of justified fear has a distinguished lineage. Writing in the fifth century BC, Thucydides drew attention to the role played by fear in politics. He identified fear as the universal spring of human action, and the frequent cause of war. Indeed, Thucydides assigns fear a central explanatory role in his celebrated account of the Peloponnesian War. Fear, he writes, was the deeprooted cause underlying that struggle: "What made war inevitable was the growth of Athenian power and the fear this caused in Sparta."[11] Similar themes appear in the writings of Cicero. In *On Duties*, he presents the case that fear, rather than malevolence, often stands at the root of antisocial behavior. He writes, "Those injustices that are purposely inflicted for the sake of harming another often stem from fear; in such cases the one who is thinking of harming someone else is afraid that if he does not do so, he himself will be affected by some disadvantage."[12] Following the demise of both the Greek and Roman Empires, the writings of Thucydides and Cicero fell into a period of neglect, as the scholastic tradition, most commonly associated with Thomas Aquinas, Francisco Vitoria, and Francisco Suarez, entered a period of ascendancy. However, the humanist preoccupation with the role played by fear in politics enjoyed a revival following the Renaissance period. Key to this revival was Alberico Gentili (1552–1608), an Anglo-Italian professor of civil law at Oxford University.

Gentili's writings are deeply grounded in humanism. They treat the normative dimension of statecraft after the Roman fashion, in terms of prudence and a notional balance of power, rather than in a "theological" vain.[13] In particular, they display a reaction against the scholastic orthodoxy that professed that war might be properly understood as a crucible for the determination of questions of guilt and merit. For the scholastics, the right to war presupposes that the side being warred against has earned this treatment on account of some moral guilt on their behalf—hence Vitoria's insistence that just wars can only be fought against an enemy that is "culpable" for some wrongdoing.[14] On this view, there is no justification for anticipatory war. It is never right, Vitoria argues, to commit evil, even to avoid greater evils. "It is quite unacceptable that a person should be killed for a crime he has yet to commit . . . It is not lawful to execute one of our fellow members of the commonwealth for future sins, and therefore it cannot be lawful with foreign subjects either."[15]

Gentili, drawing heavily upon Roman legal sources, casts the matter entirely differently. He likens war to a legal process in which two litigants— two sovereigns—have committed to resolve their differences by means of armed contest.[16] There is no room in this construction for considerations of guilt and culpability, or even of objective justice. According to Gentili, theological concerns should not impinge upon our political judgments.[17] Instead, he is keen to stress how issues of expediency and utility may contribute to the justification of war, and emphasizes fear in this regard. "I call it a useful defense," he writes, "when we make war through fear that we ourselves may be attacked."[18] Lest there is any doubt as to what he means, he adds that states may take defensive action as soon as they have a "just cause for fear," and need not wait, as the scholastics would have it, until an attack is imminent or actually incoming.[19]

Gentili's influence is clearly discernible in the writings of Francis Bacon (1561–1626), a sometimes lawyer, parliamentarian, philosopher, and politician with whom his last days at Oxford coincided. Certainly, Gentili's influence is evident in Bacon's contempt for the "schoolmen" of the scholastic tradition and the emphasis he places on the notion of just fear as a cause for anticipatory war. Bacon set out the basic parameters of the right to anticipatory war in the essays *Of Empire* and *Of Delays*, as well as in his 1624 pamphlet *Considerations Touching Warre with Spain*. The latter piece is the more substantial of the two and was presented by Bacon as a contribution to the pro-war camp in the English court during a period of tense relations with Spain.[20] The pamphlet mostly consists of a scathing critique of the schoolmen's refutation of anticipatory war and their insistence that war can only be undertaken against an enemy guilty of committing some wrongdoing.[21] Bacon insists that such a focus on a precedent assault or injury is wrongheaded, and derived from the schoolmen's misplaced concern with questions of moral guilt and culpability. In a passage that brings to mind Gentili's account of expedient defense in *De Iure Belli Libri Tres*, Bacon denounces the

Scholastic refusal of anticipatory war. He writes, "Some schoolmen, (otherwise reverend men, yet fitter to guide penknives than swords) seem precisely to stand upon it; That every offensive war must be Ultio: A Revenge, that presupposeth a precedent assault or injury."[22] Against this view, he argues, "A just fear will be a just cause of a preventive war; But especially if it be part of the case, that there be a nation, that is manifestly detected to aspire to monarchy and new acquisitions; Then other states (assuredly) cannot be justly accused, for not staying for the first blow."[23]

Citing Gentili's lead, Bacon echoes Demosthenes in scorning those who would refrain from waging preventive wars, comparing such men to "country fellows in a fence school, that never ward till the blow be past."[24] Such an approach is mere foolishness to Bacon's mind: restraint in these matters does nothing to repulse extant threats and serves only to invite disaster. Instead, we must always be prepared to meet some dangers early, before they are imminent.[25] Where the matter at hand is the good of the state, states must not bind themselves to take defensive action only after they have already been struck, but may take anticipatory action as soon as they have good cause to fear that their well-being may be threatened in the foreseeable future. The reason for this is that it is often better to initiate a war (that is sure to come anyway), instead of allowing your opponent to choose the time and place of battle.

Bacon was concerned, however, that the idea of just fear, a highly subjective category, is open to abuse. Bacon cautions that fear can sometimes "dazzle men's eyes [rather] than open them." A suspicious disposition, he writes, may sometimes cloud man's mind and lead him toward paranoia rather than prudence.[26] For these reasons, he argues that a fear based on little more than "umbrages, light jealousies, apprehensions-a-far-off" is never sufficient to give rise to justified war. Rather, what is required is a "clear foresight of imminent danger."[27] But what might count toward clear foresight of an imminent danger?

Bacon mentions three possible examples of what might count toward clear foresight of an imminent danger. The first arises where one state is seen to embark on some self-aggrandizing design that is likely to endanger the balance of power, and, eventually, the well-being of one's own state. Bacon approves in this respect of Antiochus's scheming against the Romans, wherein he pleaded with the allies of Rome "to join with him in a war against them, setteth before him, a just fear, of the overspreading greatness of the Romans, comparing it to a fire that continually took, and spread from kingdom to kingdom."[28]

The second possible example of foresight of imminent danger emphasizes the threat continually posed by states that are, by their very character, hostile or rogue actors. That is, those states that "aspire to great monarchies, and to seek upon all occasions to enlarge their dominions" are always to be regarded as a source of danger, as Bacon argues the Turks were in his day. "In deliberations of war against the Turk," he writes, "it hath been often, with great judgment, maintained: That Christian princes and states have always a sufficient ground of invasive war against the Enemy; not for the cause of religion but upon a just fear."[29] The Turkish Empire, Bacon explains, is fundamentally hostile to Christian states and princes and so must always be regarded as a threat to their well-being (even in what we nominally term times of peace). There are obvious parallels here to the recent proclivity of the U.S. government to label certain states, such as Iraq, as rogue states.

The third instance refers to occasions where states are observed committing acts perceived to be hostile to one's state. What kind of actions does Bacon have in mind? He suggests that we might consider any form of navy blockade, trade disruptions, military mobilizations, or alliance building as indication enough that a state poses a threat that warrants some response.[30] Additionally, he would include the historical record of a state when assessing whether or not precipitate action should be undertaken against it. Thus, he argues that Spain's catalogue of attempted aggressions against England (going back to 1588 and the Spanish Armada) must count toward considering Spain an imminent danger to England in 1624.[31]

Ultimately, Bacon understands the right of anticipatory war to hinge on the question of whether or not a state has reasonable grounds to suppose that it might be threatened in the foreseeable future—that is, whether or not it has a justified fear of some potential future threat. As we have seen, he attaches the condition of imminent danger to this formulation, but it is so vaguely applied as to do little more than rule out wars fought on the basis of minor anxieties rather than proper, substantive fears. Further, when it comes to fleshing out what might be considered reasonable grounds for such fears, Bacon is very loose and permissive. He speaks in terms of the balance of power, and suggests that states can fear other actors on the basis of their actions or on the grounds of their hostile or rogue character. In supplying these examples, however, he is not so concerned with circumscribing the idea of just fear, but of providing examples of how we might understand it. Thus, these examples are not definitive; they are only intended to give the reader a sense of what Bacon means by the idea of just fear. Still, Bacon does provide at least some sense of what kind of a threat might give rise to a right to defensive action. This is clearly a permissive statement in favor of anticipatory war that makes much of the notion of fear, although it does insist that fear must always be grounded in observable phenomena in the international sphere if it is to give rise to a right to defensive war.

Unknown Unknowns

The next key figure to treat the notion of just fear was Thomas Hobbes (1588–1679). Born in his own words as a "twin of fear" in the year that the Spanish Armada set sail for England, Hobbes was deeply unsettled throughout his whole life by the political turmoil that marked seventeenth-century Europe.[32] He devoted his working days to understanding (and theorizing how we might escape from) the political conditions that gave rise to such unrest. Interestingly, he knew Bacon quite well, having been closely acquainted with him in the 1620s, the period when Bacon was strongly aligned with the pro-war camp in the court of King James. It is thought that Bacon's writings were a major influence upon Hobbes during this period.[33] Hobbes's frequent allusion to the notion of just fear supports this view.

Hobbes relates the notion of just fear to the right of both individuals and states to ensure their own security. He took as his starting point Hugo Grotius's thesis that the foundation of human order and morality is the right of every person and every state to ensure their own self-preservation.[34] According to Grotius (1583–1645), the whole schema of natural law is built upon and derives from this right. What form, then, did the right to self-preservation take for Grotius? He conceived of the right in rather restrictive terms, such that it permitted individuals and states the right to forceful defense only in those cases where the threat was imminent or, in his words, "present, and as it were, contained in a point."[35] Hobbes, as we shall see, endorsed Grotius's thesis that the right to self-preservation is foundational to human order, but rejected his narrow understanding of what that right entails.

Hobbes writes in *Leviathan* that the first natural right is the "liberty each man hath, to use his own power, as he will himself, for the preservation of his own nature; that is to say, of his own life; and consequently, of doing any thing, which in his own judgment, and Reason, he shall conceive to be the aptest means thereunto."[36] However, where Grotius understood the right to self-preservation to provide a solid and unproblematic basis for morality, Hobbes perceived it to give rise to another set of challenges. Despite our initial agreement regarding the general right of self-preservation, Hobbes contends, there is still no common understanding as to what this right might entail and when it applies. Though all men afford one another a notional right of self-preservation, they may still disagree as to what it might sanction in a concrete situation. The problem, as Hobbes puts it in *De Cive*, is that men may agree on the right of self-preservation in principle, but can reach no consensus on what it might properly entail in practice. In the end, then, each man must act as his *own judge* and determine what constitutes a threat to his well-being and what the right to self-preservation permits him to do in response.[37] The quest for survival is, then, bound to subjective reasoning regarding what might constitute a threat to oneself. This formula studiously leaves open the possibility that an individual may rightfully resort to defensive action on the basis of little more than a "just fear" of some distant threat—so long as he or she *perceives* that it is necessary to their self-preservation.[38]

The implications of this position are far-reaching. If every person is entitled to interpret the right to self-preservation as he or she sees fit, the effect of this must be "almost the same as if there were no right at all."[39] In other words, the right to self-preservation translates into a "right of all men to all things" and thus becomes a mockery of itself.[40] As a result of this, man's natural condition is one of struggle and conflict; a war of all against all, as Hobbes would have it.[41]

Hobbes extends the same reasoning to the international realm, allowing states an unfettered right to self-preservation and all that they deem necessary to this end. Given the anarchic nature of international politics, which Hobbes famously depicts as a perpetual state of war, this is a prescription for a far-reaching right to anticipatory war.[42] The logic is simple: where states coexist in a pre-civil state of nature such as the international realm, without the security provided by a higher authority, they must provide for their own self-preservation. Thus they possess a license to resort to force whenever they deem it necessary and in whatever way they see fit (just as the individual would before the institution of civil society). In other words, claim of a justified fear of some impending assault or injury provides states with a warrant to ensure their own survival by whatever means necessary. This reasoning easily leads to anticipatory war: from "diffidence of one another, there is no way for any man to secure himself, so reasonable, as Anticipation; that is, by force, or wiles, to master the persons of all men he can, so long, till he see no other power great enough to endanger him."[43] In a nutshell, given that there is no escaping the subjectivity of security calculations, the prince may rightly resort to precipitate action on behalf of his state in those cases where he *perceives* a potential challenge to the state's well-being or survival.[44] The key, then, for Hobbes, like Bacon and Gentili before him, is that states possess a right to anticipatory war where they have a "just fear" of potential injury or assault.[45]

There is a sharp radical edge to Hobbes's views on wars undertaken on the basis of just fear. This point relates to the fact that the logic of the Hobbesian state of nature (as it exists in the international realm) actually serves to generate fears. In the international state of nature, as previously noted, princes construct their own understanding of what constitutes a threat and act on the basis of this understanding. The attentive prince must always, however, be aware that his knowledge of the world is partial and limited. Consequently, he must always be plagued by the fear that there may well exist, unawares to him, extant threats to his society of which he has never even conceived. Thus, fear for Hobbes, as Michael Williams writes, is "not reducible solely to a fear of the potential actions of others. It is constituted by a more fundamental fear of the unknown—and in some basic ways unknowable—nature of reality as a whole."[46] The former U.S. Secretary of Defense, Donald Rumsfeld, provided a fine example of this reasoning in June 2002 when he told a NATO press conference of the possibility of threats that he considered "unknown unknowns."[47] This kind of reasoning is mired in a paranoid mindset that drives decision-makers to act on the basis of imagined future scenarios rather than current circumstances. The result is a self-fulfilling prophecy. As Williams writes, "Acting within the logic of worst-case scenarios, Hobbesian individuals [and states] create an anarchic state of nature in part out of their fear of future harm rather than their calm appraisal of current realities."[48] In light of this, Hobbes's acceptance that a just fear might give rise to a grounds for war is a surrender to the perception of the international realm as a constant state of war of all against all: given the "condition of epistemological indeterminacy" that marks the state of nature, fear must be an ever-present and self-perpetuating reality.[49]

In conclusion, although Hobbes developed Bacon's idea of just fear as a basis for war, he was ultimately quite skeptical of the idea that there can be such a thing in international affairs as a distinct and identifiable moment of just fear. Rather, Hobbes perceived the international realm as an arena of uncertainty where (just) fear is the constant state. This conclusion effectively negates the very idea of just war that assumes the possibility of some limited peace in international affairs—something approximating Augustine's *tranquillitas ordinas*. Hobbes's position, by contrast, denies the possibility of peace and stresses the ontological primacy of war in the international realm. Where the spectrum of anticipation is concerned, his thoughts on the matter of how proximate or extant a threat must be to provide grounds for a right to defensive war are clearly more radical than Bacon's. Yet a wide gulf separates even Bacon's position from the legalist paradigm commonplace.

Toward the Middle Ground

Walzer advises that the classic argument for preventive war is a pernicious logic to accept in the condition of international anarchy. Not only does it set the bar too low for the recourse to force, thereby tempting states to solve their problems by military rather than diplomatic means, it also fails to recognize the gravity of the decision to resort to force in the first place.[50] Yet if the classic argument for preventive war is too generous in its assessment of how proximate a threat must be to generate a right to defensive action, the legalist paradigm doctrine of preemption errs in the opposite direction. It is too restrictive and subsequently fails to provide for a meaningful right to self-defense. Bacon's classic argument for preventive war, although too extreme, provides an interesting contrast to such unreasonable conservatism, according to Walzer. He subsequently treats it as a dialectical counterpoint to the overly restrictive legalist paradigm doctrine of preemption. Adopting Bacon's commitment to a meaningful right to self-defense as his antithetical point of departure, Walzer seeks to "edge along" the spectrum of anticipation, in the direction of the middle ground, until he finds the *point* where a threat is sufficiently substantive to be objectively verifiable.[51]

Walzer's assumption is that this *point*, wherever it lies on the spectrum, will provide the most finely attuned marker of the moment at which a threat is sufficiently extant to justify defensive action. By proceeding in this manner, Walzer virtually ensures that this point will be located in the middle ground between the legalist paradigm doctrine of preemption and Bacon's position. This is the same vicinity that Grotius, the German jurist Samuel Pufendorf (1632–94), and the Swiss jurist Emmerich de Vattel (1714–67) occupy.

Pufendorf states quite categorically in *Of the Law of Nature and of Nations* that "fear alone does not suffice as a just reason for war unless we determine with a morally evident certitude that there is an intention to hurt us."[52] Although an "uncertain suspicion of danger" may furnish a state with grounds for defensive armament or mobilization, "it cannot create a right [to] be the first to bring force to bear." For as long as the state that is the object of fear has not taken deliberate action against another, and is not found to be obviously preparing to do so, it must be granted the benefit of the doubt and left unhindered.[53] This line of thought explicitly rejects the notion of just fear as a basis for war, refutes Hobbesian skepticism, and restores a narrower conception of the right to self-defense to center-stage. Both Grotius and Vattel also differentiated themselves from Francis Bacon's classic argument for preventive war by refusing to sanction wars fought to counter a neighbor's "augmentation." Vattel concedes that while nations ought to be wary where their neighbors appear to be augmenting their power, this by itself is never a sufficient ground for war.[54] Grotius is equally firm on this matter. "The Dread of our Neighbour's encreasing Strength," he writes, "is not a warrantable Ground for making War upon him."[55] Uncertain fears, he argues, never provide a sound basis for waging war. However, despite rejecting Bacon's argument relating to augmentation, Grotius and Vattel both concur with his more general point that states need not wait until a threat is right upon them before they take defensive action. Both concede the possibility of anticipation in cases where the putative danger is still some way off in the "distance," and in this way maneuver themselves toward the middle ground on the spectrum.[56] The manner in which they formulate and set out this position is instructive when it comes to understanding Walzer's revised standpoint.

Vattel and Grotius both contend that for a threat to give rise to a right to defense, it must reflect *both* an *intention* to injure as well as the *capacity* to do so. Vattel puts it succinctly when he writes, "Power alone does not constitute a threat of injury; the will to injure must accompany the power."[57] In a similar vein, Grotius argues that a threat sufficient to give rise to a right of defense must comprise "not only forces sufficient, but a full *Intention* to injure."[58] That is, only where both intention and capability are present might a potential antagonist be deemed to constitute a threat to the security of its neighbors, thereby furnishing any nation in its line of fire with a right to anticipatory self-defense. Grotius is content to rest his discussion of anticipation here, but Vattel recognizes the difficulty inherent in any category relating to the knowledge of another state's intentions. He subsequently looks to devise a list of indicators that may be taken as evidence of hostile intentions on the part of another nation.

The first indicator occurs where another state is observed making "preparations" for undertaking aggressive maneuvers.[59] There is no question, Vattel states, but that a prince is "clearly entertaining designs of oppression and conquest if he betrays his plans by preparations or other advances."[60] We are at liberty to interpret a neighboring prince's designs as hostile when, "in the midst of a profound peace," he looks to construct "fortresses upon our frontier, fits out a fleet, increases his troops, assembles a powerful army, [and] fills his magazines."[61] This requirement would seem to correspond quite closely to Bacon's suggestion that a state might more easily be considered a threat if it has already taken some steps toward preparing an act of aggression.

Second, echoing Bacon again, Vattel suggests that the case against a state making such preparations be further strengthened where the state in question is reputed to be of dubious moral character. The restraints are loosened and the calculus shifted in favor of anticipatory war when we are dealing with what we today call rogue states. These are states that Vattel classifies as "restless and unprincipled nation[s], ever ready to do harm to others, to thwart their purposes, and to stir up civil strife among their citizens."[62] As examples of such states, he suggests Philip II's Spain, and Louis XIV's France. Faced by the prospect of such a state increasing its power or offensive capabilities, one must assume the intentionality of the threat and the presumption in favor of anticipatory war is strengthened to such an extent that justification of such a war is almost a formality.[63]

To this, Vattel adds one further criterion that does not relate to either power or intention. This final criterion refers instead to an admixture of the probability and gravity of the threat. "One is justified in forestalling a danger," Vattel writes, "in direct ratio to the degree of probability attending it, and to the seriousness of the evil with which one is threatened."[64] If the evil in question is only trivial or likely to be relatively inconsequential, Vattel elaborates, there is no cause for prompt action. However, if the "safety of the State" is at stake, states acquire greater license to act early. On those occasions where it is "impossible or too dangerous to wait" until the threat is truly upon us, states may reasonably resort to anticipatory action.[65]

Sufficient Threat

Returning to Walzer's quest to locate the point at which a threat ought to generate a right to self-defense, we might fairly say that he eventually reaches a position very close to Vattel's. Indeed, he cites Vattel's discussion of the Spanish Succession approvingly, even going so far as to validate Vattel's rejection of Bacon's argument regarding augmentation.[66] Augmentation, Walzer claims, is not necessarily an indicator of political design or intent to threaten on the part of the growing power, and therefore any war fought on that basis must be considered premature and morally problematic. There is a great difference, Walzer tells us, "between killing and being killed by soldiers who may or may not represent a distant danger to our country." He continues, "In the first case, we confront an army recognizably hostile, ready for war, fixed in a posture of attack. In the second, the hostility is prospective and imaginary, and it will always be a charge against us that we have made war upon soldiers who were themselves engaged in entirely legitimate (nonthreatening) activities. Hence the moral necessity of rejecting any attack that is merely preventive in character, that does not wait upon and respond to the willful acts of an adversary."[67] Walzer thus makes it clear that anticipatory war is only justified in instances where the emergence of a serious and objectively verifiable threat is evidenced in the "willful acts of an adversary."[68] Elaborating upon this, he adds that "the line between legitimate and illegitimate first strikes is not going to be drawn at the point of imminent attack but at the point of *sufficient threat*."[69]

The notion of sufficient threat is a vague formulation—and Walzer acknowledges as much—but it is intended to convey three criteria for legitimate self-defense and anticipation. First, one's enemy must display a manifest intent to injure. Second, one's enemy must have undertaken a degree of preparation that renders their intent a positive danger. Third, the enemy's actions must have created a situation in which waiting, or doing anything other than fighting, exposes one's state to grave peril and magnifies the risk.[70] Walzer spells out the implications of these revised criteria. He writes, "Instead of previous signs of rapacity and ambition, current and particular signs are required; instead of an 'augmentation of power', actual preparation for war; instead of the refusal of future securities, the intensification of present dangers. Preventive war looks to the past and future, Webster's reflex action to the immediate moment, while the idea of being under a threat focuses on what we had simply best call the *present*. I cannot specify a time span; it is a span within which one can still make choices, and within which it is possible to feel straitened."[71]

This position is remarkably similar to that formulated by Vattel. Indeed, the phraseology in the passage just cited is drawn from book III of *The Law of Nations of the Principles of Nature*.[72] The only point on which Walzer deviates from Vattel is the matter of "previous signs of rapacity and ambition": where Vattel considers them relevant to whether or not defense is justified in a given instance, Walzer would rather discount them. In all other respects, Walzer's views on the moment at which a threat ought to generate a right to self-defense are almost perfectly aligned with Vattel's thoughts on anticipatory war.

In Walzer's own words, this position suggests a "major revision" of the legalist paradigm, for it means that a threat sufficient to generate a right of defense can be manifested not only in the absence of a military attack or invasion but even in the (probable) absence of any immediate intention to launch such an attack. The general formula is presented thus: "States may use military force in the face of threats of war, whenever the failure to do so would seriously risk their territorial integrity or political independence."[73]

Bush, Blair, and the Case of Iraq

In the course of making a case for anticipatory war against Iraq in early 2002 to March 2003, President Bush and Prime Minister Blair engaged very energetically with the core issues at stake in the literature just surveyed. In putting forward a justification for what was variously described as a preventive or preemptive war, Bush and Blair pressed for a new approach to how we understand and deal with threats in the new security environment ushered in by the events of September 11, 2001. While this move comprises a major development in both British and American foreign policy that extends well beyond any one specific case, it was almost entirely presented in the context of the war in Iraq. The nature of the threat posed by Iraq, Bush and Blair advised, was like nothing known before. On its own terms it required urgent attention, but it also highlighted the need for a revised understanding of what constitutes a threat sufficiently serious to give rise to a right to self-defense.

This section will unpack Bush and Blair's justifications for anticipatory war against Iraq with a view to locating their position on the question of how extant a threat need be to justify defensive action relative to the literature surveyed previously in the chapter. It submits that Bush and Blair's justifications for anticipatory war against Iraq may be understood as a challenge to the conventional understanding of the right to national self-defense in international society. Despite being couched in the terminology of the Caroline standard, Bush and Blair's justifications present a more permissive account of the right to anticipatory war than is to be found in either the legalist paradigm or even Walzer's revised notion of sufficient threat. In order to appreciate the innovation proposed by way of these subtle maneuvers, we must first summarize the justifications as they were put forward by Bush and Blair. When this summary is complete, we can turn to examining the precise nature of the innovations proposed by Bush and Blair.

Bush and Blair's justification for anticipatory war against Iraq was predicated upon the representation of Saddam Hussein's regime as a rogue actor and a "grave and growing danger" or threat to America and its allies, as well as to international peace and security more generally.[74] This understanding was nurtured by both Bush and Blair throughout the course of 2002 and in the early months of 2003, as they sought to characterize Iraq as just the sort of threat that both required and justified anticipatory action. Iraq, they claimed, gathered the dangers of weapons of mass destruction (WMD), rogue states, and global terrorism all "in one place."[75] This, Bush argued, provided cause for concern on two counts. In the first place, should Iraq acquire a nuclear bomb, it would be capable of blackmailing other states and pursuing an aggressive agenda without fear of U.S. interference. Secondly, Iraq could transfer whatever WMD it possesses to global terror networks such as al-Qaeda, who would be willing to use them against the United States and its allies.[76]

Bush elaborated on the first of these two concerns in a speech delivered in Cincinnati in October 2002.[77] If Iraq were to obtain a significant stockpile of WMD, he cautioned, it would be capable of pursuing its rogue agenda under the cover of what is often casually referred to as a nuclear shield. A substantial arsenal of WMD would provide Iraq with the means to indulge in nuclear blackmail and retain impunity from U.S. interference. In the words of President Bush, "Saddam Hussein would be in a position to threaten anyone who opposes his aggression. He would be in a position to dominate the Middle East [and] he would be in a position to threaten America."[78] Were Iraq to acquire a nuclear weapon (or a sufficient stockpile of chemical and biological weapons), Bush claimed, it would then possess the capabilities to threaten international peace, and the United States and everyone else would be powerless to do anything about it.

Bush and Blair's second major concern was that Iraq might convey WMD technologies to al-Qaeda, who have stated their intention to use them against the United States and its allies. Bush, in particular, gave voice to this concern on many occasions. For instance, in his 2003 State of the Union address, he expressly claimed that Saddam Hussein's Iraq threatened the United States by virtue of the fact that it was a potential conduit of WMD to terrorist networks intent on attacking America. "Secretly, and without fingerprints, [Saddam] could provide one of his hidden weapons to terrorists, or help them develop their own," Bush warned. "Before September 11th, many in the world believed that Saddam Hussein could be contained. But chemical agents, lethal viruses and shadowy terrorist networks are not easily contained. Imagine those nineteen hijackers with other weapons and other plans—this time armed by Saddam Hussein. It would take one vial, one canister, one crate slipped into this country to bring a day of horror like none we have ever known."[79] This was not the only time Bush issued this warning. On September 12, 2002, he cautioned the United Nations General Assembly of the possibility that Iraq might, in the future, choose to supply WMD to terrorist networks.[80] Just two weeks later, on September 26, he spoke of the possibility that "each passing day could be the one on which the Iraqi regime gives anthrax or VX—nerve gas—or some day a nuclear weapon to a terrorist ally."[81] Blair was also exercised by the fear that Iraq would transfer WMD to terrorist groups. He told the House of Commons on March 18, 2003, that he was concerned that Iraq would supply WMD to "extreme terrorist groups who profess a perverted and false view of Islam."[82]

Despite the tentative nature of these concerns, both Bush and Blair claimed that the perceived threat from Iraq warranted and justified anticipatory military action on their part. "We cannot stand idly by and do nothing while dangers gather," Bush explained to the United Nations General Assembly in September 2002. The threat from Iraq, he claimed, must be confronted.[83] Blair made it very clear to the Trade Union Convention (TUC) delegates present at his Blackpool address that he shared President Bush's stance. He claimed that Britain would be within its rights to take early action aimed at thwarting the threat from Iraq before it materializes into actual hostilities. He warned, "Because I say to you in all earnestness: if we do not deal with the threat from this international outlaw and his barbaric regime, it may not erupt and engulf us this month or next; perhaps not even this year or next. But it will at some point. And I don't want it on my conscience that we knew the threat, saw it coming, and did nothing."[84]

In the face of the threat posed by Saddam Hussein's Iraq, Blair argued that Britain would be better off acting early to head off the threat posed by Iraq, than waiting to see how it develops. Waiting would not prevent war from breaking out, but only defer it to a later date when it is likely to be more destructive. Bush pushed this line of argument quite strongly when addressing Congressional leaders in September 2002: "the dangers we face [from Iraq] will only worsen from month to month and from year to year. To ignore these threats is to encourage them. And when they have fully materialized it may be too late to protect ourselves and our friends and allies."[85] It would make much more sense, Bush argued, to challenge the threat from Iraq before Saddam acquired the bomb: "America must not ignore the threat gathering against us. Facing clear evidence of peril we cannot wait for the final proof— the smoking gun—that could come in the form of a mushroom cloud."[86]

In summary, Iraq was represented by Bush and Blair as constituting a threat which, though not obviously imminent, justified defensive action. The representation of Iraq as such a threat was based, as we have seen, on assumptions regarding Iraqi capabilities and intentions. In turn, these assumptions were premised upon the characterization of Iraq as a rogue state imbued with aggressive designs, the stated belief that Iraq was in the process of acquiring a WMD capability which would serve its aggressive designs, and hypothetical and general fears relating to the possibility that Iraq may one day opt to work in league with terrorist organizations to bring great destruction upon the United States and its allies. Built into this case for conceiving Iraq as a threat is an unorthodox position regarding when a threat justifies the right to defense.

New Threats, New Thinking: Innovation

The arguments presented by Bush and Blair for the timely use of force against Iraq are notable for many reasons, not the least of which is the manner in which they constituted a proposal to broaden the right to anticipatory war in international society. Bush and Blair both contended that the world has changed in the wake of 9/11 and that the conventional doctrine of self-defense no longer suffices in a security environment dominated by the nexus of WMD, rogues states, and terrorism. New threats have emerged that require a fresh approach to the idea of anticipatory war. New threats, as the NSS proposes, require new thinking. What new thinking did Bush and

Blair's arguments offer? Without doubt they represented a departure from the legalist paradigm/Caroline standard position, but what did they propose in its stead? Their case for invading Iraq proposed new thinking concerning what ought to be considered a threat serious enough to justify defensive action. This new thinking comprised three main aspects.

Jettisoning Imminence

The first aspect of this new thinking relates to the manipulation of the Caroline standard, particularly the jettisoning of the imminence requirement. Bush and Blair located their arguments for anticipatory war against Iraq firmly within the frame of Webster's formula.[87] Where Bush is concerned, his staff did most of the talking for him on this issue. National Security Advisor Condoleezza Rice, for example, argued that the position advocated by the Bush administration was consistent with Daniel Webster's "famous defense of anticipatory self-defense."[88] In a similar manner, the White House director of policy planning, Richard Haass, explicitly referenced the Caroline standard when making the case for anticipatory war against Iraq in a speech delivered in January 2003.[89] More directly linked to the president, perhaps, the arguments pertaining to anticipatory war put forward in the NSS wore the idiom of the Caroline standard quite openly. Blair's arguments did likewise.

But if Bush and Blair were willing to anchor their arguments for anticipatory war against Iraq within the Caroline standard, they also sought to innovate upon this framework. In particular, they demonstrated a determination to jettison the notion that a threat must be imminent before it warrants or justifies defensive action. This idea was first floated in relatively moderate terms in the NSS: "We must adapt the concept of imminent threat to the capabilities and objectives of today's adversaries."[90] However, the full extent of this proposed adaptation was made clear by President Bush in an appearance on *Meet the Press* in February 2004. "I believe it is essential that when we see a threat, we deal with those threats before they become imminent," Bush declared. "Its too late if they become imminent."[91] Put simply, Bush's argument amounts to a claim that a threat need no longer be considered imminent before it is deemed sufficiently grave to justify defense. The reasoning behind this position is straightforward: given the nature of today's threats, the category of imminence just does not make any sense. Today's threats do not rely on military mobilization and are not preceded by visible warning signs. As Bush phrased it, "Terrorists and terror states do not reveal . . . threats with fair notice."[92] To insist on the establishment of an imminent threat before sanctioning defensive action would thus be an act of misguided folly that fails to appreciate the unconventional nature of the threats we face today. Across the Atlantic, Blair made a similar case. He suggested that the very idea of trusting in a threat to register as imminent before taking action exposes the world to a "risk" he is not prepared to run. "This is not a time," he argued, "to err on the side of caution; not a time to weigh the risks to an infinite balance."[93] This is a time for early action.

Bush and Blair were both aware of the significance of the position they assumed, and how it runs counter to conventional legal wisdom on the right to self-defense. In Bush's case, the NSS provides solid grounds for this claim. Even as it seeks to undermine the requirement of imminent threat, the NSS concedes that legal scholars have typically "conditioned the legitimacy of preemption on the existence of an imminent threat."[94] Blair also displayed a cognizance of what was at stake. He spoke at Sedgefield in quite sweeping tones of his position on preemption in terms of an attempt to overhaul the traditional Westphalian orthodoxy in international relations.[95] The crux of Bush and Blair's argument, then, rests in the charge that the very nature of the threats we face today means that we can no longer wait for them to register as imminent before taking action; such an approach would mistake suicide for virtue. In this way, their arguments may properly be understood as a proposal to amend the right to anticipatory war by extending it beyond the parameters of the Caroline standard.

Hypothetical Threats

The second notable aspect of Bush and Blair's new thinking follows directly from the jettisoning of the requirement of imminence. It challenges conventional thinking by presenting Iraq as a threat on the basis of little more than vague fears concerning what Iraq could choose to do with WMD *if it were* to acquire them. Both of Bush and Blair's major concerns, relating to the possibility that Iraq might choose to use WMD or even pass such technology onto terrorist networks, reflect a *hypothetical and general* threat and fail to refer to any solid evidence that such occurrences might actually be in process.[96]

Blair's speech at the Lord Mayor's Banquet on November 11, 2002, is typical in this regard. "I have got absolutely no doubt at all that unless we deal with both of these threats they will come together in a deadly form," he told diners. "Terrorism and weapons of mass destruction are linked dangers . . . Iraq has used weapons of mass destruction . . . Just reflect on it and the danger is clear."[97] Blair's Sedgefield speech provides another fine example of this style of argument. Blair took the opportunity at Sedgefield to speak to his constituents about his "fear" that terrorism and WMD might "come together" at some unspecified time in the future.[98] His speech focused specifically on the *possibility* that Saddam Hussein, if left in power, might have someday supplied WMD to a terrorist group. In a speech laden with doomsday scenarios, Blair cautioned, "We know that they [the terrorists] would, if they could, go further and use chemical, biological or even nuclear weapons of mass destruction. We also know that there are groups of people, occasionally states, who will trade the technology and capabilities of such weapons . . . We have been warned by the events of September 11, and we should act on the warning."[99] This argument links Iraq, mentioned earlier in the speech, to global terrorism only in the most hypothetical or contingent manner possible: Blair declared that he feared Iraq might choose to supply WMD to terrorists, but he did not offer any factual basis for supposing that such an event was actually in train.

Such arguments, Neta Crawford points out, ultimately rely on little more than fears.[100] Bush's speech on March 2002 in North Carolina followed the same pattern. In particular, it echoed Blair's stress on hypothetical threats, while drawing attention to the dangers of inaction: "At the same time, the civilized world must take seriously the growing threat of terror on a catastrophic scale. We've got to prevent the spread of weapons of mass destruction, because there is no margin for error and there is no chance to learn from any mistake. The United States and her allies will act deliberately—we'll be deliberate—but inaction is not an option . . . I have made it clear that we will not let the most dangerous regimes in the world team up with killers and, therefore, hold this great nation hostage."[101] This argument, just like Blair's, is based on fears rather than evidence. Apparently, the possibility that Saddam *could* threaten international peace is sufficient for Bush to label Iraq a threat and treat it accordingly.

It is interesting to note, then, that some scholars have compared Bush and Blair's argument in this respect with the classical idea of just fear.[102] Indeed, one can point to a number of occasions upon which Bush and Blair, or their officials, clearly invoked this trope. For instance, in a speech delivered on October 2002, the then National Security Advisor Condoleezza Rice quoted George Shultz's support for the policy of anticipatory war: "If there is a rattlesnake in the yard, you don't wait for it to strike before you take action in self-defense."[103] The parallels with Gentili's assertion that we must always be prepared to "kill a snake as soon as we see one . . . for thus we protect ourselves before it attacks" are striking.[104]

Intentions, Capabilities, and Rogue States

The third notable aspect of Bush and Blair's case for war against Iraq was the manner in which it constructed the threat posed by Iraq. They relied on a complex weave of assumptions concerning Iraqi capabilities and intentions. For most observers, Bush and Blair's focus upon Iraqi WMD reflected an overriding concern with the question of Iraqi capabilities. Yet, their argument that a WMD-armed Iraq would pose a threat to international peace was not based entirely on the assumption that it possessed the capabilities to do so. It was equally as reliant upon the claim that Iraq was a regime animated by hostile intentions as it was upon the supposition that Iraq might someday soon possess the capabilities to threaten international peace. The manner by which Bush and Blair sought to make the case that Iraq was animated by hostile intentions is rather interesting. It rested on two main lines of argument: the first one sought to establish that Iraq was a rogue state that by definition harbored aggressive ambitions, while the second focused on Iraq's alleged acquisition of WMD.

By characterizing Iraq as a rogue state, Bush and his administration effectively, if somewhat obliquely, made the case that Iraq harbored hostile intentions with respect to international peace. Consequently, every time Bush referred to Iraq as a rogue state, he was engaged in ascribing hostile intentions to Iraq.[105] Rogue states are generally considered to be resistant to deterrence and, subsequently, are considered prone to unpredictable and dangerous behavior. [106] The fact that Iraq was considered a rogue state was crucial to certain arguments advocated by Bush. Bush did not claim to be concerned about WMD per se, but by the fear that "Iraq's weapons of mass destruction [were] *controlled by a murderous tyrant* who [had] already used chemical weapons to kill thousands of people."[107] WMD, Bush implied, are only a concern when they fall into the hands of a rogue state, such as Saddam's Iraq.[108] "The fundamental problem with Iraq," he argued, "remains the nature of the regime itself."[109] Blair made a similar argument when facing a Parliamentary Liaison Committee in July 2003. Were Iraq not considered a rogue state, he told his interlocutors, its acquisition of WMD might not be considered such a threat. "You might take a different attitude" to a regime that was "otherwise benign but had WMD," he suggested, than you would to "a regime that was so savage and repressive and had WMD."[110] For Blair, a state's possession of WMD is a concern only when that state is rogue, as he deemed Iraq to be at this time.[111] Jack Straw, Blair's foreign secretary, argued along similar lines in a speech delivered at the International Institute of Strategic Studies, London. He spoke of the need to differentiate between the threat posed by Iraq and other would-be proliferators. No other country, he claimed, "shares Iraq's history of deploying chemical weapons in a war of aggression against a neighbor, or against innocent civilians as part of a genocidal campaign. It is this deadly combination of capability and intent which makes Saddam dangerous."[112] Iraq, one can infer, was considered to pose a threat to international peace only because it possessed *both* the *capabilities* to threaten the international order, by means of its WMD arsenal, and a rogue leadership with a perceived *intent* to do so.

But on what grounds was Iraq deemed a rogue state? Two considerations figured prominently here. The first related to Iraq's historical record of aggression and human rights violations, while the second referred to Saddam's efforts to procure a WMD capability. With respect to the first consideration, Bush and Blair were quite exercised to establish Iraq's rogue status by making much of its back catalog of human rights abuses and violations of international law. To this end, both leaders cited the history of Saddam Hussein's Ba'athist regime, its criminal record, as it were, on numerous occasions in order to establish Iraq's rogue credentials.[113] On almost every occasion that Blair spoke about the threat posed by Iraq, he made reference to Iraq's record of WMD use during the Iran-Iraq war and the repression of the Kurds in the 1980s. Much was also made of Saddam's record of initiating aggressive wars; Blair pointed to Iraq's aggressions against Iran and Kuwait as evidence of Iraq's belligerent nature. His 2002 Blackpool address to the TUC is typical in this regard. Blair took this opportunity to catalog Saddam Hussein's record of violent behavior, in order to support the charge that Iraq was a rogue state. Saddam, he told his audience, "has twice started wars of aggression. Over one million people have died in them. When the weapons inspectors were evicted from Iraq in 1998 there were still enough chemical and biological weapons to devastate the entire Gulf region . . . Uniquely Saddam has used these weapons against his own people, the Iraqi Kurds. Scores of towns and villages were attacked . . . In one attack alone, on the city of Halabja, it is estimated that 5,000 were murdered and 9,000 wounded in this way. All in all in the North around 100,000 Kurds died, according to Amnesty International."[114]

References such as this to what Bush termed the "treacherous history" of Saddam Hussein's Iraq are interesting.[115] They suggest that Iraq's violent past provides a good reason for suspecting it of harboring dastardly designs, marking it out as a rogue state, and treating it accordingly.[116] Inferring hostile intentions from a state's criminal record in this manner is a fraught issue, as suggested in the first section. Although Bacon and Vattel were willing to countenance such inferences, Walzer explicitly disavowed them. On this specific issue (as indeed more generally), Bush and Blair's arguments are rather more permissive than Walzer's position, but fall in line with Bacon and Vattel's practice.

With respect to the second consideration, Bush and Blair also consistently argued that Saddam Hussein's Iraq was in the process of making preparations for war. These preparations, they argued, established the proof of Iraqi hostile intentions beyond any doubt and, by extension, copper-fastened Iraq's status as a rogue state. Hence Bush and Blair's repeated assertions that Iraq was racing to develop a WMD arsenal, and particularly a nuclear capability. Vice President Dick Cheney gave the clearest expression of this argument. Speaking to the Veterans of Foreign Wars in August 2002, he stated, "The Iraqi regime has in fact been very busy enhancing its capabilities in the field of chemical and biological agents. And they continue to pursue the nuclear program they began so many years ago. These are not weapons for the purpose of defending Iraq; these are offensive weapons for the purpose of inflicting death on a massive scale, developed so that Saddam can hold the threat over the head of anyone he chooses, in his own region or beyond."[117] Additionally, Colin Powell's crucial February 2003 presentation to the UN Security Council amounted to an extended elaboration of Iraq's alleged preparations for aggression, including its connections with terrorist organizations as well as its development and concealment of WMD.[118] The fact that doubts have been cast on the veracity of these claims does not alter the fact that the Bush administration considered this kind of material relevant to the case for war against Iraq.

Bush and Blair's Proposal for Innovation Reviewed

In many ways, Bush and Blair's thoughts regarding when a threat justifies the right to defense are quite close to Walzer's position of sufficient threat. Like Walzer, they reject the requirement of imminence and contend that a state should possess the right to act in the time span wherein "one can still make choices, and within which it is possible to feel straitened."[119] They also contend that the assessment of any given threat must be based on capabilities *and* intentions, rather than capabilities alone. Yet Bush and Blair's approach is looser in terms of how it reaches the conclusion that a state is a rogue state and therefore animated by hostile intentions. Unlike Walzer, but in line with Vattel and Bacon, Bush and Blair take into consideration the moral history or criminal record of a state when contemplating whether it poses a threat or not. Walzer is explicit on this matter that the past actions of states should not condemn it in the present, as the past should have no place in our thinking on current matters of war and peace. Bush and Blair, however, were insistent in their representation of Iraq as a rogue state with hostile intentions and a delinquent past. In this respect, then, Bush and Blair were more permissive than Walzer. They were also more permissive than Walzer in their amenability to consequentialist reasoning and the language of risk. While Walzer displays caution when it comes to waging war on the basis of probabilities and projected risks, Bush and Blair embrace this form of reasoning. Their reliance on what I have referred to as hypothetical and general fears only underscores this lean toward Bacon's end of the spectrum, though perhaps where they end up is closest to Vattel's notion of prudential statecraft. In terms of the spectrum, Bush and Blair's position, then, might aptly be described as lying just beyond Vattel's position on Bacon's end of the continuum. This represents quite the departure from the legalist paradigm (Caroline standard) position.

Conclusion

The point of departure for this chapter was the observation that in the course of making a case for anticipatory war against Iraq, Bush and Blair engaged very energetically with the problematic of the limits of national self-defense. Over the course of putting forward a case for what was variously described as either a preemptive or a preventive war against Iraq, both leaders highlighted the need for a revised understanding of what constitutes a threat sufficiently serious to give rise to a right to self-defense, and pressed for a new approach to dealing with threats in the security environment ushered in by the events of September 11, 2001. In engaging with these issues, Bush and Blair tapped into the centuries-old just war discourse regarding when a threat is proximate or serious enough to justify self-defense.

This raises the question of how Bush and Blair's arguments correspond to just war thinking on the right to anticipatory war. This chapter has contended that Bush and Blair promoted a very lenient doctrine of anticipatory war that significantly lowered the threshold for the recourse to force, at least relative to the legalist paradigm. Working on the basis that the nature of threat facing the world in the wake of the terrible events of September 11, 2001, is radically different to anything known before, Bush and Blair articulated a right to anticipatory war that is substantially more permissive than Daniel Webster's oft-quoted Caroline standard. Indeed, Bush and Blair's position is also more permissive than Walzer's revised notion of sufficient threat, falling somewhere between Vattel's middle ground and the point of just fear on the spectrum of anticipation. This is an interesting development for it suggests a broader and more far-reaching conception of the right to war than is typically recognized in international law and twentieth century just war thought. In conclusion, this chapter has examined the interface between Bush and Blair's justifications for anticipatory war against Iraq and the just war tradition. It has presented the case that Bush and Blair's justificatory reasoning represents a clear engagement with the just war tradition, serving to innovate upon it. Chapter 3 will turn to Bush and Blair's justifications for punitive war against Iraq, with a view to exploring whether they betray a similar logic.

CHAPTER 3

Punitive War: Enforcing the Law and Ridding the World of Evil

Introduction[1]

The practice of punitive war, or wars of punishment, is a subject that typically meets with a stony silence in recent just war tradition.[2] Indeed, as Chapter 1 has demonstrated, for much of the twentieth century, a legalist approach to the jus ad bellum held sway, whereby the right to war was defined almost exclusively in terms of the right of states to resist aggression.[3] Accordingly, the very idea of punitive war was discredited, even scorned by latter-day theorists.[4] It may be surprising, then, to realize that in the wake of September 11, 2001, the notion of punitive war has acquired a certain currency among a number of contemporary just war theorists, Jean Bethke Elshtain and Oliver O'Donovan chief among them. Even more surprisingly, perhaps, the notion of punitive war figured prominently in the justifications President Bush and Prime Minister Blair offered for the invasion of Iraq and the overthrow of Saddam Hussein's regime. Punishment was clearly not the only justification they offered for this military action, or even the main one. Bush and Blair also advanced justifications relating to anticipatory war (see Chapter 2) and humanitarianism (see Chapter 4), which attracted more attention and comment, but punishment was certainly present, and it was important.[5] This chapter examines the arguments pertaining to punitive war against Iraq as presented by Bush and Blair in order to acquire some understanding of the departure they represent (or signal) from the legalist paradigm.

This chapter argues that the contemporary accounts of punitive war advanced by Bush and Blair do not relate or correspond to the legalist conception of just war, at least not in any robust sense. Rather, the train of these arguments calls to mind certain classical articulations of the jus ad bellum.

This indicates the possibility that the classical just war tradition may provide a point of reference to aid our examination of the punitive "turn" apparent in both the recent just war literature and Bush and Blair's justifications for invading Iraq. This chapter explores these linkages. With this end in mind, any common grammar, points of contact, and parallels between Bush and Blair's arguments on the one hand, and classic expressions of the just war on the other, will be examined.

The outline of this chapter is as follows. The first section reviews the recent punitive turn in just war literature, paying special attention to the writings of Jean Bethke Elshtain and Oliver O'Donovan. It suggests that their revival of the language of punishment has been mirrored in Bush and Blair's justifications for the invasion of Iraq. The second section examines this possibility by focusing upon how the discourse of punishment figured in Bush and Blair's justificatory rhetoric in the run-up to war in March 2003. It submits that two distinct approaches to punishment, both connected by Bush and Blair to the premise that there was a just cause for invading Iraq, can be discerned in their rhetoric: the first relates to punishment as a means of law enforcement, while the second relates to the punishment of evil. The third section explores whether these approaches to punishment have any parallels within the classic just war tradition. Just like Chapter 2, then, this chapter is concerned to locate Bush and Blair's justifications for the invasion of Iraq within the just war tradition, and to explore the nature of this engagement.

The Punitive Turn in Just War Literature

It makes sense to begin our discussion with the most recent literature on this subject. Oliver O'Donovan's latest book, *The Just War Revisited*, purports to reexamine the just war tradition in light of the War on Terror and the tragedy of September 11. Building upon a neoscholastic foundation, he attempts to recast the jus ad bellum as a "praxis of judgment," essentially an updating of the Pauline idea that the prince must act as the minister of God to execute His wrath upon the evildoers.[6] He states that any account of the just war must flow out from the central proposal that armed conflict is to be "re-conceived as an extra-ordinary extension of ordinary acts of judgment."[7] War, in this view, is an extension into the international sphere of governmental responsibility for the maintenance of law and order. As such, it ought to reflect the very same processes and norms that are enacted on a daily basis in courtrooms and magistrate's offices across the land. Such an account suggests, firstly, that conflict can be "brought within the scope of the authority on which government may normally call, and, secondly, that it can be undertaken in such a manner as to establish justice."[8] Of course, this is a rather expansive conception of the just war. It betrays a "natural law rather than a positive law orientation," and proposes that states might have responsibility for, and jurisdiction over, other communities.[9] It is certainly more expansive than the legalist paradigm that O'Donovan laments as an emaciated reading of justice and war. The primary argument running through *The Just War Revisited* amounts to a call for a reorientation of the just war tradition away from the legalist paradigm and back toward some recognition of the praxis of judgment. Such a proposal explicitly promotes the "recovery of the penal attitude." This recovery, if achieved, would once again identify punitive war as the paradigmatic just war.[10]

Besides O'Donovan's work, the other major original contribution to just war tradition in recent years is Jean Bethke Elshtain's *Just War against Terror: The Burden of American Power in a Violent World.* Just as O'Donovan seeks to revive the neoscholastic approach, Elshtain sets out her stall in Augustinian terms. Not only does she trace the origins of the just war tradition back to Saint Augustine, but she articulates a vision of the role of government that is derived from the Bishop of Hippo's theological framework. She writes that the primary responsibility of government is the same today as it was in the days of Rome: to provide for basic security and ordinary civic peace.[11] More revealingly, Elshtain also draws on the Pauline refrain that the prince is the minister of God in support of her claim that the act of governing is a godly vocation. In Elshtain's words, the duty of government is a "solemn responsibility for which there is a divine warrant."[12] This charge may sometimes extend to the punishment of wrongdoers by means of warfare. In Elshtain's words, "St. Paul claims that earthly dominion has been established to serve God and to benefit all human beings. It is the rightful authority of earthly kings and kingdoms to punish wrongdoers."[13] Indeed, so far as Elshtain is concerned, the Pauline refrain, and the Christian tradition of which it is a part, informs us that "government is instituted by God." This does not mean that "every government and every government official is godly, but rather that he or she is charged with a solemn responsibility for which there is a divine warrant."[14] In line with this, the just war tradition "offers a way to exercise that responsibility."

The accounts of just war presented by O'Donovan and Elshtain go far beyond the twentieth century legalist commonplace. Both authors look past the strictures of aggression and self-defense when formulating their views on the right to war, and are prepared to take account of a much broader moral picture. Crucially, the imperative of punishment is central to both of these contemporary restatements of the idea of the just war. But what is meant by punishment here? Most of us have some intuitive understanding of punishment associated with incarceration, jailhouses, gallows, and courtrooms, yet if we are to understand President Bush and Prime Minister Blair's arguments relating to punitive war, we need a more informed account of punishment than this. This chapter presents two different conceptions of punishment and relates them both to Bush and Blair's case for war against Iraq, relating this in turn to Elshtain's and O'Donovan's arguments and the just war tradition more generally. The first conception of punishment relates to the function of law enforcement while the second is attached to the idea of evil, and the imperative to punish it wherever we may find it. Both conceptions of punishment figured prominently in the justifications Bush and Blair offered for the invasion of Iraq, as the next section will demonstrate.

Bush and Blair's Punitive War against Iraq

The first understanding of punishment is closely related to the idea of law enforcement and is best understood as a complex of higher-order and lower-order goals. The lower-order goals comprise its functional aims, or internal logic. With this in mind, we might refer to retribution, deterrence, and rehabilitation as the standard lower-order goals of punishment. The issue of higher-order goals is more complex. They relate more broadly to the purpose that the practice of punishment serves in the social order. In this respect, we understand the practice of punishment as effectively fulfilling a dual function: it serves to reaffirm the integrity of societal laws and norms and encourages compliance with them. In a word, the practice of punishment provides a means of law enforcement and, in so doing, contributes toward upholding the social order.[15]

Law Enforcement

The idea of punishment, understood in these terms, is clearly present in the justificatory reasoning with which Bush and Blair chose to legitimate the invasion of Iraq. The war, they told us, was fought as a means of law enforcement, of holding Iraq to account for its violations of international law and the writ of the United Nations. Bush and Blair premised their arguments for invading Iraq on the charge that Iraq had violated numerous UN Security Council resolutions pertaining to WMD. As Lori Fisler Damrosch and Bernard Oxman, the editors of the *American Journal of International Law*, argue, the case for war against Iraq focused on Iraq's "flouting of numerous compulsory resolutions of the United Nations Security Council (UNSC) concerning de-militarization and disarmament between 1991 and 2003."[16] Bush and Blair pressed the case quite forcefully that Iraq must be punished for its indiscretions and criminal defiance of these resolutions, so that international law and the UN system might be reaffirmed and vindicated. If Iraq escaped punishment for its misdeeds, the credibility of international law and the whole UN system would be plunged into doubt. This war, then, would serve to vindicate and uphold the integrity of international law by censuring one of its most egregious violators—Iraq under Saddam Hussein.

Bush and Blair repeatedly called on the Security Council to uphold the inviolability of its own resolutions and prevent them from becoming dead letters by punishing Iraq—a major violator of these resolutions.[17] As Bush saw it, when the UN eventually failed in this regard, it was left to the United States and its allies to step in and preserve whatever scant authority Security Council resolutions still possessed by enforcing them unilaterally. "Last September I went to the UN General Assembly and urged the nations of the world to unite and bring an end to this danger [posed by Iraq and its WMD]," Bush claimed. "On November 8th, the Security Council unanimously passed Resolution 1441, finding Iraq in material breach of its obligations and vowing serious consequences if Iraq did not fully and immediately disarm. Today, no nation can possibly claim that Iraq has disarmed . . . Yet, some permanent members of the Security Council have publicly announced they will veto any resolution that compels the disarmament of Iraq. These governments share our assessment of the danger, but not our resolve to meet it . . . The United Nations Security Council has not lived up to its responsibilities, so we will rise to ours."[18]

Blair echoed this argument in his address to the House of Commons the following day. "To pass Resolution 1441 and then refuse to enforce it," he claimed, "would do the most deadly damage to the UN's future strength, confirming it as an instrument of diplomacy but not of action, forcing nations down the very unilateralist path we wish to avoid."[19] He lamented the UN's failure to enforce its own writ, and pledged that Britain, along with the United States, would now act on its behalf.

This argument that UN resolutions pertaining to Iraq's WMD must be enforced, by military means if necessary, was regularly espoused by Bush and Blair both before and after fighting broke out in Iraq. Blair argued on numerous occasions that the legal basis for military action in Iraq was UN Security Council Resolution 1441 and that Britain "went to war to enforce UN resolutions."[20] Before the war began, Bush publicly warned Saddam Hussein that "the demands of the UN Security Council must be followed . . . These requirements will be met, or they will be enforced."[21] Bush's national security advisor, Condoleezza Rice, also sought to justify war in Iraq by reference to Iraq's record of flouting UN resolutions. She claimed that "the Iraqi regime's violations of every condition set forth by the UN Security Council for the 1991 cease-fire fully justifies, legally and morally, the enforcement of those conditions."[22] If we refer back to earlier comments concerning the role punishment fulfills in society—reaffirming the integrity of the law and enforcing compliance with it—we might note that it is actually quite similar to the function Bush and Blair stated that the use of force would fulfill in Iraq.

The language of punishment seems even more apt when we consider exactly how, according to Bush and Blair, invading Iraq would contribute toward reaffirming the integrity of international law and enforcing compliance with it. Here, Bush and Blair appealed to the various logics of deterrence, retribution, and rehabilitation—the lower-order goals of punishment. For instance, Blair spoke the language of deterrence on the eve of war, March 18, 2003. "To fall back," he warned, "into the lassitude of the last twelve years, to talk, to discuss, to debate but never act; to declare our will but never enforce it; to combine strong language with weak intentions, a worse outcome than never speaking at all. And then, when the threat returns from Iraq or elsewhere, who will believe us? What price our credibility with the next tyrant?"[23] War against Iraq, Blair implied, would give future would-be-rogue states food for thought when they consider treading the same path as Saddam Hussein. Bush also argued that the war against Iraq would send out a "warning" to those rogue states already on a collision course with the United States. "By acting" in Iraq, he claimed, "we will send a signal to outlaw regimes that, in this new century, the boundaries of civilized behavior will be respected."[24]

The language of retribution was present in many of Bush's speeches, too. Speaking to the UN General Assembly in September 2002, Bush recounted the horrendous crimes committed by Saddam Hussein's Ba'athist government and argued that this regime must "be held to account" for its crimes.[25] The imperative to make Saddam pay for his crimes, based on the notion of repaying harm with harm, is retributivist. In contrast to Bush, Blair shied away from the notion of retribution, tending instead to emphasize the rehabilitative effect a war upon Saddam Hussein's Iraq might have upon that country. Blair argued in September 2002 that a war against Iraq would bring about the fall of Saddam Hussein and thereby massively benefit the people of Iraq. The people of Iraq, he claimed, "would be better off without Saddam. They deserve to be led by someone who can bring Iraq back into the international community where it belongs, not languishing as a pariah."[26] The goal of the regime change in Iraq was thus represented as a means of fostering rehabilitation in Iraq. (Interestingly, the object of rehabilitation, as presented by Blair, would be the Iraqi people, rather than the Iraqi state; the idea being that the removal of the Ba'athist regime would open the way for the rescue and revitalization of the Iraqi people.) In any case, it is apparent that the notion of rehabilitation, as well as those of retribution and deterrence, figured in Bush and Blair's arguments for war against Iraq. These notions are all closely bound up with the practice of punishment and their deployment in many of Bush and Blair's speeches contributed to the case that Iraq must be punished for its violation of international law. Of course, Bush and Blair also aired some more unorthodox (to the contemporary just war theorist at least) arguments pertaining to a second conception of punishment, one which revolves upon the notion of evil.

Ridding the World of Evil

The second conception of punishment present in Bush and Blair's arguments for military action against Iraq is attached to the concept of evil, and the imperative to punish it wherever it may be found. Yosal Rogat is quoted by Hannah Arendt on the topic of evil: "Evil," he writes, "violates a natural harmony which only retribution can restore."[27] Rogat's view that evil is the enemy of order is one that is reflected in historical thinking on evil. Evil has typically been represented as a state of adversity that is corrosive of all order. Such disorder can only be countered by the will to punish evil wherever we encounter it, for punishment serves as a restatement of the proper order. The nineteenth-century American strategist, Captain Alfred Thayer Mahan's address to the First Hague Peace Conference captures this trope quite perfectly. He stated, "Until it is demonstrable that no evil exists, or threatens the world, which cannot be obviated without recourse to force, the obligation to readiness must remain; and, where evil is mighty and defiant, the obligation to use force—that is, war—arises."[28] This idea was given fresh expression in 2003, in the context of the war in Iraq, by two White House insiders, Richard Perle and David Frum. In *End to Evil*, Perle and Frum locate the war in Iraq as part of the American duty to eliminate evil in this world.[29] This argument also echoed in many of the speeches of President Bush and Prime Minister Blair between 2001 and the outbreak of war in Iraq.[30] Indeed, President Bush has fixated upon evil, and the Manichean notion that it is a tangible presence in our world, so much that he has been dubbed by some critics as "the president of good and evil."[31]

Indeed, both Bush and Blair spoke the language of good and evil in the course of their efforts to justify the invasion of Iraq to a skeptical international community. Within hours of the 2001 terrorist strikes upon New York and Washington, Bush and Blair declared that the regular order of things had been disrupted and "chaos" had been introduced into world affairs.[32] With this chaos, they proclaimed, came evil. Blair spoke of the attacks as evidence of a "new evil in our world," while Bush simply stated that America had been the victim of "evil."[33] Both leaders committed to tackling this evil and rooting it out. Speaking on September 14 at a memorial service for the victims of the 9/11 attacks, Bush pledged that America would "answer these attacks and rid the world of evil."[34] Blair followed suit and promised that he, too, would "not rest until this evil is driven from our world."[35] The invasion of Iraq would later be justified as part of this struggle to eradicate evil from this world.

Bush, in particular, was not shy about using the language of good and evil in the build up to the war in Iraq. He spoke about evil in three hundred and nineteen separate speeches, which he delivered between the time he took office, January 20, 2001, and June 16, 2003.[36] Bush's address to the 2002 convocation ceremony at West Point provides a typical example of the president's attempts to raise the question of evil in our world today. He reassured the graduating class, "Some worry that it is somehow undiplomatic or impolite to speak the language of right and wrong. I disagree . . . *We are in a conflict between good and evil, and America will call evil by its name. By confronting evil and lawless regimes, we do not create a problem, we reveal a problem. And we will lead the world in opposing it.*"[37] Five months before the West Point speech, Bush had indeed proved his willingness to call evil by its name when he labeled Iraq, along with North Korea and Iran, as evil. Indeed, Bush made it very clear on numerous occasions that he believed the label of evil applied to Saddam's Iraq.[38] This allowed Bush and Blair to present the war in Iraq as part of a greater struggle between good and evil.

On March 19, 2004, exactly one year after American forces undertook to invade Iraq, Bush spoke of the war in Iraq as a struggle against evil for goodness and freedom. This was a fight, he insisted, "between civilization and terror, because there is no neutral ground between good and evil, freedom and slavery, and life and death."[39] In this fight, America stood for "the dignity of life, tolerance, freedom, and the right of conscience" while Iraq represented subjection, misery, and evil.[40] Civilization itself was at stake, according to President Bush, and the United States and her allies were fighting on its behalf. Those that died in this war, Bush intoned, died fighting a "great evil" in the name of "liberty" and "freedom."[41] Theirs was the "highest calling of history."[42] Bush, more than any other American president, except perhaps Ronald Reagan, likes to compare America's role in the world to a "divine assignment" to fight evil and do good.[43] Blair also proclaimed the war in Iraq to be part of a greater fight for freedom and justice.[44] It was fought, he told us, so that some "lasting good" might emerge from the "shadow of evil" cast upon the world by the events of September 11, 2001.[45] It was fought to remove "the shadow of Saddam" from world affairs.[46]

In representing the war as an epic struggle against evil, Bush and Blair utilized religious language. Evil is a term laden with theological implications, as its association with the *devil* of the Christian faith suggests.[47] In the Christian faith, it is understood to represent some opposition or adversity to God's will. Evil in this sense, Terry Eagleton offers, is a "Satanic parody of the Divine, a nullification of God's wishes and His glory in Creation."[48] This sense of religious quest finds a certain resonance in the statements of Bush and Blair, suggesting a religious justification for the war in Iraq. Blair, for instance, has stated publicly that he believes there are lessons in the Old Testament that we would do well to apply in politics today. In 1993, he wrote a foreword to a collection of essays on Christianity and Socialism that was edited by Christopher Bryant. "Christianity is a very tough religion," he writes. "It is judgmental. There is right and wrong. There is good and bad. We all know this, of course, but it has become fashionable to be uncomfortable about such language. But when we look at our world today and how much needs to be done, we should not hesitate to make such judgments. And then follow them with determined action."[49]

Blair, then, is a leader who favors Christian values in the public sphere.[50] Furthermore, as Peter Stothard has observed, Blair's sense of religiosity acquired even greater prominence in the period leading up to the invasion of Iraq, a time when Blair was under intense pressure both domestically and internationally.[51] Yet Bush is the more obvious case when it comes to religiosity in public affairs. As recently as 2003, he told Bob Woodward that he considers himself to be an instrument of the "Lord's will" on Earth, and prays daily for the strength to be "as good a messenger of His will as possible."[52] This is not the only occasion on which Bush professed the belief that he fulfills some divine function. In *A Charge to Keep*, his pre-election manifesto, Bush reflects upon the task of leadership as a Divine calling, quoting the Charles Wesley hymn, "My calling to fulfill, O may it all my powers engage, To do my Master's will."[53] As Michael Sherry comments, Bush certainly "presented himself and his nation—between which he made little distinction—as instruments of God's wrath against sinners."[54] It seems that, for both Bush and Blair, the task of ridding the world of evil could easily be understood in religious terms.[55]

Regardless of whether or not Bush and Blair's arguments should be understood in religious terms, it is clear that they sought to justify the war in Iraq as an exercise in persecuting evil. This is apparent from their pledges to confront evil and drive it from this world. It is possible, then, to discern a strong confluence between Bush's reference to his role as the "messenger of God's will" on Earth and the Pauline refrain, referred to by Elshtain and O'Donovan, that "the prince does not bear the sword in vain; he is the minister of God to execute his wrath on the evildoer." Interestingly, this refrain does not figure in any robust sense in standard twentieth-century just war thought, as represented by the legalist paradigm. The same may be said of the first conception of punishment—related to law enforcement and the vindication of order—as it surfaces in Bush and Blair's arguments for invading Iraq. Instead, the train of Bush and Blair's arguments, as they relate to both conceptions of punishment, is redolent of certain *classical* articulations of the right to war.

Punishment and the Classical Just War Tradition

Turning to the first conception of punishment treated earlier—the conception of punishment that corresponds to law enforcement—we find that it has some specific resonances within the just war tradition. As Anthony F. Lang points out, the manner in which Bush and Blair approached the possibility of punitive war as a means of enforcing international law calls to mind certain elements of the jus ad bellum formulated by Hugo Grotius.[56]

Law Enforcement

Hugo Grotius (1583–1645) was a prominent figure both on the Dutch political scene and in the European intellectual circles in the seventeenth century.[57] He wrote a number of texts, *The Rights of War and Peace* among them, which have since come to be regarded as foundational to Western political thought, and is often referred to as the father of international law. According to Grotius, just wars must always aim toward the vindication of some violated order by responding forcefully to the transgressor's wrongful actions. In this sense, they must always be punitive in character. Just wars, he states, must always be directed toward "the enforcement of rights," and that once they are undertaken, they "should be carried on only within the bounds of law and good faith." He cites Demosthenes that "war was to be used against those who could not be constrained by judicial processes," in support of this position.[58] There is a clear parallel between these arguments and the justifications advanced by Bush that the war against Iraq was the last resort in enforcing international law upon an outlaw dictator.

The importance of punitive war within Grotius's conception of just war is rendered abundantly clear in chapter 20, book 2 of *The Rights of War and*

Peace. The starting point of Grotius's discussion of punitive war is the premise that those who violate the natural law as dictated by natural rights deserve to be punished.[59] This is because "he who commits a Crime, seems voluntarily to submit himself to Punishment, there being no great crime that is not punishable."[60] From this arises the further jurisdictional question of who may undertake to execute this punishment, and on what basis. The answer to this question is simple for Grotius: any state may undertake to punish a delinquent state on behalf of international society on the basis that by violating the natural order the delinquent state has rendered itself inferior to all other parties, and is therefore subject to their justice (provided that the executor of justice is not guilty of similar crimes). In his own words: "For natural Reason informs us, that a malefactor may be punished . . . It suggests indeed so much, that it is the fittest to be done by a Superior, but yet does not shew that to be absolutely necessary, unless by Superior we mean him who is innocent, and detrude the Guilty below the Rank of Men, and place them among the Beasts that are subject to Men."[61] A similar logic is evident in Bush and Blair's claim that they possessed a mandate to punish Saddam Hussein's Iraq on behalf of the international community. The Iraqi regime, Bush claimed, had "lost its legitimacy," and, accordingly, its immunity from punishment, when it proceeded to violate international law.[62] It follows from this, that any state (the United States and UK included) with a mind to take action against Iraq would be within its rights to do so.

Grotius is also explicit that this right extends to punishing subjects of other states, including other state leaders, even where their crime was not directed against one's own state. He argues that governments may rightfully seek "to exact Punishments, not only for Injuries committed against themselves, or their Subjects, but likewise, for those who do not peculiarly concern them, but which are, in any persons whatsoever, grievous violations of the Law of Nature or Nations."[63] There are obviously close ties between this conception of punitive war and the contemporary model of humanitarian intervention. These close ties are most evident in a passage in which Grotius explores whether there might be a just cause for undertaking war on behalf of the subjects of a ruler, in order to protect them from wrong at his hands. He reasons, "If the injustice be visible, as if a Busiris, a Phalarus, or a Thracian Diomedes should exercise such tyrannies over Subjects as no good man living can approve of, the Right of human Society shall not therefore be excluded . . . And therefore . . . I may make war upon a man, tho' he and I are of different Nations, if he disturbs and molests his own Country, as we told you in our Discourse about Punishments, which is an affair often attended with the Defense of Innocent Subjects."[64]

Interestingly, Grotius perceived himself in the minority in putting forward this view in the seventeenth century. He understood his position to be in direct contention with Vitoria and Molina, who both held that war on behalf of a third party is illicit for reasons of jurisdiction.[65] Vitoria and his scholastic brethren claimed that license to punish is conditional upon proper civil jurisdiction, while Grotius countered that it may be understood as derived from the law of nature. The right to punish third parties resides, he argues, not on the basis of any civil jurisdiction, as his opponents would have it, but "of that natural Right which was both before the Foundation of Governments, and even is now still in Force in those Places, where men live in Tribes or Families, and are not incorporated into States."[66]

Of course, Grotius's argument for just war as punitive war comes with a number of caveats. In the first place, he demands that punishment be a measured endeavor. That is, it must not be wanton or inflicted without care for restraint and limitation.[67] Secondly, it should not be undertaken to avenge every crime committed; some should be passed over and not avenged.[68] In fact, Grotius counsels that wars undertaken to inflict punishment ought to be presumed unjust, unless the crimes are "very heinous and manifest."[69] The reason for this is his inherent distaste for war and zeal for fighting. War is a cruel thing, he reminds his readers, and it drags in its wake a mass of wrongs and insults.[70] The implication is that it is best avoided if possible. Thirdly, it is never permissible to punish others solely on the basis that they subscribe to a faith other than one's own. Difference of religion does not merit punishment.[71] Finally, it must be demonstrable that any proposed punitive war will have positive effects, in terms either of deterrence, correction, or rehabilitation, in addition to retribution and the higher order functions of law enforcement and vindication of order.[72] These references to deterrence, correction, and retribution only reinforce the parallels between Grotius's conception of punitive war and Bush and Blair's arguments previously discussed.

Bush and Blair's arguments for a punitive war of law enforcement against Iraq trade in many of the tropes and moves associated with the Grotian jus ad bellum, as I have just outlined. This is not, of course, to say that Bush and Blair were deliberately invoking the spirit of Hugo Grotius. Rather it is only to claim that they seemed, whether knowingly or not, to "tap into" the discourse of the Grotian jus ad bellum when making the case for war against Iraq.[73] In a similar vain, an affinity can be discerned between Bush and Blair's arguments pertaining to the punishment of evil and the Pauline conviction running through much of the just war tradition that the prince is the minister of God on earth to execute His wrath on the evil-doer.

Ridding the World of Evil

Of all the classical figures of the just war tradition, Augustine of Hippo (354–430 AD) was probably the most devoted to Pauline theology. Augustine spent his life in close proximity to war and religious strife. He had first-hand experience of violence through his dealings with the Donatist sect of North Africa and, following the sack of Rome by Alaric and his Visigoth army in 410 AD, a keen awareness of the fragility of the order imparted by the Roman Empire. Indeed, his adopted hometown of Hippo in North Africa was on the verge of being sacked as he lay on his deathbed in 430. At one point in his life he was drawn to the Manichean sect in his quest for spiritual enlightenment, but it was the witness of St. Paul that would eventually prove the greatest influence on him. [74] As such, he followed traditional Christian assumptions about the state and the other political institutions of this world, representing them as remedial institutions constituted by God to manage fallen man.[75] The state and political institutions exist, in Augustine's words, "to inspire fear and thus put a check on the bad, so that the good may live peacefully among the bad."[76] They achieve this by means of coercion and punishment, directed toward the negative end of limiting the ability of the bad to upset the public order. As Augustine articulates it, "The might of the emperor, the judge's power of the sword, the executioner's hooks, the soldier's weapons, the correction a master gives his slave . . . There is certainly much value in restraining human foolhardiness by the threat of law, both so that the innocent can live in security among the unscrupulous, and also for the unscrupulous themselves, that as long as fear of punishment might limit their opportunities, then appeals to God might heal their wills."[77] Augustine, then, is explicit that the use of institutionalized force is often necessary to restrain the wicked from their sinfulness, and thus ensure that some degree of civic peace is possible.

For Augustine, the *possibility* of civic peace, or *tranquillitas ordinas*, is provided for by God.[78] However, God has relinquished responsibility for the maintenance of this civic peace to the prince who acts as His minister on earth. It follows from this that it is the prince's duty to act in God's stead in the earthly realm and to punish evildoers and those who would threaten the civic peace. This duty extends even to the practice of war. As Augustine writes in *Contra Faustum*, "It is important to know from what causes and by whose authority men take up war: the natural order of mortal things, ordained for peace, demands that the authority for making war and inflicting punishments should rest with the ruler."[79] It is in this context, then, that we should read Augustine's reference to St. Paul's letter to the Romans (13:4): "He beareth the sword not in vain: for he is the minister of God, and avenger of

His anger on the evildoer."[80] On this view, punitive war is the solemn responsibility of the prince who derives his authority by way of divine warrant.

The idea that government is divinely instituted, and that the charge of war may be derived from this, is also present in the thought of Thomas Aquinas (1225–74). Aquinas led a much more cloistered life than Augustine: he joined the Dominican order at a young age and spent most of his life traveling and lecturing between Italy and France. In his writings, he treats the right to war as a rightful function of government founded on proper authority. In this regard, the justification for war is directly analogous to that for domestic punishment, and both share their roots in the prince's divinely instituted obligation to govern the commonwealth for the common good. Aquinas makes this clear in *Summa Theologiae* (IaIIae, 40.1):

> Rather, since the care of the commonwealth is entrusted to princes, it pertains to them to protect the commonwealth of the city or kingdom or province subject to them. And just as it is lawful for them to use the material sword in defense of the commonwealth against those who trouble it from within, when they punish evildoers, according to the Apostle (Romans 13:4), "He beareth the sword not in vain: for he is the minister of God, a revenger to execute wrath upon him that doeth evil"; so too it pertains to them to use the sword of war to protect the commonwealth against enemies from without.[81]

Consequently, the prince possesses a divinely instituted mandate to use force to coerce the wicked.[82]

This Pauline framework surfaces once again in the late Middle Ages in the writings of Francisco de Vitoria (1485–1546) and Francisco Suarez (1548–1617). Vitoria and Suarez have a number of things in common: both men were Jesuits, both taught at the University of Salamanca, and both shared a concern with Christian teachings on war. In their hands, the prince's solemn responsibility to exercise punitive war is compared to an act of judgment. A "prince who wages a just war," Vitoria writes, "acts the part of the judge in the contention which is the cause of war."[83] Suarez expands upon this point. The "power of declaring war," he argues, is "a power of jurisdiction, the exercise of which pertains to punitive justice, which is especially necessary to a state for the purpose of constraining wrongdoers; wherefore just as the sovereign may punish his own subjects when they offend others, so may he avenge himself on another prince or state which by reason of some offence becomes subject to him."[84] Both Vitoria and Suarez are keen to attach the caveat that this right to war as a form of judgment is only operative in those instances where the prince's own commonwealth is the injured party on whose behalf justice is sought. Both are explicit that there is no universal jurisdiction for punitive war to enforce God's will or the natural law.[85] It is the jus ad bellum that flows from this conception of the use of force that O'Donovan invokes when he speaks of the just war as a praxis of judgment.

This understanding of war as a praxis of judgment undertaken on God's behalf is clearly evident in Bush's assertion that he perceives himself as the messenger of God's will on Earth. Indeed, it reverberates on a more general level in many of Bush's statements concerning Iraq. For instance, Bush's claim in March 2003 that the war in Iraq was fought to "bring justice to a dictator" very clearly represents the use of force as an extrajudicial mode of judgment.[86] Just, then, as the Grotian conception of a just war of punitive law enforcement resonates in Bush and Blair's stated determination to uphold the writ of international law, traces of the Pauline conviction that is present in Augustinian and scholastic just war thought can be perceived in Bush and Blair's representation of the war in Iraq as part of an undertaking to punish evil in this world.

Conclusion

This chapter has been concerned to locate Bush and Blair's punitive justifications for invading Iraq within the context of the just war tradition. It commenced with the observation that the idea of punishment has been disregarded or ignored by much recent just war thought. There can be little doubt, however, that Bush and Blair advanced a number of arguments for the war in Iraq that reflected the idea of punitive war. These arguments variously resonate with both a broadly Grotian account of the just war as a punitive mode of law enforcement, as well as the Pauline commitment (common to much of the scholastic and Augustinian literature, and recently restated by Elshtain and O'Donovan) that the prince is the minister of God on earth to execute His wrath upon evildoers. In contrast, then, to the disregard for the broader punitive element of just war displayed by much of the twentieth century literature, Bush and Blair's arguments, as well as those of Elshtain and O'Donovan, suggest a revivification of certain classical understandings of punishment associated with the tradition. This is an interesting development that suggests, as with the expansion of the right to anticipation examined in Chapter 2, that a loosening of the jus ad bellum may currently be taking place. We will subject this possibility to further scrutiny in Chapter 4, when we examine the humanitarian justification for the invasion of Iraq. It is to this task that we turn now.

CHAPTER 4

Humanitarian War: Can War Be a Force for Good in the World?

Introduction

The third justification President Bush and Prime Minister Blair offered for the invasion of Iraq was phrased in humanitarian terms. The matter of humanitarian war is historically closely associated with the practice of punitive war. As Chapter 3 discussed, it was referred to by Hugo Grotius in connection with the question of who exercises jurisdiction in cases where the natural law is violated. More recently, humanitarian war has been treated in terms of an exception to the general rule of nonintervention in international society. This is still the standard legal approach to what is usually known as "humanitarian intervention." Humanitarian war, this approach suggests, is justified as a *via negativa* in exceptional cases where some instance of horrific human rights abuse enjoins that the default ban on international border-crossing is overridden. Yet when Bush and Blair sought to justify the invasion of Iraq in March 2003 by reference to humanitarian arguments, both leaders stressed a much more robust conception of humanitarian war. They variously sought to justify the war as a means of promoting a more just world order and exporting democracy and human rights to Iraq and the Middle East while still relating their case to the language of the just war tradition. The liberation of Iraq, Bush told us, is a just cause. This chapter examines Bush and Blair's humanitarian justifications for the invasion of Iraq, paying special attention to its correspondence with the just war tradition.

This chapter argues that the idea of humanitarian war presented by Bush and Blair actually reflects quite closely the classical idea of the just war, as it is presented by James Turner Johnson. This prompts a number of interesting questions relating to whether it is actually the restrictive twentieth century approach to humanitarian intervention, rather than Bush and Blair's justifications for invading Iraq, which is out of step with the classical thrust of the just war tradition. It also begs us to further examine Johnson's recovery of the classical just war idea. This mostly pertains to the question of whether a presumption against war or against injustice resides at the core of just war thinking. This question points us toward the difficult matter of how we relate current just war thinking to the historical development of the just war tradition. In this regard, it will build upon the contributions of Chapters 2 and 3 on this issue.

This chapter aims to accomplish two objectives. Firstly, it aims to present an account of Bush and Blair's humanitarian justifications for invading Iraq, and to locate these justifications within the context of twentieth century just war thought. Secondly, it is concerned to examine how we might relate this twentieth century just war thought (as well as the arguments offered by Bush and Blair) to the broader historical development of the tradition. Johnson's reflections on these questions provide the pivot for this examination. Much of the second half of this chapter is dedicated to analyzing the manner by which Johnson seeks to account for the historical development of the tradition, and the place that Bush and Blair's arguments (and indeed twentieth century just war thought) occupy within it.

The layout of this chapter is quite straightforward. The first section examines the humanitarian justifications offered by Bush and Blair for the invasion of Iraq. It contends that the character of these justifications differed markedly from the conventional treatment of humanitarian war in twentieth century just war thought, which is dealt with in the second section. This section discusses the twentieth century approach to humanitarian war/intervention as an exception or *via negativa*. It relates this approach to the broader, prevailing notion that the use of force is always morally problematic and that a presumption against war stands at the beginning of just war reasoning. The third section discusses Johnson's rejection of this approach, paying particular attention to his claim that it represents a perversion of the just war tradition properly understood. The final section turns to Johnson's reconstruction of the tradition. It aims to analyze both the manner by which he accounts for the historical development of the just war tradition and his efforts to locate twentieth century just war thought within this narrative. The basic objective of this chapter is to consider how Bush and Blair's humanitarian justifications for invading Iraq correspond with different approaches to the just war tradition.

Bush and Blair: Justifying Humanitarian War in Iraq

Bush and Blair both presented a humanitarian justification for the invasion of Iraq. Blair often alluded to this justification as the "moral case for war."[1] His point in so doing was to emphasize that this was an argument that was grounded in considerations of justice rather than national interests narrowly defined.[2] Although Bush refrained from referring to humanitarian arguments as the moral case for war, he too couched the humanitarian justification for the invasion of Iraq in terms of a broader agenda. His secretary of state, Colin Powell, even spoke of the humanitarian cause in Iraq as concomitant to the American duty to export freedom and democracy to the "dark places" of the earth.[3] This "missionary zeal," as some commentators have referred to it, was evident in both the NSS and Bush's major foreign policy addresses pertaining to Iraq.[4] The NSS contains a clear statement of the Bush administration's conviction that the United States must "stand for" the promotion of freedom, justice, and democracy across the world. It states: "The United States must defend liberty and justice because these principles are right and true for all people everywhere . . . No people on earth yearn to be oppressed, aspire to servitude, or eagerly await the midnight knock of the secret police. America must stand firmly for the non-negotiable demands of human dignity . . . We will champion the cause of human dignity and oppose those who resist it."[5] The United States is thus committed "to help make the world not just safer but better."[6] It would, the NSS claims, assume responsibility for "leading" freedom to triumph over its foes and bringing "the hope of democracy" to "every corner of the world."[7]

Using Force to Build a More Just World

These sentiments were accentuated and expanded upon by Bush in many of his major foreign policy addresses pertaining to the invasion of Iraq. At West Point, for instance, he made it clear that the United States would act to promote freedom around the world. America aims to "extend a just peace, by replacing poverty, repression, and resentment around the world with hope of a better day. America has a greater objective than controlling threats and containing resentment. We will work for a just and peaceful world" beyond the war on terror.[8] Ivo Daalder and James Lindsay observe that this amounts to an assertion that the United States "should use its strength to change the status quo in the world."[9] This view is supported by Bush's statement on February 10, 2003, that he was determined to tackle tyranny and make the world a more peaceful, gentler place where "freedom and liberty" command universal respect.[10]

Where Iraq was concerned, this translated into a will to remove Saddam Hussein from power, and thereby to liberate the Iraqi people. Bush claimed in January 2003 that America has a commitment to human dignity and human rights that leads it into the world to bring succor to the afflicted and justice to their oppressors. This same commitment, he promised, would lead

America into Iraq. Addressing the Iraqi people as part of his 2003 State of the Union speech, Bush committed to their liberation: "And tonight I have a message for the brave and oppressed people of Iraq: Your enemy is not surrounding your country—your enemy is ruling your country. And the day he and his regime are removed from power will be the day of your liberation."[11] By intervening in Iraq, Bush hoped that America (and its allies) would aid the Iraqi people in shucking off the bonds of Ba'athist oppression and provide them with the "chance to live in freedom and choose their own government."[12] The ordinary people of Iraq would be free from the fear of torture and intimidation, and would once again have ownership over their own future.

Of course, the plight of Iraq cannot be viewed independently of the broader issues mapped out by the NSS and Bush; the ideals of democracy and human dignity would both be equally served by a war that liberated the Iraqi people. Whereas Saddam Hussein's Ba'athist regime contributed to a freedom deficit in the Middle East, a liberated Iraq would "show the power of freedom to transform that vital region" and serve as a beacon of democracy to light the way for other troubled peoples.[13] In this sense, by acting against Saddam Hussein and liberating Iraq, America would be leading "freedom's cause" and helping to make this an "age of progress and liberty."[14] Of course Bush was always careful to add that America acts only as the handmaiden of providence in this regard, for liberty, as he put it, is not America's gift to the world but God's gift to humanity.[15]

Challenging the Status Quo

What comes across quite clearly in many of these arguments put forward by Bush is the idea that, where Iraq is concerned, "the status quo has become unacceptable."[16] Between January and March 2003, he continually exhorted people to recognize that for as long as Iraq is captive to Saddam Hussein, it would remain a brutal police state that threatens its neighbors and represses its people. Bush claimed that such a state of affairs is repugnant and, for the sake of the Iraqi people, must not be allowed to stand. He reasoned, "The first to benefit from a free Iraq would be the Iraqi people themselves. Today, they live in scarcity and fear, under a dictator who has brought them nothing but war, and misery, and torture . . . Bringing stability and unity to Iraq will not be easy. Yet that is no excuse to leave the Iraqi regime's torture chambers and poison labs in operation. Any future the Iraqi people choose for themselves will be better than the nightmare world that Saddam Hussein has chosen for them."[17]

Blair shared Bush's assessment that the state of affairs in Iraq (prior to intervention) was unacceptable. According to Blair, the state of affairs in Iraq was so appalling that the status quo must be considered corrupt and devoid of any legitimacy. The containment policy that had been directed toward Iraq since the conclusion of the 1991 Gulf War only exacerbated an already appalling state of affairs within Iraq.[18] In this instance, then, the status quo facilitates, even perpetuates, horrendous injustice in Iraq.[19] As Christopher Bluth writes, "Containment was failing and its continuation was not acceptable given its consequences for the Iraqi people. Saddam's was a brutal regime and to leave it in place would mean continued untold suffering for Iraq."[20] To allow the status quo to persist would, it follows, be to condemn the people of Iraq to further suffering. It is no great leap from this position to argue that war against Saddam might better serve the interests of the Iraqi people than would the status quo.

This is precisely the argument to which Blair devoted much of his February 2003 Labour Party address. On this occasion he framed his case in terms of a response to those marchers who protested against war in Iraq on the grounds that it would cause great suffering for the Iraqi people:

> Yes, there are consequences of war. If we remove Saddam by force people will die and some will be innocent . . . But there are also consequences of "stop the war." If I took that advice, and did not insist on disarmament, yes, there would be no war. But there still would be Saddam. Many of the people marching say they hate Saddam. But the consequences of taking their advice means that he stays in charge of Iraq, ruling the Iraqi people . . . There will be no march for the victims of Saddam, no protests about the thousands of children that die needlessly every year under his rule, no righteous anger over the torture chambers which if he is left in power, will be left in being . . . So if the result of peace is Saddam staying in power, not disarmed, then I tell you there are consequences paid in blood for that decision too. But these victims will never be seen. They will never feature on our TV screens or inspire millions to take to the streets. But they will exist nonetheless. Ridding the world of Saddam would be an act of humanity. It is leaving him there that is in truth inhumane.[21]

This must be understood as a simple utilitarian argument based on the calculation (worked out in terms of the suffering of the Iraqi people) that the costs of leaving the status quo in place outweigh the costs of military action. Blair reprised this argument just over one week later, begging the Commons, "Let us not forget the tens of thousands imprisoned, tortured or executed by his barbarity every year. The innocent die every day in Iraq, victims of Saddam, and their plight too should be heard."[22]

These arguments are notable by virtue of the fact that the status quo is denied any privileged standing. Rather, it is posited as something to be overcome. This is consistent with Blair's response to the events of September 11, 2001, when he called upon all global leaders to seize the moment and "re-order the world around us."[23] Where Iraq was concerned, Bush and Blair both associated the status quo with the continued operation of the Ba'athist torture chambers and poison labs, and the prolonged suffering of innocent Iraqi people. Faced with the endurance of this torrid state of affairs, Bush and Blair argued that the use of force to reorder Iraq must surely be a preferable option.

What is lacking in this argument is any sense that the use of force poses unique moral challenges for those who opt to use it. Instead, this argument treats war no differently to any other instrument of policy, regarding it as just another means of effecting political results. As Anthony Burke notes, by weighing the shortcomings of the status quo against the potentiality of reordering Iraq (and the world) along more democratic and just lines, Bush and Blair promote a "relatively sanguine view of the role and legitimacy of force in international life."[24] They represent war as the "continuation of morality by other means" and endow it with some functional worth as a conduit of liberal values and a force for good in the world.[25] It is a small step from here to Wilsonianism, that brand of crusading, interventionist foreign policy usually associated with the presidency of Woodrow Wilson. The drift in this direction is clearly evident in Bush and Blair's stated willingness to countenance humanitarian war even in a case such as Iraq where there was no identifiable "humanitarian catastrophe." [26] Their proclaimed willingness to use force to deal with what would previously have been considered nasty *but tolerable* instances of daily oppression stressed their commitment that we may use force to reorder the world (and particularly its less palatable societies) along more just and democratic lines.[27]

Twentieth Century Just War Thinking and Humanitarian War

The very idea of crusading Wilsonianism runs directly counter to twentieth century orthodoxy in the just war tradition. According to the mainstream of the just war tradition in the twentieth century, the practice of humanitarian war is tightly circumscribed. So much so, in fact, that it is typically represented as a *via negativa*. A cursory glance at the literature on humanitarian war and the right to force in international society will reveal an almost uncontested tendency among scholars to treat humanitarian war in negative terms as an exception to the general rule of nonintervention.[28] J. Bryan Hehir provides the categorical statement of this position when he writes that "the character and composition of the international system requires presumptive restraint on intervention." Although intervention may occasionally be necessary, he continues, "it should not be made easy" and the burden of proof must always rest with the intervening party.[29]

The Humanitarian Exception

The twentieth century approach to humanitarian war as an exception to the general rule of nonintervention was given its paradigmatic expression by Michael Walzer in 1977.[30] Drawing on the writings of J. S. Mill, Walzer argues that the practice of humanitarian intervention is best approached as a "negative demonstration" of the reasons underpinning the principle of nonintervention in international affairs.[31] In most cases, he writes, states ought to respect the principle of nonintervention for it is the best safeguard of important values relating to self-determination and communal liberty in the society of states. Yet, cases sometimes arise where the only way to uphold these values usually fostered by a practice of nonintervention is to take the opposite course of action and intervene. One such set of circumstances arises when there occurs within a community some violation of human rights so horrendous as to make all talk of communal liberty or self-determination seem "cynical and irrelevant."[32] Walzer cites enslavement and massacre as two examples of sufficiently horrendous cases of human rights abuse; the marker of acts such as these is that they always "shock the moral conscience of mankind."[33] He elaborates upon these cases:

> If the dominant forces within a state are engaged in massive violations of human rights, the appeal to self-determination in the Millian sense of self-help is not very attractive. That appeal has to do with the freedom of the community taken as a whole; it has no force when what is at stake is the bare survival or the minimal liberty of (some substantial number of) its members. Against the enslavement or massacre of political opponents, national minorities, and religious sects, there may well be no help unless help comes from outside. And when a government turns savagely upon its own people, we must doubt the very existence of a political community to which the idea of self-determination might apply.[34]

In these instances humanitarian intervention is justified. Yet, Walzer is very clear that this is not a general right, but is rather an exception to a general right. It is imperative, Walzer argues, that international society demonstrate a "kind of a priori respect for state boundaries" and understands that intervention may only ever be justified "as if it were an exception to a general rule, made necessary by the urgency and extremity of a particular case."[35] Indeed, Walzer even stipulates that the burden of justification lies with those who would intervene and it is "more onerous than any we impose on individuals or governments pleading self-defense."[36]

Walzer returned to this argument in an article published in *Dissent Magazine* in 2002, "The Argument about Humanitarian Intervention." This piece further stresses Walzer's assertions that instances of misrule and tyranny must be "extreme" if they are to justify humanitarian intervention. Every violation of human rights, he argues, is not a justification: "The common brutalities of authoritarian politics, the daily oppressiveness of traditional social practices—these are not occasions for intervention."[37] Only the worst instances of human suffering, where the stakes are so high that the international community cannot reasonably affect disinterest, should provoke intervention; everything else is best left to the troubled society to deal with by itself in its own way.[38] Moreover, where intervention does take place, it must be animated by "minimalist" goals.[39] He specifically argues against the idea that interventions should be undertaken to promote "democratic or liberal or pluralist or (even) capitalist" values in the more brutal corners of this world. Rather, intervention is best conceived as a "limited" task that aims only at ensuring that some basic level of order attends the process of self-determination within communities.

A similarly restrained approach to humanitarian war marks the work of Nicholas Wheeler and Alex Bellamy. Wheeler, for example, argues that humanitarian war is only justified in exceptional cases where a genuine "supreme humanitarian emergency" exists.[40] This ensures that the bar for the use of force is set very high, ruling out the possibility that humanitarian wars might be fought to end "ordinary routine abuse of human rights."[41] In a similar vein, Alex Bellamy refers to intervention as "the humanitarian exception to the legal ban on the use of force" and stipulates that it may only be justified in "humanitarian emergencies."[42] Bellamy and Wheeler both display substantial concern, then, that the right to intervention is suitably circumscribed by thresholds and safeguards.

A Presumption against War

The restrained approach to humanitarian war adopted by Walzer, Wheeler, and Bellamy reflects a more general presumption against the use of nondefensive force in international affairs. Their deliberate concern to circumscribe the right of intervention with thresholds and limits is emblematic of a broader caution regarding the role of nondefensive force in international society.[43] International law and church thinking present two of the clearest expressions of this skepticism concerning the utility of war as a tool of foreign policy. International law establishes a broad prohibition on the use of force for any purpose that is not conceived as self-defense or collective security, as the UN Charter affirms. Church thinking on war and peace exhibits a similar disposition. As the National Conference of Catholic Bishops (NCCB) wrote in their influential 1983 pastoral letter, the unprecedented gravity of the nuclear threat leads us to assume that a "presumption against war" must stand at the "beginning of just war thinking" today.[44] "Only if war cannot be rationally avoided," they continue, "does the teaching then seek to restrict and reduce its horrors. It does this by establishing a set of rigorous conditions which must be met if the decision to go to war is to be morally permissible. Such a decision, especially today, requires extraordinarily strong reasons for overriding the presumption in favor of peace and against war."[45] This general presumption against nondefensive force evident in international law and church doctrine precipitates a skepticism regarding humanitarian war. International law, for example, affords no general permission for humanitarian war. Instead, its legality is conditional upon a customary law exception to Article 2(4) of the UN Charter.[46] Meanwhile, the NCCB's pastoral letter fails to acknowledge any right of humanitarian intervention, arguing that the only just cause for war in the modern world is self-defense.[47]

Viewed against the restrained approach to humanitarian intervention just essayed, Bush and Blair's "moral case for war" against Iraq appears divorced from the mainline of the just war thinking in the twentieth century. Certainly, their arguments do not sit easily with the *presumption against the nondefensive use of force* that appears to rest at the heart of recent just war thought. Yet, some contemporary scholars of the just war tradition, most notably James Turner Johnson, argue that the idea of a *presumption against the nondefensive use of force* (which he refers to in a more general idiom as a "presumption against war") is itself a twentieth-century conceit that is alien to the just war tradition properly understood.[48]

Challenging Twentieth-Century Just War Thinking

According to Johnson, underpinning the "presumption against war" is a conviction that the use of force is always morally problematic.[49] At the very least, it requires special justification, while some go so far as to say that it is an inherently immoral exercise.[50] At the heart of this moral problematic is the conviction that modern war must inevitably tend toward disproportionality and nuclear armageddon. Given the destructive capacity of modern military hardware, and the serious possibility that any conflict could escalate into a nuclear exchange, war has ceased for the most part to provide a reasonable means of settling disputes and promoting justice and order in world affairs. Johnson spells out the logic of this approach: "On this reasoning the destructive capabilities of contemporary weapons are made the core of an argument that any use of force today must necessarily be disproportionate and hence unjust. It follows that there can be no reasonable hope of success, and that contemporary war can never reasonably be a last resort for serving justice, order, and peace, because it will by its nature create injustice, disorder, and more war." [51] We must start, then, with the assumption that war is so destructive today that it can never be justified; only in the most extreme cases is there any possibility that war might serve the just ends of society. Consequently, the purpose of the jus ad bellum must be understood as providing criteria to guide whether the presumption against war should be overruled in particular cases or not. A prima facie case against war as an instrument of justice in the international realm is thereby established, and the middle ground between pacifism and the just war tradition is located. The result was (disparagingly) labeled the *jus contra bellum* by Johnson's mentor, Paul Ramsey.[52]

Following Ramsey, Johnson alleges that this middle ground is only achieved at the cost of perverting the classical idea of the just war. To think of the just war tradition as beginning with a presumption against the use of force is, Johnson argues, to make it over "into something very different from what it is."[53] This approach places undue emphasis upon the prudential categories of the jus ad bellum—proportionality and hope of success—such that they smother the concerns of just cause and aim of peace before they can be properly considered. Rather than treating the prudential categories as checks upon what Johnson calls the deontological core of the jus ad bellum—legitimate authority, just cause, right intention, and aim of peace—the "presumption against war" approach treats them as de facto barriers blocking the possibility of just war reasoning. This runs contrary to the true nature of the just war tradition. "It is a serious distortion of the meaning of just war tradition," writes Johnson, "to magnify the importance of the prudential concerns included in the jus ad bellum so that they diminish the importance of the fundamental requirements of just cause, proper authority, and right intention."[54] The result of this distortion is to make it more difficult to resort to war, while simultaneously sanctifying the status quo to some extent. Essentially, the status quo is conflated with *peace*, which is itself recast in overly minimalist terms as the absence of war. The lesson that war, although ugly, is not the ugliest of things is forgotten, as is the wisdom that the so-called peace (the status quo) can sometimes be crueler than war.

Much of Johnson's recent work has been devoted to the argument that the just war tradition *properly understood* approaches the relationship between force, peace, and justice in a fundamentally different manner. A *faithful* reading of the tradition, Johnson argues, suggests that peace should not be accounted for in such minimalist terms that it is confused with the status quo or the absence of war.[55] Just war thinking in its classic form is cognizant of the limits of the status quo and always mindful of the injustices it conceals. Crucially, it accepts that it is sometimes necessary to employ force against the status quo so that a more just order may be achieved. Viewed in this way, war is not perceived as an intrinsically immoral exercise, or even just the ugliest of things; instead it is an instrument of justice. In Johnson's words:

> It takes its moral character from who uses it, from the reasons used to justify it, and from the intention with which it is used . . . To be sure, force is evil when it is employed to attack the justice and peace of a political order oriented toward these goods, but it is precisely to defend against such evil that the use of force may be good. Just war tradition has to do with defining the possible good use of force, not finding exceptional cases when it is possible to use something inherently evil (force) for the purpose of good.[56]

This instrumental understanding of the use of force produces a more relaxed reading of the right to war than the presumption against war model. Rather than starting with the presumption that the use of force is itself morally problematic, this concept of the just war is centered upon a "presumption against injustice."[57] It associates the just war with the responsible use of force directed against wrongdoing and injustice. The just war tradition properly understood, Johnson concludes, is all about "the use of the authority and force of the rightly ordered political community . . . to prevent, punish, and rectify injustice." There is, he writes, simply put, "no presumption against war in it at all."[58]

If one accepts Johnson's strong claims that the very notion of a presumption against war is a perversion, and that we should instead perceive a "presumption against injustice" as lying at the heart of the just war tradition, Bush and Blair's humanitarian justifications for war against Iraq actually fit in quite well with the classical just war idea.[59] Perhaps, then, Bush and Blair's justifications for humanitarian war against Iraq are not so alien to the just war tradition in its classic form as we might have thought. If Johnson's reading of the tradition is to be accepted, it is instead the twentieth century approach to humanitarian intervention that is out of line with the just war tradition in its classic form.

Johnson's Reconstruction of the Just War Tradition

Johnson's reconstruction of the just war tradition is based loosely upon a reiteration of the jus ad bellum as articulated by Thomas Aquinas. Johnson considers Aquinas a central figure in the historical development of the tradition and deems his writings to constitute a "classic statement" of the just war.[60] At the heart of Aquinas's understanding of the just war lies the conviction (borrowed directly from Augustine) that "A just war is customarily defined as one which avenges injuries, as when a nation or state deserves to be punished because it has neglected either to put right the wrongs done by its people or to restore what it has unjustly seized."[61] Accordingly, for a war to be justified, it must satisfy three conditions: right authority, just cause, and right intention. The order sequence in which these conditions are listed reflects a logical order, according to Johnson (though Aquinas never actually argues this): "only one in sovereign authority could justly employ force, and he could do so only in pursuit of justice and for the end of peace."[62] This simple tripartite structure provides the framework for Johnson's treatment of the historical development of the just war tradition.[63] Within this framework, he emphasizes two thematic lines that he perceives as animating the tradition: the idea of vindicative justice and that of Christian love (also sometimes referred to as charity). Conceived within these parameters, the just war tradition reflects an interventionist ethic that supposes a radically different approach to humanitarian war than twentieth century thinking provided for.

Right Authority

According to the jus ad bellum stipulated by Aquinas (and echoed by Johnson), the first condition is that war may only be waged by a prince with the requisite authority to do so. As Aquinas phrases it, "Since the care of the commonwealth is entrusted to princes, it pertains to them to protect the commonwealth of the city or kingdom or province subject to them. And just as it is lawful for them to use the material sword in defense of the commonwealth against those who trouble it from within, when they punish evildoers . . . so too it pertains to them to use the sword of war to protect the commonwealth against enemies from without."[64] In other words, only the prince may wage war on account of the fact that it is he who is responsible for the kingdom. Aquinas's reasoning here rests on "an inference from the domestic situation in which the magistrate is justified in using force for the common good to the international situation in which the sovereign is justified in using force to respond to externally based wrongs."[65] Proper authority is thereby related to the Aristotelian notion of the common good of the community; the result of this being that the just war is viewed as an act of judgment undertaken by the prince on behalf of his polity.[66] It is in this light that we should read Johnson's bold proclamation that the just war tradition is "first and foremost about the place the use of force may have in the exercise of the responsibilities of good government . . . These are positive responsibilities: to ensure the common good, to protect against threats, and to support the order that makes just societies possible."[67]

In making this argument, Johnson places great emphasis on the notion of vindicative justice, lending weight to Alfred Vanderpol's claim that it constitutes the essence of just war thinking.[68] Johnson derives his understanding of vindicative justice from the writings of Aquinas in particular, but also Vitoria and Suarez.[69] As classically articulated, vindicative justice relates to the responsibility of princes to exercise authority in the service of order and justice. This denotes that the prince is the repository of three primary duties: to maintain order within a given community by defending against internal wrongdoing and external attack, to restore justice by punishing those responsible for wrongdoing, and to reclaim any persons or property wrongly seized by avaricious neighbors.[70] The prince is thereby charged with the object of, in Augustine's words (also cited by Aquinas and Vitoria), "securing the peace by coercing the wicked and helping the good."[71] Consistent with the Pauline precept that the prince is the minister of God to execute His wrath upon the evildoer, this conception of authority empowers the prince to use the sword to establish (or reestablish) a just and peaceful political order. It is with sentiment in mind that Aquinas remarks that it pertains to the prince to use the sword of war in order that we may have true peace. As he succinctly puts it, "Those who wage war justly aim at peace, and so they are not opposed to peace, except to the evil peace."[72] The just war, on this view, is a war fought on princely authority with the object of vindicating proper relations between communities where they have been disrupted by some instance of wrongdoing. As Suarez writes, war is justified when taken "under legitimate and public authority, with the intention of holding an enemy to his duty and of reducing to its due order that which was disorderly."[73]

Indeed, this line of argument runs through the writings of Vitoria and Suarez. Vitoria, for instance, is explicit in comparing the role of the warring prince to that of the domestic judge. "The prince who wages a just war," he writes, "becomes ipso facto the judge of the enemy, and may punish them judicially and sentence them according to the offence."[74] James Brown Scott writes that this comparison is central to Vitoria's thinking on the rights of war. Vitoria's doctrine, Scott argues, is properly understood as a judicial system for international society where the princes are posited as judges responsible for prosecuting any violation of natural rights on the writ of the law of nations. "Hence it is that Vitoria's prince may redress rights and punish wrongs just as may a judge of civil or criminal jurisdiction . . . On an international scale, the prince is the executor of the judgment which he has rendered."[75] If anything, Suarez amplified this idea that princely authority functions as a means of judgment. The power of declaring war, Suarez states, is a "power of jurisdiction." He explains, "Wherefore just as the sovereign may punish his own subjects when they offend others, so may he avenge himself on another prince or state which by reason of some offence becomes subject to him; and this vengeance cannot be sought at the hands of another judge, because the prince of whom we are speaking has no superior in temporal affairs; therefore, if that offender is not prepared to give satisfaction, he may be compelled to do so by war."[76] There is a certain continuity, then, between this position and Grotius's argument that any state may undertake to punish a delinquent state on behalf of international society.[77] The core of this argument is the view that the prince may preside in judgment over the wrongdoing of others, and it is on this basis that he may lead his community or kingdom to war.

Just Cause

The idea of wrongdoing comes to the foreground in Aquinas's second condition for the justification of war—just cause. Those against whom war is to be waged, Aquinas offers, "must deserve to have war waged against them because of some wrongdoing."[78] This formulation emphasizes that the fundamental character of the just war relates to the correction of some outstanding act of injustice.[79] This too is absorbed by Vitoria and Suarez in their accounts of the just war. "The sole and only just cause for waging war," according to Vitoria, "is when harm has been inflicted."[80] Likewise, Suarez demands that it is "necessary that [the enemy] shall have committed some wrong on account of which they render themselves subjects" before the prince acquires a right to wage war against them.[81] He elaborates upon this conclusion in a lengthy passage that illuminates how the idea of just cause is closely entangled with the previous condition of proper authority:

> A war may also be justified on the ground that he who inflicted an injury should be justly punished, if he refuses to give satisfaction for that injury . . . Just as within a state some lawful power to punish crimes is necessary to the preservation of domestic peace; so in the world as a whole, there must exist, in order that the various states may dwell in concord, some power for the punishment of injuries inflicted by one state upon another; and this power is not to be found in any superior; therefore, the power in question must reside in the sovereign prince of the injured state, to whom, by reason of that injury, the opposing prince is made subject; and consequently, war of the kind in question has been instituted in place of a tribunal administering just punishment.[82]

The condition of just cause as presented by Aquinas, Vitoria, and Suarez is close in meaning to the notion of "cause of action" that is to be found in the Anglo-American legal tradition. It refers to a wrong that gives grounds for complaint and just claims for redress.[83] Accordingly, the purpose of the just war is, as John Finnis puts it, to right wrongs and to heal the "disorder" introduced into the international system by the wrongdoer's conduct. War, on this view, serves a "re-ordering function."[84]

The rationale for taking the burden upon oneself to affect such reordering is derived for Johnson from the idea of Christian love. Johnson's treatment of Christian love is one of the most intriguing aspects of his writings on the just war tradition. Although he is critical of Paul Ramsey for overstating the centrality of love to the tradition, claiming that no benchmark figure from within the tradition argued explicitly from love to the idea of just war, Johnson still draws extensively on this trope. Consequently, despite his reservations, love nonetheless emerges in Johnson's writings as one of the key thematic lines in the historical development of the just war tradition. It provides the key to understanding the idea that force may ever be employed in pursuit of justice, and the guide-rails for how that force should be used.

Christian love, or charity, as Johnson uses it, is a precise term, which has roots in Augustinian theology as well as the neoscholastic approach to just war thinking associated with Vitoria and Suarez, among others. It refers to the virtue that arises from the "perfect love of God," and supposes a harmonious ordering of man's regard for self, others, and the divine.[85] It demands that people display a "dutiful concern" for others to the extent that one is enjoined to love one's neighbor as oneself.[86] Only by offering oneself up in this way can one display disinterest in worldly goods and true devotion to God. There must, then, be some willingness to place the welfare of others ahead of oneself and to adopt a self-offering disposition. The ideal of Christian love thus comprises an ethic of other-regard backed by the faith that serving others will produce a "well-ordered concord" guaranteed by the grace of God.[87] This ideal is encapsulated in the image of Jesus suffering on the cross, offering himself up in order to redeem mankind. Paul Ramsey contends that this idea of Christian love contains within it the very essence of the just war tradition: the soldier is required to do only what love requires and permitted to do only what love declares to be right.[88]

Writing in the fifth century, Augustine utilized the idea of Christian love in response to the objections of earlier Christian fathers that war is contrary to the teachings of Jesus. Citing the Sermon on the Mount, these early pacifists declared war inconsistent with the New Testament's pacific injunction to refrain from violence and turn the other cheek.[89] Against this, Augustine asserts that an ethic of other-regard as suggested by Christ's death on the cross may occasionally require "more than personal, witnessing action."[90] It may sometimes require war; nonresisting love has sometimes to grapple with evil. The imperative of charity sometimes dictates that one should go to war to correct another's sins and to return them to righteousness. In such instances, war is motivated and indeed justified by a self-giving regard for others and a desire to halt another person's wayward descent into sinfulness. Thus conceived, war becomes a "work of Christian love."[91]

The very idea that war may serve as an instrument of love presupposes that it is conducted in the right spirit. This entails that there must be no trace of "animosity" or "cruelty" in the decision to fight, only concern for the plight of one's fellow human being in light of his/her errant ways.[92] Augustine illustrates the logic of this position is illustrated by reference to fatherly discipline. A father, he argues, does no wrong by punishing his son, as he does so out of care for the child's welfare rather than any will to hurt him. "When the father strikes [his son], he does so out of love. The boy does not want to be beaten; but his father takes no account of his wishes; his concern is for his benefit."[93] What underpins the father's actions is a desire to guide his son toward proper conduct and a determination to discipline him so that he might fare better in this world. He only resorts to the rod in order that his son is not spoiled. According to Augustine, this is the paradigmatic example of Christian love applied in the fallen world. It is harsh but benevolent. It is Augustine's contention that the spirit of "benevolent severity" that marks fatherly discipline should also guide princes in their war making.[94]

On the surface, the irony of this position is striking: war and all its attendant brutality is held up as an instantiation of Christian love as modeled on Jesus's sacrifice on the cross. The key to understanding this seemingly perverse logic is the emphasis on subjectivity. According to this view, it is one's inward disposition rather than one's outward deeds that determines the rightfulness of one's conduct. Vitoria cites Augustine's letter to Marcellinus to this effect. It contends that Jesus's instructions to turn the other cheek are more relevant to the training of the heart than to our external activity:

> Forbearance and benevolence should be kept secretly in one's own mind, while publicly we should do whatever seems likely to benefit those we wish well. In short, we should always hold fast to the precepts of forbearance in *the disposition of our hearts*; and in our will we should always have perfect benevolence in case we return *evil for evil*. For people are often to be helped, against their will, by being punished with a sort of kind harshness . . . If the earthly commonwealth observes Christian precepts in this way, then even wars will be waged in a spirit of benevolence.[95]

There is a radical distinction here between one's physical actions, and the inward intentions that motivate such actions. This allows Augustine (and Vitoria) to claim that the New Testament injunction to refrain from violence applies only to one's inward intentions, not one's outward deeds. Provided that one fights in the right spirit, animated by love for one's enemies even as one smites them, there is nothing problematic about war. War, as Suarez observes, is obviously "not opposed to the love of one's enemies; for whoever wages war honorably hates, not individuals, but the actions which he justly punishes."[96] Understood in this light, war is a practice of "care, not cruelty," and is justified accordingly.[97]

But to whom is this care owed? Where war is concerned, the sphere of obligation or care is not restricted to conationals or fellow citizens. Pauline universalism contributes here to ensure that Christian love is extended to all people, believers and nonbelievers included. We are meant to love and care for all men, writes Augustine, and not just our neighbors. This position has universal implications; as Herbert Deane notes, it posits that there is "no one in the whole human family to whom kindly affection is not due by reason of the bond of a common humanity."[98] This commitment to universalism is later picked up by Suarez, among others, who argues that, "No matter how many diverse peoples and kingdoms the human race may be divided into, it always has a certain unity, not merely as a species, but even a sort of political and moral unity, which is indicated by the natural precept of mutual love and mercy which extends to everyone, even to foreigners of any nation."[99]

The parable of the Good Samaritan can be considered instructive with respect to the position staked out by both Augustine and Suarez. As the story of the Good Samaritan celebrates, charity entails leaping to the defense of any innocent person who cannot easily defend themselves, regardless of whether or not we share ties to them.[100] Thus, Augustine's friend and mentor, Ambrose of Milan, declared that any person who declines to come to the aid of a waylaid neighbor should be considered at fault: other-regard requires that we come to the rescue of the needy and the vulnerable wherever it is at all possible. In a similar vein, Augustine himself perceived "a moral duty for those who possess power to protect those who are relatively impotent when they are being threatened by others more powerful than they."[101] This commitment to the oppressed crystallized in the sixteenth century, in the context of the Spanish conquest of the Americas, as a duty to "protect the innocent" from injustice. Of particular note on this subject is the thinking of Francisco Vitoria.

Vitoria's significance relates in part to his assertion that it is lawful for an external force to wage war in order to save the innocent from their oppression.

The proof of this position, Vitoria reasons, is provided by the fact that God commanded each man to care for his neighbor, where "neighbor" is defined broadly as one's fellow human being.[102] Vitoria addresses this reasoning specifically to the case of the American Indians (whom he referred to as "barbarians"). These barbarians, he writes, are properly understood as victims of the tyranny of their own rulers—most notably their inclination to "human sacrifice practiced on innocent men [and] the killing of condemned criminals for cannibalism."[103] Vitoria asserts that foreign princes may intervene where such practices are commonplace on the grounds that the "barbarians are all our neighbors, and . . . anyone, especially princes, may defend them from such tyranny and oppression." Such an intervention would constitute a "lawful defense of the innocent."[104] He expands upon this reasoning in a passage in his 1537 *Relectiones*:

> Christian princes can declare war on the barbarians because they feed on human flesh and because they practice human sacrifice. The proof is as follows. First, if they eat or sacrifice innocent people, princes can defend the latter from harm, according to the passage: "Deliver them that are carried away unto death, and those that are ready to be slain see that thou hold them back" [Proverbs, 24:11] . . . It is no reply to argue that they neither seek nor wish this help; it is lawful to defend an innocent man even if he does not ask us to, or even if he refuses our help, especially when he is suffering an injustice in a matter where he cannot renounce his rights, as in the present case. No one can give another the right to kill him, whether it be to eat him or sacrifice him. Besides it is certain that the victims of these practices are often unwilling, for example children.[105]

Vitoria concludes that princes are within their rights to wage war upon the barbarians to force them to give up these rituals of human sacrifice and cannibalism. Suarez and Luis Molina present similar arguments supporting the idea that Christian love sometimes requires princes to wage wars so that the innocent may be protected from injustice.[106] Interestingly, both Vitoria and Suarez clearly remark that the right to wage a war to protect the innocent does not translate into a right of occupation, dominion, or conquest.[107]

Vitoria figures prominently in Johnson's treatment of Christian love and just cause, as does Paul Ramsey.[108] Writing in the twentieth century, Ramsey also draws upon the implications of love to make the case that state leaders should sometimes wage war so that the innocent may be protected from injustice. He does so by way of an argument pertaining to the relationship between force and politics. Force, he submits, may be employed in the political realm in order to promote the ideal of an ordered justice, as dictated by

Christian love. Ramsey is keen to impress upon his readers that all state leaders have an obligation to use force to prevent injustice and restore justice where they can.[109] Indeed, there is a marked leaning in his work toward what Johnson labeled a presumption against injustice. This is most apparent in his 1965 essay on intervention. "No authority on Earth," he writes, "can withdraw from 'social charity' and 'social justice' their intrinsic and justifiable tendencies to rescue from dereliction and oppression all whom it is possible to rescue."[110] Where circumstances allow, state leaders are obliged to work toward achieving the "charitable extension of an ordered justice" even where this demands the use of force. Put more simply, state leaders must commit their states to the promotion of a just world where it is practicable, and they must display particular regard for correcting and overturning injustice in the international sphere. This produces a praxis of intervention backed by an internationalist ethic.

In Johnson's hands, then, Christian love draws together the writings of Ramsey, Suarez, Vitoria, and Augustine, and serves as a key thematic line in the historical development of the just war tradition. Crucially, it is presented as producing a strongly interventionist ethic that does not distinguish between neighbor and stranger. Christian love or charity requires the prince to wage war wherever doing so is likely to halt injustice and direct people back to God's will. What is most fundamental in this conception of the right to war, Johnson writes, is that it justifies the use of force not out of self-interest but solely for the sake of others.[111] It is a "duty of Christian love," Johnson writes, "to defend the innocent when attacked."[112]

Right Intention: The Aim of Peace

The third idea which Aquinas identifies as necessary for recourse to war follows closely from the emphasis placed on subjectivity by the idea of Christian love—this is the requirement that "those who wage war should have a righteous intent."[113] Johnson argues in his most recent writings that right intention and the aim of peace tend to be overlooked in contemporary just war thinking. He considers this a major problem as this requirement is central to the very idea of the just war as he perceives it.[114] But what is right intention? Johnson again follows Aquinas's lead here. Aquinas offers two possible meanings for right intention. The first meaning relates to the subjective motives for acting. Drawing on Augustine, it equates right intention with the absence of base *motives*—"the desire to do harm, the cruelty of vengeance, an unpeaceable and implacable spirit, the fever of rebellion, the lust to dominate, and similar things"—declaring that any war would be rendered unlawful by such corruption.[115] Secondly, and more interestingly, right intention might be taken to stipulate that war must be undertaken with an *intention* or will to affect righteous change; a war must have the object of "securing peace, of punishing evildoers, and of uplifting the good."[116] Put more simply, those waging war, Aquinas writes, "should intend either to promote a good or avert an evil."[117] It is this second understanding of right intention that Johnson dwells upon in his recent writings. He is concerned in this respect to treat war as a possible force for good in the world.

The possibility of wars waged to promote a good contains within it an opening to what Jonathan Barnes calls the doctrine of "ameliorative warfare," which holds that the justice of a given war is determined not by the antecedent misdeeds of one's enemy but by the anticipated results of going to war.[118] This approach is most often associated with Alexander of Hales (1185–1245), who writes that the justice of war in any instance lies in "the support of the good, the coercion of the bad, peace for all."[119] Thus, the end of war is related to "the pursuit of a supreme moral ideal."[120] Johnson's own reading of the just war tradition follows this opening to ameliorative war, to some degree. This is most apparent in the great weight he attaches to the idea that war can sometimes serve utility, thus relating the justification of force to the positive ends that a war can serve rather than the wrong that it is intended to redress. In this context, a typical account of right intention is expressed in *The War to Oust Saddam Hussein*, where Johnson argues that the justification of the Iraq war lies in the benefits that it might yet bring to Iraq. He describes the war in Iraq as an effort to install good and just governance in Iraq, rather than merely as a response to the threat posed by Saddam Hussein's arsenal of WMD, and argues that it may be justified on these grounds. Underpinning the requirement of right intention is the conviction that force may be employed to make the world a better place. In this respect, it pays only scant respect to the status quo. Instead, it requires a willingness to challenge the status quo wherever doing so might produce some net benefit in terms of peace, order, and justice. The "ideal" of the just war tradition, Johnson concludes, is not to maintain the status quo, but to actually foster a more just and orderly peace.[121]

This gentle nod in the direction of progressivism lends Johnson's reconstruction of the just war tradition a strongly interventionist feel. This is not something he shies away from. In his own words:

> Just war reasoning tends to support the idea of intervention for humanitarian purposes. The classic tradition makes no distinction as to whether the person or people in sovereign authority may use force in response to a violation of the peace at home or abroad; rather, while the moral responsibilities of government

have, first of all, to do with securing the just and peaceful order of the sovereign's own political community, they extend also to protecting the frame of orderly, just, and peaceful relations among political communities, for without this, the good of each individual community is at risk.[122]

By privileging the thematic lines of Christian love and vindicative justice in his reconstruction of the "classic tradition," Johnson produces a particular reading of the just war tradition that is by character "interventionist" and broadly speaking favorable toward the practice of humanitarian war.[123]

Conclusion

When Bush and Blair sought to justify the invasion of Iraq by means of humanitarian arguments, both leaders stressed a much more robust conception of humanitarian war than the twentieth century approach sanctions. They offered a conception of humanitarian war that arguably privileged a "presumption against injustice" over a "presumption against the use of force." They variously sought to justify the war as a means of promoting a more just world order and exporting democracy and human rights to Iraq while still relating their case to the just war ideal. Bush and Blair's approach to humanitarian war against Iraq, it seems, was more consistent with the classical idea of the just war as Johnson presents it than more standard twentieth century just war thinking. Johnson himself recognizes this, claiming that Bush and Blair's humanitarian case for war was "strong" and in line with the spirit of the just war idea.[124] It would seem then, on this basis, that it is the twentieth century approach to humanitarian war (rather than Bush and Blair's arguments for invading Iraq) that is out of step with the historical thrust of the just war tradition. This is certainly an idea that Johnson is keen to support, constantly claiming that the circumscribed approach to intervention adopted by, for example, the NCCB, is a wrong turn in terms of the development of the just war tradition.[125]

Where, then, does this leave us? Having surveyed the three justifications Bush and Blair offered for the invasion of Iraq, and located them within the context of the just war tradition, we are in a position to make some more sweeping comments. I will restrict myself to three main points here. First, the broader conception of humanitarian war presented by Bush and Blair in the context of the Iraq debate rests easily alongside the punitive and anticipatory justifications discussed in Chapters 2 and 3. Viewed collectively, all three lines of justification may be viewed as innovative engagements with the just war tradition and all three suggest a more expansive approach to the jus ad bellum. They variously present a right to war that is not restricted to the idea of defense against aggression but is couched in far-reaching, expansive, moralistic tones. Classical tropes relating to good and evil, the rescue of the innocent, and the imperatives of fear figured particularly prominently in the debate over Iraq and now appear to have some renewed life in contemporary just war thought. This suggests that the strictures of the legalist paradigm are being disregarded and that a loosening of the jus ad bellum may currently be taking place. This is an interesting possibility. If it is indeed the case, it would represent a signal shift in direction for the just war tradition, as the history of the jus ad bellum over the past two centuries arguably reflects a progressive narrowing and restriction of the right to war in international society.

Second, given that the terms in which we discuss the social world are to some extent constitutive of that world, the potential loosening of the jus ad bellum should be taken as more than just a shift in rhetoric, epiphenomenal in character.[126] It has very real implications for praxis. After all, the manner in which we argue about war "helps to constitute the character of [that] practice."[127] Certain modes of conduct are enabled and others restrained by the "perlocutionary force" of the manner in which we seek to justify our wars.[128] This is most apparent when we consider how framing our just cause arguments in strong, moralistic terms diminishes expectations regarding adherence to jus in bello norms. Where the jus ad bellum is phrased in terms of a broadened concept of justice that speaks to ideas of good and evil and the Christian faith, there is a greater likelihood that the jus in bello imperative of restraint may be eclipsed. This tendency towards a denial of the *jus in bello* is indeed alarmingly evident in much of the discourse surrounding the war in Iraq as well as the War on Terror currently being pursued by the United States and its allies. The stated willingness of the United States to discard restraints and employ dubious means of war, such as "coercive intelligence collection" in Camp X-Ray and various other detainment facilities or the deployment of white phosphorous in centers of enemy activity such as Fallujah, testifies to this. As a captain in the U.S. Marines confirmed just prior to the 2005 military offensive on Fallujah, the "gloves" have most certainly come off in the prosecution of the War on Terror.[129] Worryingly, it is a dynamic that has been all too apparent in Iraq, at least if the words of Lt. Col. Gary Brandl of the U.S. Marines are to be taken seriously. When rallying American troops for the aforementioned assault on Fallujah, Brandt told his men that "the enemy has got a face. He's called Satan. He's in Falluja. And we're going to destroy him."[130]

Acknowledging the perlocutionary force of our jus ad bellum arguments in this way should prompt us to reflect upon the manner in which we speak about the right to war today. In particular, it should raise the issue of whether we should allow any room for subjective, broad-based moral claims and considerations (such as those that refer to good and evil) in the present-day jus ad bellum. Scholars such as Jutta Brunee and Stephen Toope argue that we should resist such a move for it risks muddying the conceptual waters and undermining the capacity of international law to restrain aggressive war.[131] Opposing this view is James Turner Johnson. The thrust of much of his work is to argue that the moral element of the jus ad bellum should not be bracketed for the sake of the creation of some legal order that relies on formal, procedural, and objective categories. To exclude the moral element of the jus ad bellum, he argues, would be a "reductionist" move that would entail turning our backs on much of what the just war tradition, as it has been passed down from Augustine to the present day, has to teach us.[132] Given the loosening of the jus ad bellum that we currently seem to be witnessing, and the revival of the language of good and evil that has accompanied it, this debate as to whether we should allow the jus ad bellum a moral element has acquired a fresh urgency of late. The revivification of the language of good and evil, along with the very idea of punitive war, has forced our hand in this regard. This, however, is a debate that I cannot enter into in any serious manner here. Perhaps it is enough that this chapter has expressed concern that where the jus ad bellum is allowed a strong, moralistic content, it may overwhelm the possibility of restraint in war, especially when the jus in bello is framed in comparatively weak juristic tones. One might note in this respect that the modern jus in bello, based as it is upon rights and protocols, necessarily appears shallow when confronted with the language of vindicative justice and Christian love. As the Bob Dylan song goes, "You don't count the dead with God on your side." One would be well advised on this basis alone to exercise caution when advocating a broader-based conception of the right to war.

Third, the potential loosening of the jus ad bellum should alert contemporary just war theorists to the possibility of change and continuity that underpin the tradition. At stake here is not just the question of how we understand just war reasoning today, but also how we relate it to the historical development of the just war tradition itself. Chapters 5 and 6 will address this issue in more detail and look to map out how we might understand the just war tradition *qua* tradition, paying particular attention to the question of how we might account for the modalities of continuity and change that animate its historical development. Chapter 5 will be particularly concerned to undertake some form of second-order analysis focused on how the idiom of the just war was taken up and engaged by three of today's leading just war theorists in the context of the Iraq debate. The aim is to acquire some understanding of how the just war tradition is referred to, and deployed, in the course of moral debate, while also indicating how the tradition might be reconstituted through this very activity. It is to this task that we turn now.

CHAPTER 5

Whose Just War, What Tradition?

Introduction

The profusion of unorthodox justifications offered for the invasion of Iraq, reviewed in Chapters 2, 3, and 4, suggests that significant developments are afoot in the just war tradition. It indicates that the jus ad bellum is in the process of being reconstituted along more broad-based lines: as classical moral tropes relating to good and evil, the rescue of the innocent, and the imperatives of fear are reappearing in just war discourse, the strictures of the legalist paradigm are being disregarded. Accordingly, the Iraq debate provides a context against which we can explore the renegotiation of the just war tradition. The general purpose of this chapter, and the next, is to examine the modalities of this renegotiation. What this requires is not an examination of whether the justifications canvassed in earlier chapters were appropriately applied to Iraq, but some form of second-order analysis focused on how the idiom of the just war was taken up and engaged by scholars and practitioners in this particular instance. The aim is to acquire some understanding of how the just war tradition is referred to, and deployed, in the course of moral debate, while also indicating how the tradition might be reconstituted through this very activity.

Of course, the very idea of the reconstitution of the just war tradition belies the notion that it is already previously constituted in some way or other, replete with its own basic "postulates" of engagement.[1] It supposes that the tradition is premised upon certain assumptions, conditions, and commitments, and bounded by certain parameters, understood as definitive of the very notion of the just war tradition. This leads us to the nub of the issue to be explored here: a review of the literature on the just war tradition reveals many diverse views on which assumptions, conditions, and commitments are key to, and definitive of, this tradition. Where one account of the just war tradition privileges a particular normative orientation as the *sine qua non* of the tradition, others will stress a certain historical origin as key, or a given chain of transmission as essential. Indeed, different views with respect to this very issue are apparent when one considers the images of the just war tradition presented by the various theorists discussed in previous chapters. The specific function of this chapter is to draw out and elaborate the various images of the just war tradition suggested by Michael Walzer, Jean Bethke Elshtain, and James Turner Johnson in the course of their engagement with the moral debates generated by the invasion of Iraq.[2] These three authors have been selected for two reasons: first, they are three of the most influential contemporary just war theorists and their respective work is a reference point in the field; second, they have all contributed substantially to the Iraq debate. Thus all three sections of this chapter will be devoted to elucidating the respective accounts of the just war tradition put forward by these thinkers.

There is much value in this task. Specifically, it achieves three ends. First, it provides us with a richer understanding of the moral debates over Iraq, as they pertained to the just war tradition. It does so by providing us with some insights as to the "platforms of understanding" that conditioned the arguments offered by the various theorists in question.[3] Second, it awakens us to the difficulties that attend any attempt to articulate a definition of the just war tradition. Thirdly, and perhaps most importantly, it informs us as to how these various attempts to impose a settled definition upon the just war tradition may (at least partially) determine the future development of that tradition by directing it down certain paths instead of others, excluding certain voices from consideration, and disciplining those voices that do get a hearing.

All of this leaves one rather large question pending. All three accounts of the just war tradition surveyed here are very different from one another. Each privileges different postulates as providing the basic premise of the just war tradition. It might appear, then, to paraphrase R. B. J. Walker, that there is no single tradition of just war, but rather a knot of historically constituted tensions, contradictions, and evasions.[4] In place of a unified or coherent just war tradition, we are greeted by a cluster of rival theories and competing visions. Faced with this plurality of competing and seemingly incommensurable accounts of the just war tradition, we must acknowledge the possibility that the conviction that there is such a thing as *the* just war tradition, singularly conceived, may be flawed. If we concede this view, it would necessitate dismissing the whole notion that we share a common just war tradition with Augustine, Aquinas, and Grotius (and even Bush and Blair, among others) as nonsensical. Such a concession would undermine the basic assumption shared by most just war theorists that there is a unitary just war tradition that somehow unites political thinkers (like Walzer, Elshtain, Johnson, Augustine, Aquinas, and Grotius) and political leaders (such as Bush and Blair) alike in a common framework of meaning. How, then, do we understand the just war tradition in such a way that it comprises a unitary field, encompassing all these divergent voices and rival visions? The final section of this chapter will attempt to frame an answer, very much in interpretative terms, to this difficult question. This is intended to prepare the way for the analysis of current—that is, post-Iraq—developments taking place within the just war tradition that will form the subject matter of Chapter 6. My immediate concern, however, is to turn to Walzer's conception of the just war tradition in order to gauge some sense of the platforms of understanding that underpin his engagement in the moral debate over the invasion of Iraq.

Michael Walzer: Speaking Just War as a Language[5]

Walzer is widely credited with playing a crucial role in the revival of the just war tradition as an academic pursuit in the latter half of the twentieth century. Indeed, *Just and Unjust Wars* is afforded canonical status by many now working on matters related to the ethics of war and is a core text at the United States Military Academy.[6] In this work, Walzer gestures toward an account of the just war tradition as a language that reflects the moral reality (or experience) of war. This section will elucidate and comment upon Walzer's understanding of the just war tradition, as it is presented in his writings. Of particular interest here is the degree of malleability (or rigidity) assumed by Walzer's conception of the just war tradition. In order to reach this point, however, we must first spend some time exploring Walzer's presentation of the tradition as a moral language.

Walzer speaks of the tradition as a set of ideas that inform "the ordinary language in which we argue about particular wars. It is the way most of us talk when we join political debates about whether to fight and how to fight."[7] These ideas, he writes, are "our common heritage, the product of many centuries of arguing about war," and they provide us with a "moral language" for carrying on those arguments.[8] Writing in autobiographical style, Walzer comments that he was first moved to argue in terms of the just war in the course of protesting against the Vietnam War in the 1970s. Where these protests were concerned, the just war provided a "vocabulary" through which to express his anger and indignation at the actions of his government. Thus he learned to use words such as "aggression," "just cause," "intervention," "self-defense," "neutrality," and "atrocities," and to appreciate that they brought a certain weight, born of their historicity, to bear on his protests.[9]

Crucially, however, he also came to understand that his protests, as well as his anger and indignation, were "shaped" by these words that the just war tradition made available to him.[10] So while it is true that this language may be used instrumentally, it also possesses "its own structure," which determines what may be argued to some extent.[11] The just war tradition, then, may properly be understood as a language through which we can access, debate, and contribute to the moral questions that every war inevitably provokes. It provides us with a "medium of shared understanding and an arena of action" with which to make sense of, and respond to, the moral experience of war.[12] The terms of the just war, Walzer writes, "reflect the real world . . . They are descriptive terms, and without them we would have no coherent way of talking about war."[13]

If Walzer understands the just war tradition as a descriptive language, he recognizes that it is also constitutive of the moral reality of war that it purports to describe. The just war tradition not only provides us with a glossary of terms to describe war, it also assigns (moral) meaning to war, and establishes our relation to it. How we "arrange and classify and think" about war in moral terms is deeply delimited, or partly determined, by the "conceptual, argumentative, and rhetorical resources" of the tradition.[14] It is, Walzer writes, how we argue about war that "makes [it] what it is."[15] He elaborates, "Reiterated over time, our arguments and judgments shape . . . the moral reality of war—that is, all those experiences of which moral language is descriptive or within which it is necessarily employed. It is important to stress that the moral reality is not fixed by the actual activity of soldiers but by the opinions of mankind. That means, in part, that it is fixed by the activity of philosophers, lawyers, publicists of all sorts."[16] This, then, is the hermeneutic circle within which Walzer operates. While he acknowledges that our arguments and judgments do not take place in isolation from the experience of combat, and have value only insofar as they render that experience comprehensible, he also wishes to argue that they contribute to how we experience combat in the first place. As a language, then, the just war tradition does two distinct things, though they can hardly be separated: first, it contributes to the moral reality of war by establishing it as a frame of reference, and, second, it provides us with a set of terms with which to make sense of that reality.

Walzer's contention that language provides a medium for understanding the world at the same time as it discloses and manifests the world for us suggests a certain affinity with the hermeneutic theory of Hans-Georg Gadamer.[17] In line with this, Walzer is keen to stress that the just war tradition is hardly a linguistic prison house from which one cannot escape. It is not an argumentative iron cage, hermeneutically sealed, in which people may find themselves trapped. To paraphrase Michael Oakeshott—another discernible influence on Walzer—it "does not impose upon an agent demands that he shall think certain thoughts, entertain certain sentiments, or make certain substantive utterances. It comes to him as various invitations to understand, to choose, and to respond."[18] On this view, a language such as the just war tradition is not a set of instructions to follow, nor is it a logic to be perfected. Rather, it is an inheritance that must be interpreted and reinterpreted, made and remade, by those who invoke it and engage its terms. Indeed, moral languages such as the just war tradition are best understood, Walzer writes, as the "products of many people talking, of real if always tentative, intermittent, and unfinished conversations . . . the work of many years of trial and error, of failed, partial, and insecure understandings."[19] They are, it follows, never finished or complete; rather, they appear as "perpetual works in progress."[20]

This approach emphasizes the evolutionary nature of moral languages such as the just war tradition by drawing attention to the fact that they must always be subject to change, revision, and even reinvention at the hands of their speakers. As James Boyd White writes, to learn and speak a language is "also to change it, for one constantly makes new gestures and sentences of one's own, new patterns or combinations of meaning. Language is in part a system of invention, an organized way of making new meaning in new circumstances."[21] Oakeshott, once again, expresses this understanding in penetrating fashion. As he puts it, every "vernacular of moral converse"—his term for a moral language—is a historic achievement of human beings:

> Each is a continuously accumulating residue of conditional relationships learned in an experience of intercourse between optative agents. It emerges as a ritual of utterance and response, a continuously extemporized dance whose participants are alive to one another's movements and to the grounds upon which they tread . . . This language is responsive to the aspirations of those who speak it . . . It is never fixed or finished, but (like other languages) it has a settled character in terms of which it responds to the linguistic inventions, the enterprises, the fortunes, the waywardness, the censoriousness, and sometimes the ridicule of those who speak it. It *is* its vicissitudes . . . It is learned only in being used.[22]

Extending this logic to the just war tradition, it seems obvious that it must always be subject to the processes of negotiation and renegotiation as its advocates seek to reinterpret and apply it to new scenarios and historical contexts. (Thus, for example, we can read the debate, introduced in Chapter 2, regarding the limits of self-defense as an attempt to renegotiate the "old rules" of the just war tradition to fit the "new threats" posed by global terrorism.)

Key here is the understanding that every engagement with the just war tradition is an act of interpretation and, to borrow Walzer's own typology, not an act of invention or discovery.[23] Interpretation requires critical introspection. It involves examining our moral languages as they are manifested in our "daily practices" with a view to elucidating them more clearly and subjecting them to internal critique.[24] It entails a working out of principles already present or latent in our daily practices, though they may hitherto have only been partially fulfilled, so that we might contribute to their progressive realization. By way of example, we might think of the manner by which the abolition of slavery was achieved in America: it was made possible by challenging every American to live up to that article of faith, already proclaimed by all, that all men are born free and equal. Interpretation always follows this course: at its core, it reflects a quest to realize more fully the principles upon which our common life is based.

Walzer's work on the just war tradition follows this model precisely. *Just and Unjust Wars* takes the form of an extended reconstruction of our understanding of the morality of war as it is reflected in the legal, moral, and political arrangements of international society. Consider, for example, Walzer's presentation of the legalist paradigm (discussed in detail in Chapter 1). It is not a work of discovery or invention; rather it is a sketch of the rules and principles that *already* structure and inform our understanding of war in international society. Its principles and terms are merely expressions of the moral realities of war that are embedded in the conventions of international society. Thus the propositions of the legalist paradigm reflect the rules governing interstate conduct. These rules, it is supposed, have been worked out over time by members of international society in their dealings with one another.[25] (Even in those cases where Walzer opts to revise the legalist paradigm—as in his desire to acknowledge the justice of humanitarian war or a more expansive right of anticipatory war—his stated aim is to reconcile the paradigm more closely with "the judgments we actually make."[26])

Not surprisingly, Walzer's interpretative approach to the just war tradition has not been to everyone's liking. It tends, in the eyes of some critics, to steer an unsure course between the perils of conservatism and relativism. Ronald Dworkin, for instance, delivers a critique of Wazer's conception of moral traditions that can be extended to Walzer's view of the just war tradition.[27] Dworkin accuses Walzer of positing moral traditions in general as little more than an "elaboration" of "conventional social arrangements."[28] Consequently, Dworkin argues, they tend toward conservatism and may be fairly adjudged to lack critical bite. Extending this critique to the just war tradition, we might contend that the tradition constitutes little more than a "mirror" of society, reflecting its shared understandings (and the compromises these entail), rather than a "yardstick" against which we measure the rights and wrongs of any chosen course of action or argument.[29] This conception of the tradition, the critique goes, is too "relaxed and agreeable": it promises a tradition that is "at peace" with society, rather than one that can stand against society as a site of criticism.[30] In other words, it reflects the practices of society back upon itself instead of holding them to some external standard. The just war tradition, thus conceived, is unlikely to provide a vehicle for speaking truth to power. A similar critique has also been offered by Brian Midgely, who accuses Walzer of stripping the just war tradition of its critical edge by severing it from its historical foundations.[31]

These are serious accusations to level at Walzer. The fact that just war thought has historically provided a site of criticism is one of its perceived strengths. According to Elshtain, for instance, the "specific strength embedded in [the tradition's] ontology of peace is the vantage point it offers with reference to social arrangements, one from which its adherents frequently assess what the world calls peace and find it wanting. From Augustine's thunderings against the *Pax Romana* to John Paul II's characterization of our present armed-to-the-teeth peace as the continuation of war by other means . . . just war thinking has . . . offered a critical edge."[32]

Walzer, however, is able to respond to this critique by pointing to the possibility of "internal criticism," which he alludes to in the preface to the first edition of *Just and Unjust Wars*. We can hold the judgments and justifications people commonly make to account, Walzer writes, by seeking out their coherence and laying bare the principles they exemplify. We can "expose the hypocrisy of soldiers and statesmen who publicly acknowledge these commitments while seeking in fact only their own advantage . . . we hold such people to their own principles, though we may draw these out and arrange them in ways that they had not thought of before."[33] Again, we might think here of the success achieved with respect to the abolition of slavery in America by this form of social criticism. Perhaps, then, it is not as toothless as its critics would have us believe.

Walzer is still, however, prone to the charge that his understanding of the just war tradition slides into historical relativism. During those periods when international society is undergoing some form of radical change, the just war tradition as it is presented by Walzer must absorb these developments and come itself to reflect them. We do not have to look far for an example of such an instance: consider how the realities of American hegemony currently impose upon the just war tradition, forcing some consideration of questions related to *jus post bellum* and the responsibilities of empire (it is Walzer who is leading the way in addressing these questions[34]). The broader point here, however, is that the just war tradition (as it is presented by Walzer) reflects a degree of historical mutability bordering on relativism. We might like to question, then, whether the just war tradition could evolve, or is in the process of evolving, to reflect the new security environment such that the jus ad bellum is phrased in more broad-based and far-reaching terms than previously. This issue will be addressed in Chapter 6. For the moment, we will keep our attention focused on Walzer's conception of the just war tradition.

While it is true that Walzer's conception of the just war tradition presupposes some degree of historical mutability or even relativism *in theory*, he suggests that the historical record does not quite bear this out. Although the tradition's capacity for change and variation is certainly real enough, and makes for a compelling tale, "the importance of that tale . . . is easily exaggerated."[35] Empirically speaking, Walzer claims, the just war tradition has remained relatively stable from generation to generation. It is a language that spans centuries, displaying a remarkable consistency over the passage of time. Thus, it is possible that we share the same basic words and means for arguing about war as did our historical predecessors.[36] Walzer supports this assertion by pointing to the commonalities shared by the various, historically separated accounts of King Henry's conduct at the Battle of Agincourt. Holinshead, David Hume, and William Shakespeare, writing at very different times and for very different audiences, all offered their thoughts on this episode. What is striking for Walzer is that these accounts are still "structured by underlying agreements" and work within the same paradigm of meaning.[37] There is, then, for Walzer, a timelessness about the just war tradition, though it is best characterized as historical, sociological, and contingent. So while it displays a potential for renovation and change, the tradition also reflects a strong element of continuity. Subsequently, we can be relatively confident that when we tap into the language of the just war, we are participating in a transhistorical dialogue with the great and the good of previous generations.[38]

Crucially, such dialogue should be understood as challenging and developing, rather than canonizing, the ideas of those who have come before us.[39] Walzer's faith in the critical capacity of dialogue is evidence of his firm belief that the tradition offers an internal perspective from which inconsistencies in its own practices, foundations, and espoused norms might be scrutinized. Dialogue, it follows, is an interpretative process that involves the working out of shared meanings in a given historical context. It provides a means through which we can determine whether the internal rules, maxims, and ideals of the tradition support certain interpretations and derivations or not. It allows us, in other words, to "mark off better from worse arguments, deep and inclusive accounts of the just war tradition from shallow and partisan offerings."[40] We will return, in Chapter 6, to Walzer's contribution to the transhistorical dialogue of the just war tradition. Now, though, I will turn to Jean Bethke Elshtain's conception of the just war tradition, as she tapped into it during the course of the Iraq debate.

Jean Bethke Elshtain's Burden of Order[41]

Jean Bethke Elshtain's *Just War against Terror* is one of the most significant statements of the just war tradition in recent years, and has provoked much comment and controversy.[42] It assumes a certain view of the just war tradition that stands in contrast to that proposed by Walzer. As we have just seen, Walzer's just war tradition reflects the "sheer continuity of usage" that the everyday practices of international society presuppose, and gives little or no attention to the origins of these practices.[43] In his own words, he is less interested in the "making of the moral world" than he is in its "present character."[44] By contrast, Elshtain's view of the just war tradition conserves a highly specific account of its origins. It stresses the historical roots of the tradition—that is, its moment of creation—as its locus point. As such it suggests a second way of understanding and approaching the just war tradition.

Elshtain specifically identifies the origins of the just war tradition with Augustine. Just war, as a continuing narrative, she writes, "starts with Augustine."[45] He may be regarded as the "acknowledged forefather" of the tradition.[46] It is his elaboration of the notion of *Tranquillitas Ordinas* and the burden of order that provides the tradition's point of departure, and most visible landmark, according to Elshtain. She submits, "When citizens evoke justice [in relation to war], they tap into the complex Western tradition called 'just war'. The origins of this tradition are usually traced from St Augustine's fourth-century masterwork, *The City of God*. In that massive text, Augustine grapples with how best to think about force and coercion in light of the fact that the Christian savior was heralded as the Prince of Peace by angels proclaiming 'peace on earth and goodwill' to all peoples."[47]

According to Elshtain, Augustine's thoughts on these matters provide the genesis of the just war tradition, "framing" subsequent centuries of theorizing on the justice of war in the fallen world.[48] It identifies the human condition with the problematic of the proper relationship between force, order, justice, and peace, and suggests the *Tranquillitas Ordinas*, rather than utopian idealism, as the proper standard for human conduct. It "requires actions and judgments in a world of limits, estrangements, and partial justice [and] fosters recognition of the provisional nature of all political arrangements."[49] Indeed, order of a provisional nature is posited as the condition for civic life, and governments are charged with the responsibility for its preservation.[50] Thus Elshtain claims, "The presupposition of just war thinking is that war can sometimes be an instrument of justice; that war can help to put right a massive injustice or restore a right order where there is disorder, including those disorders that . . . call themselves 'peace.'"[51] The primary responsibility of government, then, is the same today as it was in the days of Rome: it is to provide for basic security and ordinary civic peace—or, in Elshtain's words, derived from Augustine, to uphold the *Tranquillitas Ordinas*.

Indeed, the Augustinian roots of the just war tradition have, in Elshtain's view, conditioned its historical development. This holds true for the evolution of the tradition from the medieval canonists, through the natural law thinkers of the early modern period, right up to Elshtain's own contribution.[52] Thus, for Elshtain, the Augustinian origins of the just war tradition constitute its primary platform of understanding. She proposes that the tradition is rational only in terms of this past—its "creative and charismatic" origins—with which it must maintain some connection.[53] It is comprehensible only as a historical project set in motion at its point of origin, and its continued force, or authority, is provided for by reference to those origins.[54] Hence Elshtain's statement that just war thinking must stay true to its Augustinian roots if it is to "remain honest."[55] Where just war thinking loses its connection to its Augustinian origins, where it deviates from the template provided by the *Tranquillitas Ordinas*, its relationship to the just war tradition is thrown into doubt. In such cases, it is probably better characterized as some variant on liberal institutionalism or a kind of generic internationalist sentimentalism rather than just war thought, properly conceived.[56] Consequently, its ongoing development must be understood as a furtherance of the creative actions with which it began, and its origins must be considered constitutive of the tradition as a whole. The tradition's past, then, is never something to be merely discarded, but rather the condition of its ongoing development. Such a conception of the tradition supposes, as Alasdair MacIntyre writes, that "the present is intelligible only as a commentary upon and response to the past."[57] Elshtain, however, would disagree with MacIntyre's belief that a tradition, while seeking to preserve the canonical status of its origins, can eventually break free of them.[58] For Elshtain, a tradition must remain true to its origins, displaying a fidelity to them that precludes their transcendence.

The danger with privileging the origins of a tradition, in the manner that Elshtain does, is that one's choice of starting point is always likely to be more or less tendentious. This is certainly the case with Elshtain's election of

Augustine as the starting point for the just war tradition. A strong case could be made for looking beyond Augustine to Cicero and Greek and Roman practice for the roots of the just war tradition. Indeed, Paul Christopher, Gregory Reichberg, and Henrik Sysse, among others, do precisely this.[59] Moreover, they have plausible grounds for doing so; Augustine's elaboration of the very idea of the just war is derived from Cicero's definition of just war, which survives substantively unaltered right through to the modern period.[60] On the other hand, an equally strong case could be made for dating the just war tradition back no further than the late Middle Ages. James Turner Johnson takes this route; he argues that the tradition does not emerge in *recognizable* form until at least 1500 AD when canonical and chivalric codes merge with theories of natural justice.[61] The problem here, however, is not really that Elshtain selects a particularly loaded starting point when better options are available, but that all starting points are, in the final analysis, necessarily and equally tendentious. The story to be told has to begin somewhere. Where we choose to begin will reflect no less (and maybe no more) than the stories we wish to tell about the tradition.[62] As Oakeshott writes, to inquire into "origins" is to "read the past backwards and thus assimilate it to subsequent or present events." It is, he continues, an enquiry that "looks to the past to supply information about the 'cause' or the 'beginning' of an already specified situation . . . governed by this restrictive purpose, it recognizes the past only insofar as it is represented in this situation, and imposes upon past events an arbitrary teleological structure."[63] In Elshtain's case, her choice of Augustine as the starting point of just war tradition reflects her will to present that tradition as an extended meditation on the question of how to maintain some minimal order in world affairs.

This is fine in so far as it goes, except that the issue of starting points is of great consequence where Elshtain is concerned, owing to the fact that she defines the tradition almost entirely in relation to its origins. The upshot of this is a foreclosed conception of the tradition that is not amenable the validity of alternative accounts of just war and may even lead us to deny their legitimacy. As Walker writes, "the identification of a point of origin . . . is always liable to turn into a powerful myth of origin. Other points of departure are rendered trivial or even unthinkable."[64] As one's tendentiously selected starting point comes to appear natural and inevitable, other equally plausible points of departure and accounts of the tradition are likely to be stifled.[65] Moreover, it will appear *proper* that these alternative accounts are stifled, for they are convicted in advance of irrelevance.[66] This is evidence that a "silencing logic" is at work.[67] With respect to Elshtain, this is most apparent when we observe the short shrift she gives Aristotelian accounts of the just war tradition, which focus on the politics of the common good. An Aristotelian politics of the common good, she offers, always sounds good, but "may prompt its adherents to evade doing what is necessary to curb violence, domestic and international; they may indulge in naïve advocacy and refuse to engage with the least pleasant realities of a world in conflict. 'Justice' and 'non-violence' too easily become mantras divorced from the realities of a world descending into a vortex of horrible threats and even more terrible realities."[68] What she dismissively labels pseudo-pacificist approaches to the just war tradition fare even worse at her hands.

In the same respect, Elshtain's presentation of the just war tradition moves the weight of that tradition away from the legalist paradigm. This is clear with respect to five key issues. First, it supposes that questions of *international justice as equal regard* lie at the heart of the tradition, rather than the imperative to respect the sanctity of borders and state sovereignty. Second, good and evil are perceived as being of central concern, whereas the legalist paradigm eschews them as indicative of a troublesome moralism. Third, the notion of punitive war moves center stage in place of the legalist paradigm's overriding focus on defense and aggression. Fourth, the state leader is posited as the minister of God charged to carry out His will on Earth rather than merely the custodian of an elevated bureaucratic office. Finally, there is, for Elshtain, something above and beyond the "morality of states" that marks the parameters and supplies much of the content of the legalist paradigm. There is some awareness of, and trust in God at the heart of Elshtain's just war tradition that is completely absent in the legalist paradigm. The point here is that the framework of thinking fostered by Elshtain's focus on the just war tradition's origins in Augustinian politics favors the posing of certain problematics, and privileges certain readings of the just war tradition, while strangling others at birth.

James Turner Johnson and the Classical Idea of the Just War

Johnson, the foremost historian of the just war tradition, presents yet another vision of the tradition. Like Walzer, he stresses the role that interpretation must play in our understandings of the just war tradition, but approaches this task very differently. His approach is marked by a determination "to seek to identify and recover the historical tradition in its setting and fundamental purpose, and to apply an understanding of just war based in knowledge of that tradition to contemporary issues."[69] This leads him to present a Burkean reading of the just war tradition that depicts it as encompassing a "classical idea" distilled from the wisdom of the ages. This "idea," which he considers the central premise of the just war tradition, marks the sum of the tradition's historical development. This is distinct from the approaches put forward by both Walzer and Elshtain, who argue, respectively, that a *shared language* and common *origins* rather than some historically produced *core idea* provide the focal postulates of the tradition. This section will attempt to draw out Johnson's conception of the just war tradition, demonstrating both its close affinity with Edmund Burke's writing on tradition and its tendency toward gatekeeping.

Johnson presents the just war tradition as a body of moral wisdom deeply and broadly rooted in the history of international society.[70] Just war tradition, he writes, "represents above all a fund of practical moral wisdom, based not in abstract speculation or theorization, but in reflection on actual problems encountered in war as these have presented themselves in different historical circumstances."[71] Accordingly, it reflects a history of "interpretation and adaptation to changing contexts."[72] This is crucial for Johnson; he submits that it is through its vicissitudes that the tradition reveals itself to us. It follows that it may best be understood through study of its historical development. Accordingly, to grasp its meaning one must engage with "the tradition out of which it comes and [enter] into dialogue with the classical statement of the just war idea within that tradition. This is important . . . because it is by engaging the historical tradition of just war that we get at the values that underlie it and the lasting concerns about human life in political community on which just war thinking is based and which it expresses."[73] In other words, to think and speak seriously about the tradition, it is necessary to "take account of the historical just war tradition and engage the thinkers who shaped it in a continuing dialogue."[74] Johnson provides two reasons to support this claim. He submits that it is necessary to engage with the historical record, first, in order to acquire a proper understanding of the tradition and the stories of change and continuity that constitute its essence; and, second, in order to preserve the integrity of the tradition—or, in Johnson's words, to keep it "true to itself."[75]

Johnson's own writings display fidelity to this conviction that the just war tradition is best engaged through its historical development. He tends to introduce the tradition by recounting its historical development in narrative form. The format he adopts is fairly standard in this regard: he selects a basic repertoire of classic works—from Augustine to Walzer—arranges them chronologically, thereby infusing them with evolutionary significance, and treats them as a preconstituted tradition that culminates in the classic idea of the just war.[76] The following passage, drawn from Johnson's most recent work showcases this approach in typical, if somewhat abridged, fashion:

> The deepest roots of [the just war] tradition reach back into the history of biblical Israel and into the thought and practice of classical Greece and Rome. A specifically Christian version of it traces at least to Augustine in the fourth and

early fifth centuries. A coherent and systematic form of this tradition came together in the Middle Ages, over roughly the three centuries from the canonist Gratian's magisterial collection, the *Decretum*, in the mid-twelfth century to the end of the Hundred Years War in the mid-fifteenth century. At the beginning of the modern period, seminal thinkers from Francisco de Vitoria (1492–1546) to Hugo Grotius (1583–1645) assumed the terms of this tradition and applied them to the political conditions of their own times.[77]

Subsequent pages detail how the tradition evolved from Grotius to Walzer, taking in the contributions of Emmerich de Vattel, Francis Lieber, Paul Ramsey, and others along the way. An extended expression of this style of presentation can be found in Johnson's first major work on the just war tradition, *Ideology, Reason, and the Limitation of War*.

Emerging from the historical datum collated by Johnson is a view of the just war tradition as bounded by the moral-cultural imperatives of Christian love and vindicative justice. As Chapter 4 demonstrated, these imperatives function as key thematic lines in Johnson's reconstruction of the just war tradition. To recap briefly, Christian love might be summarized as a self-sacrificing form of other-regard modeled on Christ's suffering on the cross on behalf of sinful man. Johnson identifies pronounced expressions of Christian love in the writings of Ambrose, Augustine, Vitoria, Suarez, and Ramsey. He depicts these benchmark thinkers as forceful proponents of the view that the idea of the just war comprises an absolute ethic of other-regard, a commitment to universalism, and a rejection of injustice. Following this, he then proceeds to synthesize the ideal of Christian love variously presented by these major figures, effectively bringing the notion of *charity* forward into contemporary thinking on just war, even relating it to the war on Iraq. The second thematic line elaborated by Johnson refers to the notion of vindicative justice. The notion of vindicative justice is related to the responsibility of princes to exercise authority in the service of order and justice. Instructive here is Alfred Vanderpol's statement, "The Prince that declares war acts as a magistrate under the jurisdiction of which a foreign nation falls, *ratione delicti*, by reason of a very grave fault, a crime which it has committed and for which it has not wished to make reparation. As the depository of authority to punish a guilty subject, he pronounces the subject and acts to execute it in virtue of the right of punishment that he holds from God."[78] Johnson traces the notion of vindicative justice exemplified by this statement through Suarez's writings more generally, as well as through the writings of Augustine, Aquinas, and Vitoria, eventually relating it to the idea of sovereign authority as it is understood today.[79]

These thematic lines combine to affect what Johnson labels the "just war idea."[80] This idea is embedded in the historical development of the tradition and functions as its basic premise or core postulate; it constitutes its very essence, or, in Johnson's words, its "historical purpose."[81] Johnson describes it as encompassing a particular orientation toward war that falls between pacifism on the one side, and political realism and a crusading mentality on the other. At its most basic, it involves a "conception of the use of force that [accepts] it as a sometimes necessary tool of good statecraft, but at the same time [sets] strict yet meaningful moral restraints on the resort to force and the practical application of such force."[82] Importantly, it stresses the conviction not only that the use of force can sometimes be justified in the international realm, but that it is sometimes enjoined as a requirement of responsible government. It supposes that "just societies may sometimes employ force to protect themselves, their citizens, and the ideals of justice on which these societies depend, as well as the broader structure of international relations in which just societies coexist, against evil and the threat of evil directed at them."[83] On this view, then, the just war tradition is primarily about the role force may play in the exercise of the responsibilities of good government.[84]

This is where it starts to get interesting. The idea of the just war functions, for Johnson, as a certain (the proper) understanding of the just war tradition against which all just war discourse and engagements might be held up and "tested."[85] Contemporary just war discourse, he writes, "needs to be tested and disciplined by reference to historical just war tradition, especially by reference to the normative content and *purposes* of that tradition in its classic form."[86] Where contemporary discourse diverges in such a way that leads it to be "at odds with the historical purpose" of the tradition as Johnson understands it, it should be treated as a wrong turn, or a perversion of the just war idea.[87] Accordingly, it should be disregarded as a betrayal of the classical inheritance that the tradition bequeaths to us. What Johnson is proposing, then, is the deployment of a "deeper" historical understanding of the just war tradition as a "critical tool" to direct contemporary just war discourse, where it has strayed, back to its proper, historically constituted course.[88] This supposes that the past may be enlisted to speak to the present as a voice of criticism. For Johnson, then, "It is simply not the case, I think, that the 'making of the moral world' can be divorced from 'its present character,' as Michael Walzer suggests . . . [R]ather, the moral world as it was made in the past continues to be with us in the present, and responsible moral discourse must have a significant dialogue with the past and the processes which made it."[89] In other words, it is important that we look to the idea of the just war as it has been produced over time in order to preserve the historical integrity of the tradition. We must, Johnson urges, seek to maintain a strong link between contemporary just war discourse and the deeper tradition, instead of continually attempting to "invent the idea of just war anew, treating its categories as shells without content to be filled with contemporary meanings."[90] For Johnson, then, the appeal to the classical idea of the just war, and the wisdom of the ages that it reflects, serves as a safeguard against the "hubris of the present."[91] It promises to keep the tradition true to itself.

This mode of argument suggests that there is a Burkean element present in Johnson's thought. Edmund Burke is often associated with the view that the wisdom of the ages, usually embodied in traditions, provides the best tutor for political practice. Thus he refers to the British constitution, which comprises nothing more than a record of past practices and decisions, as the best guide British leaders could wish for when confronting the challenges that they would surely face in the future. According to Burke, it promises wisdom above reflection, the learning of the ages.[92] Such learning is the key to stability and indeed future progress; without it we could not possibly hope to surpass or even equal the achievements of the past. People, he writes, "will not look forward to posterity, who never look backward to their ancestors."[93] Conversely, any reflection that eschews the wisdom of the ages embodied in tradition is to be treated with suspicion. Indeed, Burke is wary of any line of thought that would disown the traditional past, and divorce us from its inheritance. Such a move is likely to undercut the foundations of society, cutting communities adrift from their own history and leaving them to flounder unaided in a present marked by turmoil and instability. For Burke, then, it is important that people remain true to the inheritance we receive in the form of tradition from past generations.

> [One] of the first and most leading principles on which the commonwealth and the laws are consecrated, is lest the temporary and life-renters in it, unmindful of what they have received from their ancestors, or of what is due to their posterity, should act as if they were the entire masters; that they should not think it among their rights to cut off the entail, or commit waste on the inheritance, by destroying at their pleasure the whole original fabric of their society; hazarding to leave those who come after them a ruin instead of an habitation—and teaching these successors as little to respect their contrivances, as they had themselves respected the institutions of their forefathers. By this unprincipled facility of changing the state as often, and as much, and in as many ways as there are floating fancies or fashions, the whole chain and continuity of the commonwealth would be broken. No one generation could link with the other. Men would become little better than the flies of the summer.[94]

Burke's concern here is that it is a great loss, and indeed a moment of great hubris, when traditions are "squandered or wantonly destroyed" by lack of attention or care.[95]

These are precisely the concerns motivating Johnson's engagement with recent developments in the just war discourse, particularly those developments relating to the emerging consensus that there is a presumption against war at the heart of the tradition. This engagement was alluded to in Chapter 4. It relates to the controversy surrounding the contention, advocated most forcefully by J. Bryan Hehir and the NCCB, that the just war tradition expresses a presumption against war. Both Hehir and the bishops' conference (now known as the USCCB—the United States Conference of Catholic Bishops) contend that there is a "strong presumption against the use of force" to be found in the just war tradition, while Johnson strenuously denies this on various occasions.[96] Johnson claims that a presumption against war is "nowhere to be found in the classical tradition as it took shape in the Middle Ages, and developed through much of the modern period."[97] Rather, the idea of a presumption against war is a relatively recent conceit, borne of the experience of total war in the twentieth century and the emergence of nuclear pacifism as a response to that experience. Hehir concedes these points, accepting that the "presumption against war" is a relatively recent innovation upon the just war tradition, while adding that it is a necessary and entirely beneficial move. "Johnson," he argues, "has often stated his view that the presumption against war is detrimental to the intention of the just war tradition and cannot be found in the classical authors. I think all would concede the last point and contest the first . . . [The] substantive reason for placing a presumptive restraint on war as an instrument of politics is, in my view, entirely necessary. Both the instruments of modern war and the devastation of civilian society which has accompanied most contemporary conflicts provide good reasons to pause (analytically) before legitimating force as an instrument of justice."[98] The question, then, is whether we should recognize a presumption against war as a welcome and useful addition to the just war tradition? Johnson's reaction to this question is telling with respect to his Burkean understanding of the just war tradition.

Johnson reacts very strongly to the emergence of a presumption against war in recent just war discourse. He argues that this emergence of a presumption against war in the just war tradition threatens to make the tradition "over into something very different from what it *properly* is."[99] Not only does it promise to confuse the proper order between the jus ad bellum and the jus in bello, as well as between the deontological and consequentialist categories of the jus ad bellum, it would also divorce contemporary just war reasoning from the classic just war idea that, as previously noted, stresses that force is not intrinsically evil, but instrumentally good or bad depending on the use to which it is put.[100] The emergence of a presumption against war in the just war tradition, Johnson argues, threatens to give the game away by treating the justification of war as an exercise in overriding a *prima facie* case against war rather than as part and parcel of the charge of responsible government and good statecraft. It promises to shift the just war over "into a position effectively pacifist in practice."[101] Such a development would divorce contemporary just war reasoning from its own heritage, thereby displaying a lack of fidelity to the idea of the just war.[102] It would squander the wisdom of the ages, as it were. On these grounds, Johnson rejects the emergence of a presumption against war in the just war tradition.

What is interesting about Johnson's argument here is the manner by which he appeals to a "deeper" understanding of the just war tradition in order to correct an instance where he perceives contemporary just war discourse to be diverging from the classical idea of the just war. In undertaking such a maneuver, Johnson presumes to locate himself at the headwaters of the tradition, in position to observe any instances when the just war idea is in danger of being diverted from its proper historical course.[103] Viewing the emergence of a presumption against war as one such instance, he reacts by depicting it as a departure or degeneration from its own beginnings. Additionally, he reasserts the classical idea of the just war by presenting it as the purest expression of the tradition's historical development.[104] It is, then, possible to perceive the Burkean elements of Johnson's conception of the just war tradition come to the surface. He is concerned to keep faith with those who have gone before, with the classic idea of the just war as it has been worked out by that lineage of great just war thinkers stretching from Augustine through to Vattel, and to extend their vision intact (and unblemished by perversions) to future generations.

There is a clear possibility of gatekeeping with such an approach. Appeals to the just war tradition as constituted by a core idea, historically understood, betoken a conservative approach. They may even serve to close down potential avenues of future development for the tradition, such as, for example, any further work that assumes a presumption against war. Thus, J. Bryan Hehir and the NCCB/USCCB have their credentials checked and found wanting at the door of the just war tradition, as conceived by Johnson. Their engagement with the historical tradition is too "spotty" for Johnson's liking, and the new assumptions and criteria they introduce alienates them from the classic just war idea.[105] Indeed, Johnson's account of the just war tradition acts to "circumscribe what counts as proper scholarship" in this field.[106] Yet this is not something that Johnson shies away from; indeed, he has emphasized his intention to "discipline" future contributions to the just war tradition on numerous occasions. His most recent monograph, *The War to Oust Saddam Hussein*, even includes a chapter, entitled "Disciplining Just War Thinking," that seeks to establish the parameters for future just war reasoning.[107] Johnson thus sets himself up as a custodian of the just war tradition, with all the hubris this entails—ironic, given Johnson's distaste for the hubris displayed by those who value innovation.

In fine, there is an inbuilt conservatism in Johnson's conception of the just war tradition. His writings reflect a pronounced antipathy toward those scholars who would discount the wisdom of the past, preferring instead to recast the just war categories as they see fit, imposing on them whatever meaning they find attractive or useful in the here and now. Against this view, Johnson repeatedly insists that taking the just war tradition seriously requires that we engage in an ongoing conversation with those who have come before us. At the heart of his writing, then, lies a respect for the authority of tradition and a rejection of the short-sighted "presentism" that marks much current just war thought.[108]

Many Just War Theories, One Just War Tradition

All three accounts of the just war tradition surveyed above are very different from one another. Each privileges different postulates as providing the basic premise of the just war tradition. Where Walzer speaks of the tradition as a moral language, Elshtain focuses on its Augustinian roots, and Johnson stresses the historically constituted core idea of just war. All three writers consequently produce divergent and sometimes seemingly incommensurable conceptions of just what the just war tradition is supposed to be. Before moving on, a brief summary of these divergences might be helpful.

Three main divergences may be discerned. First, while Walzer produces a conception of the just war tradition that is almost sociological in character—in that it is presented as a reflection of the moral experience of war in international society—Elshtain and Johnson's accounts respectively stress the roots and development of the tradition within a body of literature. When Johnson and Elshtain seek to bring the wisdom of the just war tradition to bear on debate, they are referring to the just war tradition as a body of thought derived from a canon of great works. Thus, Johnson seeks to illuminate contemporary discussions of humanitarian war by passing reference to the works of Vitoria and Suarez, while Elshtain constantly endeavors to inform these same debates with some Augustinian content. Walzer, on the other hand, perceives the just war tradition to have some life beyond a historical literature; it resides in the everyday practices and arrangements of international society. Second, and following from the first point, Johnson and Elshtain's conceptions of the just war tradition are much more engaged with the historical constitution of the tradition. They both display a great amount of concern to engage the ideas of those whom they see as their historical precursors within the tradition. Thus, Elshtain wears her commitment to an Augustinian frame of thought on her sleeve, while Johnson urges just war theorists to engage in dialogue with all those thinkers who have gone before us. Walzer, on the other hand, is blasé about the necessity of such an exercise. His concern, he states, is not with the historical making of the tradition, but with its present manifestation. Consequently, he does not look to bring the writings of past greats directly into contemporary debate, preferring instead to direct a form of internal critique at the practices of states and other members of international society.[109] Third, and finally, Elshtain and Johnson's accounts of the tradition are prone toward gatekeeping in a way that Walzer's conception of the tradition avoids. As such, both Elshtain and Johnson betray a proclivity to circumscribe what qualifies as a legitimate engagement with the just war tradition. For example, they exclude from the realm of just war tradition certain voices—such as those of Hehir and the NCCB/USCCB—which they feel do not meet the criteria of *bona fide* just war reasoning. Walzer's version, on the other hand, can accommodate a plurality of visions. His account of the just war tradition as a moral language is rather more open-textured than that presented by either Johnson or Elshtain. Where, then, does this leave us?

Faced with this plurality of competing and seemingly incommensurable accounts of the just war tradition, we must acknowledge the possibility that there is no such a thing as the just war tradition, singularly conceived. For a start, the idea of a multiplicity of just war traditions renders it impossible to speak directly of *the* just war tradition without qualification. Put simply, it suggests that we cannot speak or write of the tradition without stating whose version of it we are referring to. There would be, on this view, as many just war traditions as there are just war theorists. Instead, then, of a unified and coherent just war tradition, we would be left with nothing more than a knot of rival theories and competing visions. If we concede this view, it casts doubt upon the notion that we share a common just war tradition with Augustine, Aquinas, and Grotius (and even Bush and Blair, among others).

This does not seem quite right, though; it does not reflect how we typically refer to the just war tradition. Nor, indeed, does it reflect how these theorists refer to the just war tradition. Even though we (and here I am including the theorists just discussed) can recognize a plurality of just war theories, we commonly tend to refer to some idea of a unitary just war tradition that encompasses all these different versions and voices. Johnson, for instance, has written that though there may be a variety of different theories of just war in play at any one time, we may still speak in terms of a singular just war tradition; he submits that there is a sufficient amount of overlap between the various accounts of the just war to justify treating them as comprising a tradition.[110] He presents the argument that there is *one* just war tradition rather than many, and that this just war tradition accommodates a multiplicity of rival and competing voices (though his recent writings suggest a desire to discipline this pluralism, as previously discussed).[111] This is an assumption that is shared by both Walzer and Elshtain. Walzer refers on numerous occasions to the tradition as a framework that accommodates both consensus and disagreement, while Elshtain acknowledges that the tradition encompasses a variety of positions (not all of which are compatible with her own).[112] But on what grounds might such claims about the unity of the just war tradition stand? Is there a solid basis for assuming its existence? And if there are good grounds for assuming its existence, how should we conceptualize it? The task of this section is to examine these questions. In the course of so doing I will offer a substantive account of the just war tradition.

There are good grounds for speaking of a unitary just war tradition. These grounds are based on three observations. In the first place, we might like to note that the various accounts of the just war tradition outlined in this chapter share a number of commonalities. The presence of these commonalities indicates a degree of coherence among these various accounts, which is suggestive of the existence of an overarching tradition. As Johnson argues, though there are many different just war theories in play at any time, there is enough overlap between them to suggest that together they comprise a common just war tradition. The most basic area of agreement is that all of these rival theories and accounts assume that there is such a thing as *the* just war tradition, indicating some shared conception of the tradition that rises above the particularities of competing just war theories. For example, despite their very real disagreements and disconnects, Walzer, Elshtain, and Johnson are all united in claiming that we can speak of a common just war tradition. Other scholars have been less obvious in their acknowledgement of the tradition. Kant, for instance, famously derided the just war tradition as a school of "sorry comforters."[113] Barbed though it may have been, this must still count as a tacit subscription to the claim, expressed more openly by Johnson and Elshtain, that there is such a thing as the just war tradition.

But on what grounds do such claims about the existence of the just war tradition stand? A shared idea that there is such a thing as *the* just war tradition is not sufficient to establish it as a reality, and nor does it give us any idea of what the tradition looks like, assuming it is a reality. Rather, it merely indicates the possibility of a conversation framed by the notion of the just war tradition. A conversation naturally invites a variety of views, and the voices and modes of expression through which to advance them.[114] It is pluralist through and through; the interchange of voices is its whole point.[115] Accordingly, it often lacks coherence extending beyond its common frame of reference, which the notion of the just war tradition provides in this instance. People may speak past one another when engaged in conversation. Indeed, conversation often degenerates into a series of misunderstandings in which different modes of expression and different voices come together absent any mutual comprehension. In the worst instances, it resembles communicative breakdown, as occurred at the Tower of Babel.[116] Once again, then, we are presented with a cacophony of incommensurable and rival voices rather than evidence of a coherent or unified just war tradition. It becomes clear, in such cases, that the common expression of belief that there is such a thing as *the* just war tradition does not provide sufficient grounds for speaking of it as a unified entity.

Our second observation may help in this regard. It is informed by Walzer's friendly critique of Oakeshott's idea of conversation: where issues of morality are concerned, Walzer writes, "conversations turn naturally into arguments."[117] This is because moral talk draws people together in a common endeavor, endowing them with a common frame of reference, and therefore certain shared understandings. This insight points the way to a further, more substantive commonality between the various accounts of the just war tradition just mentioned. This commonality refers to the shared possession of a historically informed moral vocabulary and mode of reasoning. This moral vocabulary and mode of reasoning enables theorists and political leaders alike to engage one another (and other thinkers from both the past and present) in dispute regarding the rights and wrongs of war. It constitutes a set of themes, tropes, texts, concepts, codes, and conventions that Walzer, Elshtain, Johnson, Hehir, and the NCCB/USCCB, among others, associate with the notion of just war and commonly pay homage to in the course of their debates. These actors habitually refer to commonly held notions such as "just cause," "aggression," "self-defense," "punishment," and "anticipation," which then structure their debates. This is no shallow or superficial structure; each of these notions contains within it some encoded meaning conditioned by its historical usage. As J. L. Austin points out, concepts have histories and come to us with "trailing clouds of etymology."[118] In this case, these are the traces left by earlier thinkers such as Augustine, Aquinas, and Grotius, among others, who have also referred to these concepts, and who have fashioned and refashioned them in various ways according to the ends to which they put them. Thus the reference to commonly held notions such as "just cause," or "aggression," brings the weight of their historical memory to bear upon any debate. They carry with them the baggage of their earlier associations with Augustinian, scholastic, or Grotian lines of argument, and the just war tradition more generally. This is apparent, as Chapters 2 through 4 demonstrated, when we consider how certain arguments, relating variously to anticipation, punishment, and humanitarianism, made in the course of the debate attending the Iraq war, resonate with certain classical articulations of the jus ad bellum. Indeed, it was the just war tradition that provided the common medium through which Bush and Blair could engage the international community in *meaningful* debate regarding the rights and wrongs of the invasion of Iraq. Far from evidencing communicative breakdown in this instance, the just war tradition provided a common resource, a bounded rationality as it were, on which all parties to the debate could draw.

This suggests that we can speak comfortably of a unified just war tradition on the basis that it comprises a bounded rationality, and reflects the common possession of a moral vocabulary and mode of reasoning that is historically associated with the idea of just war. Yet there is more to it than this. This leads us, then, to our third observation. It is this: no moral vocabulary or mode of reasoning is freestanding; moral vocabularies always presuppose the existence of an interpretative community (that engages itself in arguing about how best to make sense of the given moral vocabulary and mode of reasoning). In this case, then, the third factor supporting the idea that there is such a thing as a unified just war tradition is the presence of such an interpretative community—which we might refer to as "the just war community"—represented here by Walzer, Elshtain, and Johnson (and Bush, Blair, and myself), engaged in attempting to understand the just war tradition. The phrase "just war community" is borrowed from Brian Orend, but it reflects Walzer's notion of the interpretative community.[119] For Walzer, an interpretative community is a body of people bound to a certain tradition by the fact that they look to find meaning and a vocabulary through which to express themselves within it.[120] Over the course of this book, I have extended this idea to those people who look to find meaning and a mode of expression within the just war tradition. Consequently, the just war community comprises that body of people who engage the tradition by arguing through (and about) the historically loaded terminology and vocabulary that is associated with it. This is a broad understanding of the just war community that allows that membership is open to anyone, be they an academic, a politician, or a member of the general public, who speaks its language.

The role of the interpretative community is actually quite central to the form that the tradition takes at any given time. Just as an argument is constituted by the contending positions of those who enjoin it, the just war tradition is, to a large degree, what its interpretative community makes of it. This means that the tradition will always be subject to negotiation and renegotiation, as its cluster of practitioners contest among themselves how it should be understood and approached. This, it must be stressed, is an act of interpretation and not an act of invention, discovery, or description.[121] It is a working out of meanings already present or latent in the tradition (though they may have been previously ignored or overlooked). Thus, the tradition comes to reflect the contestation, dispute, disagreement, and flux that mark the debates of its interpretative community.[122] Accordingly, it is not a static or fixed entity; rather, it is a permanently shifting field that reflects the interactions of its exponents. The disagreements and disputations of Walzer, Elshtain, and Johnson regarding the proper characterization of the just war tradition actually constitute, then, on this view, the warp and woof of the tradition. They provide the impetus behind its shifting form, if not its substance.

To recap briefly, I have offered three observations to support the assertion that there is such a thing as a unitary just war tradition rather than merely a knot of competing just war theories and voices. These observations related, respectively, to the common assumption that there is such a thing as the just war tradition, the association of this tradition with a specific moral vocabulary and mode of reasoning that carries with it historical connotations to the idea of just war, and the presence of an interpretative community engaged in arguing the form of the tradition. What we are left with, then, is a self-reflexive tradition that is only as vital as its interpretative community.[123] This vision calls our attention to the mutability of the tradition, its open-ended nature and capacity for change and development.

Conclusion

The moral debates attending the war in Iraq witnessed sharp exchange regarding the right to war today. Much of this debate was carried through the moral vocabulary of the just war tradition, as Chapters 2 through 4 demonstrated. However, a close reading reveals that many of the contributions to this debate betray different interpretations of the just war tradition. This is indicative of the difficulties attendant to any attempt to define the just war tradition. Indeed, many of today's most celebrated just war theorists appear divided over just what the tradition is. Walzer, Elshtain, and Johnson have each submitted accounts of the just war tradition that display little in common, except mutual disagreement. They all privilege different postulates of engagement, or platforms of understanding, as constitutive of the tradition, and consequently produce very different visions of the just war. Faced with this plurality of competing and seemingly incommensurable accounts of the just war tradition, we were forced to acknowledge the possibility that there is no such a thing as *the* just war tradition, singularly conceived. That is, we were forced to consider that instead of a unified and coherent just war tradition there is actually just a knot of rival theories and competing visions. The task confronting this chapter, then, was to ascertain whether there is some solid basis for speaking of a unified just war tradition.

This chapter argued that there are indeed good grounds for speaking of a unitary just war tradition. These grounds are based on three observations. The fact that theorists typically refer to *the* just war tradition rather than to a plurality of just war theories provides our first such observation. Despite their disagreements, Walzer, Elshtain, and Johnson join together in insisting that we can speak of a common just war tradition. This constitutes evidence of some shared conception of the just war tradition that rises above the particularities of competing just war theories. The second observation that we can point to in support of the just war tradition is the common possession of a historically informed moral vocabulary and mode of reasoning. The fact that just war theorists as diverse as Walzer, Elshtain, and Johnson—and, indeed, Augustine, Aquinas, and Grotius—all subscribe to a common vocabulary and grammar consisting of words such as "aggression," "punishment," and "anticipation," which are historically associated with the notion of just war—suggests a shared (and historically constituted) mode of reasoning. Of course, no moral vocabulary or mode of reasoning is freestanding; it presupposes the existence of an interpretive community that engages itself in arguing about how best to interpret the tradition. Our third observation, then, is the presence of such an interpretive community—represented here by Walzer, Elshtain, Johnson, and perhaps myself—so engaged. Together these three observations indicate that there is indeed something behind the notion of a unitary just war tradition; that is, they suggest that it is indeed possible to speak of a unitary just war tradition rather than a multiplicity of competing theories and visions.

Out of this emerges an image of the just war tradition as comprising a moral vocabulary and mode of reasoning, historically associated with the idea of just war, and an interpretative community engaged in arguing about how best to make sense of it. This is a rather substantive account of the tradition, and is a useful addition to the existing literature in this regard. While it is a richly textured definition that strives for conclusiveness, it also provides a very open account of the tradition, one that is designed to avoid the snare of gatekeeping, which Johnson and Elshtain's efforts arguably fall into. In addition to capturing the plurality of the just war tradition, the account provided here is sensitive to the stories of continuity and change suggested by the tradition's ongoing development. In particular, it calls attention to the fact that the tradition, viewed this way, is rather open-textured and possesses a rich capacity for renovation and evolution. How might this express or manifest itself? Chapter 6 will examine the tradition's capacity for change and evolution as it was evidenced in the course of the moral debate pertaining to the invasion of Iraq in March 2003. It will address the question of how change and evolution were proposed, contested, and also sometimes negated within the just war tradition during this debate. With this in mind, it will revisit the various justifications offered for the invasion of Iraq—already discussed in Chapters 2, 3, and 4 under the respective headings anticipation, punishment, and humanitarianism—in order to evaluate how they impacted upon the just war tradition, and affected its renegotiation.

CHAPTER 6

The Right to War after Iraq: Change, Continuity, and Contestation

Introduction

Thus far, I have presented the case that the jus ad bellum debate generated by the invasion of Iraq was phrased in much broader terms than one might have expected, especially given the narrow form the right to war had assumed over the course of the twentieth century. Chapter 1 recounted the rise of the restrictive legalist paradigm and submitted it as constituting the dominant mode of jus ad bellum discourse since the conclusion of the First World War. Following this, Chapters 2, 3, and 4 related how the various justifications offered (by Bush and Blair) for the invasion of Iraq disregarded this mold and suggested, respectively, that the ends of anticipation, punishment, and humanitarianism provided grounds for the use of force against Iraq in March 2003. Additionally, these chapters demonstrated how these various justifications resonated with a number of tropes, themes, and commitments usually associated with certain classical articulations of just war. Collectively, then, these chapters comprise an extended analysis of the innovative and potentially consequential manner in which the just war tradition was engaged by Bush and Blair as they sought to legitimate an extremely divisive war. Chapter 5 extended this analysis by examining the manner by which the just war tradition is referred to, and deployed, in the course of moral debate, while also indicating how the tradition might be reconstituted through this very activity. In doing so, it sought to draw out and elaborate the various assumptions, conditions, and commitments that we construe as the defining postulates of the tradition. It concluded that the just war tradition is best approached as a self-reflexive tradition comprising a moral vocabulary and mode of reasoning, historically associated with the idea of just war, and an interpretative community arguing about how best to make sense of it.

All of this leads us to the present, and final, chapter. If Chapter 5 called our attention to the rather open-textured nature of the just war tradition, and its rich capacity for renovation and evolution, it also prompted the question of how this might express itself. This chapter will examine the tradition's capacity for change and evolution as manifested in the moral debate prompted by Bush and Blair's determination to invade Iraq. With this in mind, it inquires what developments the Iraq debate has precipitated within the just war tradition today and how these developments are being negotiated. The focus, therefore, is upon the interpretative community and the debates that raged within it regarding the invasion of Iraq.[1] The just war tradition is, after all (as Chapter 5 noted), what its interpretative community makes of it. This is the point that David Armstrong and Theo Farrell are making when they refer to the just war tradition as a "site" rather than a "source" of legitimacy.[2]

This chapter, then, will examine how proposals for change and evolution were submitted and contested within the just war community during the Iraq debate. By studying the debates taking place within this community, we should achieve some appreciation of (1) the developments the Iraq debate has occasioned within the just war tradition today and (2) how these developments are being negotiated. With this end in view, this chapter will revisit the various justifications offered for the invasion of Iraq in order to evaluate whether they might have affected some change upon the jus ad bellum. The first three sections will deal respectively with the debates regarding anticipation, punishment, and humanitarianism. The concluding remarks of this chapter will address whether these debates have indeed enacted change upon the just war tradition. The underlying aim is to present an account of the stories of change, continuity, and contestation that constitute the tradition's ongoing evolution.

Anticipation

As Chapter 2 recounted, Bush and Blair provoked major debates within the just war community in the period immediately preceding the invasion of Iraq by articulating a more far-reaching right to anticipatory war with which many just war theorists have appeared uncomfortable. Indeed, it reached far beyond the bounds of the legalist paradigm and challenged, as Kofi Annan noted, the most basic rules governing the use of force in international affairs.[3] The radical element in Bush and Blair's formulation was rooted in a relaxed understanding of how proximate or extant a threat must be before a state acquires the right to take defensive measures. This section is dedicated to examining what developments Bush and Blair's proposal for an extended right to anticipatory war has precipitated within the just war tradition today, and how these developments are being negotiated. This entails three tasks. First, we must recap briefly the nature of Bush and Blair's proposal and the challenge it posed to the just war tradition. Second, we must examine how Bush and Blair's proposal has fared. That is, has it been contested, accepted, or rejected by the just war community, and how has this process taken shape? Finally, what if anything does all of this tell us about the stories of change, continuity, and contestation that constitute the life force of the just war tradition? It is to these tasks that we turn now.

Bush and Blair's Challenge to the Just War Tradition

First, how did Bush and Blair's arguments regarding anticipatory war challenge the just war tradition? As Chapter 2 demonstrated, Bush and Blair's arguments were a departure from the conventional just war tradition position on anticipatory war. They framed a broader right of anticipation than has been permitted by, for example, Michael Walzer, the Caroline standard, the UN Charter, Hugo Grotius, and most classical figures in the just war tradition. This was summed up by the following proclamation, issued in the NSS: "Our enemies have openly declared that they are seeking weapons of mass destruction, and evidence indicates that they are doing so with determination. The United States will not allow these efforts to succeed . . . as a matter of common sense and self-defense, America will act against such emerging threats before they are fully formed."[4] Crucially, however, this challenging proposal was framed in terms of the legalist paradigm discourse.

The NSS, as Michael Byers notes, explicitly adopted, and then sought to extend, the criteria articulated by Daniel Webster.[5] The NSS took, Byers writes, "George W. Bush's newly articulated policy of prevention or precaution and recast it within the widely accepted, pre-existing framework of preemptive self-defense."[6] Condoleezza Rice pursued much the same strategy in her speeches. In the course of echoing the NSS and setting forth a more far-reaching notion of preemption than the Caroline standard allowed, Rice sought to claim that her position was consistent with Webster's "famous defense of anticipatory self-defense."[7] The approach adopted by both Rice and the NSS reflected a wish to locate their arguments within the context of the legalist paradigm discourse. Only by doing so could they innovate upon this discourse and modify it.

This is precisely what they sought to do. Various commentators have described the approach adopted by the Bush administration (and also the

Blair government) as one designed to affect legal change or at least some modification in the prevailing normative discourse regarding the right to anticipatory war.[8] Miriam Sapiro, for example, charges that the Bush administration is attempting to reformulate the doctrine of self-defense, such that it might stretch to cover the option of preventive war. The administration is, she argues, engaged in nothing less than endeavoring to "shift the benchmarks that define the parameters of legitimate self-defense."[9] Of course, this is nothing that the Bush administration, or indeed the Blair government, would deny. They have made the case on numerous occasions that the existing legal-normative architecture pertaining to the right of (anticipatory) self-defense is inadequate to cope with the nature of today's threats.

Today's world, numerous members of the Bush administration and the Blair government have told us, faces a new kind of threat, one that is not amenable to traditional defensive measures. This threat, which is presented as an amalgam of rogue states, terrorism, and WMD, cannot be answered by the conventional strategies of deterrence and reactive self-defense. As the threat posed by the potential axis of rogue states and terrorist organizations could materialize without advance warning and with catastrophic results at any moment, the only possible counter to it is early action. As the NSS frames it, "Given the goals of rogue states and terrorists, the United States can no longer solely rely on a reactive posture as we have in the past. The inability to deter a potential attacker, the immediacy of today's threats, and the magnitude of potential harm that could be caused by our adversaries' choice of weapons, do not permit that option. We cannot let our enemies strike first."[10] The only plausible response, the argument goes, is to accept that the world has changed, that a new form of threat has emerged, and that the rules governing the right to self-defense must be amended to meet this challenge.[11] This message has been pared down over successive reformulations to the parsimonious slogan that "new threats require new thinking."

What new thinking, then, do the Bush and Blair governments propose? As Chapter 2 noted, the primary revision of the rules that they propose is a modification of the Caroline standard such that the requirement of imminence is jettisoned. Again, it is important to note that this proposal is couched in terms of the existing legal-normative framework and is posed as a modification, rather than a refutation, of it. For proof of this, consider the following statement (already cited in Chapter 2) from the NSS: "Legal scholars and international jurists often conditioned the legitimacy of preemption on the existence of an imminent threat—most often a visible mobilization of armies, navies and air forces preparing to attack. We must adapt the concept of imminent threat to the capabilities and objectives of today's adversaries."[12]

Such a move, were it accepted, would expand the right to self-defense by lowering the threshold for anticipatory war. The requirement of imminence typically figures as an evidentiary requirement—that is, it offers proof that a threat is indeed a clear and present danger and not just a routine anxiety—and laying it aside would ease the way to any recourse to force. This would constitute, to return to Annan's point, a fundamental challenge to the most basic rules governing the use of force today. This leads us, then, to our second question. That is, how has this proposed amendment to the rules fared? Has it been accepted or rejected, contested or renegotiated?

The Response from the Just War Community

How has Bush and Blair's proposal for a revised and expanded right to anticipatory war been accepted within the just war community? This is a vital question because the just war tradition is, in the final analysis, given shape and form by its own interpretative community. Accordingly, the success or failure of Bush and Blair's proposal is conditional upon the response it receives within the just war community. What reaction, then, has this proposal provoked from the just war community?

The first point to make is that it has generated a substantial response. Alex Bellamy, James Turner Johnson, and Peter Dumbrowski and Rodger Payne have all written on the reactions to Bush and Blair's arguments. They all comment on the sheer volume of the response; a lot of people have, it seems, been moved to engage with Bush and Blair's arguments pertaining to the right of self-defense. This leads us to our second point: many of these people have contested Bush and Blair's starting point. For example, Richard Falk and Gareth Evans both reassert the UN Charter rather than the Caroline standard as the baseline for any discussion of self-defense and anticipation.[13] Still, the general trend has been to suggest both the Caroline standard and the UN Charter as the relevant markers for the bounds of self-defense.[14] The insistence on referring to the UN Charter must be taken as a reaffirmation of Article 51 and a rejoinder to the unilateralist aspects of the Bush doctrine. It stands as a subtle correction to Bush's views in particular.

If, however, the just war community betrays some divisions regarding the correct starting point for a discussion of self-defense and anticipation, there is less disagreement regarding Bush and Blair's conviction that the world is facing new threats that require new thinking. This claim has met with almost unanimous agreement, even from those who are skeptical of the Bush and Blair agenda. Neta Crawford, for instance, agrees with the idea that, because we are faced with a new security environment, we require a new doctrine of self-defense but rejects Bush and Blair's attempts to lower the threshold for recourse to force.[15] Terence Taylor has also spoken, in measured tones, about the need for legal-normative thinking on self-defense to "evolve to meet today's threats and challenges."[16] Others have been more wholehearted in their support. John Yoo, Ruth Wedgwood, Gerald Bradley, Robert Litwak, Lee Feinstein and Anne-Marie Slaughter, Whitley Kaufman, Alan Buchanan and Robert Keohane, Michael Schmitt, Michael Walzer, Michael Ignatieff, and James Turner Johnson all spring to mind in this respect.[17] Johnson's statements are particularly forthright with respect to the urgency of the threats we face today relative to those faced by previous generations. Consider his statement on WMD, for example: "The WMD threat is qualitatively, as well as quantitatively, different from the upraised sword or even a mobilizing army or the sailing of a naval fleet. The potential destruction of these weapons . . . is so great and so difficult to prevent once the use of them is under way that new emphasis shifts to the matter of whether there is intent to do us harm."[18]

Johnson subsequently accepts that current just war thinking regarding the use of force does not "fit well" with the challenges posed by today's threats.[19] Intriguingly, the report issued by the UN High Level Panel on Threats, Challenges, and Change (UNHLP) also takes this view. It states explicitly that the world faces a host of new threats that require novel mechanisms to deal with them. More specifically, the report submits that "the attacks of 11 September 2001 revealed that States, as well as collective security institutions, have failed to keep pace with changes in the nature of threats."[20] It is essential, it continues, that the international community reexamine the rules regarding the right of self-defense in this climate.[21] This is evidence, as Alex Bellamy notes, that the view that the concept of self-defense requires a "rethinking in the wake of September 11" now commands a wide consensus."[22]

Of course, as Crawford's dissenting opinion suggests, just because one accepts the view that the world faces new threats that old structures cannot handle does not mean that one must support Bush and Blair's proposed solution to this predicament. Brian Orend's stance on this matter is quite interesting. He refuses to issue a blanket prohibition on anticipatory war and does not rule out Bush and Blair's revised account of self-defense, but he also suggests that it is not an entirely satisfactory proposal.[23] He does not offer an alternative proposal, but, for those of a mind to do so, he stresses the importance of an open-minded and casuistical approach: "Just war rules need to offer firm and clear guidance, yes, but to remain relevant over time some aspect of flexibility and openness to considering new situations is an absolute must."[24] In general, the just war community has displayed a good degree of openness and flexibility in responding to Bush and Blair's arguments and has put forward some interesting responses and counterproposals.

In particular, there has been a healthy debate concerning the continued utility of drawing a hard-and-fast distinction between the terms "preemptive war" and "preventive war." Commentators such as Skidelsky and Sapiro have resisted the Bush administration's attempts to blur the lines between these two categories of anticipatory war. The invasion of Iraq, Skidelsky claims, was a "preventive war dressed up as a pre-emptive one."[25] Sapiro similarly argues that the invasion was a preventive war that the Bush and Blair governments sought to legitimate as an act of preemptive defense.[26] Both Skidelsky and Sapiro state their intent to retain the distinction between preemption and prevention in their treatment of anticipatory war. Alan Dershowitz, Lawrence Freedman, and Francois Heisbourg also call attention to the fact that the NSS, and Bush and Blair's rhetoric more generally, elides the distinction so carefully drawn in international law and traditional just war thinking between preemptive defense and preventive war.[27] This elision is, of course, a direct result of Bush and Blair's determination to adapt the category of imminence so as to reflect the nature of today's threats. Their decision to jettison the requirement of imminence effectively proposed the collapse of any distinction between preemption and prevention.

While scholars such as Skidelsky and Sapiro have resisted such a move, others have been less hostile. Gerald Bradley, speaking in New York at a Pew Forum symposium on the just war tradition, argued broadly in favor of the stance adopted by the NSS. Imminence, he declared, is a concept that we have inherited from past generations, but it is presently in need of respecification. In Bradley's own words, "I think we need to look at imminence as a concept and consider whether a different conception of it may be appropriate for our time."[28] Schmitt is more categorical in his support. He is critical of those who would retain the requirement of imminence in its traditional form: "Those who urge fidelity to an outdated restrictive interpretation of imminency fail to grasp the realities of twenty-first century conflict. In an era when the enemy may be a shadowy non-state group intent on remaining invisible until it strikes its blow, a requirement to withhold defensive action until that blow is about to land would render the right to self-defense meaningless. Exacerbating matters is the fact that, given WMD proliferation, any miscalculation as to when an attack will occur could be fatal."[29] There is, then, a lively and ongoing debate regarding whether or not the concept of imminence needs to be recalibrated, or even abandoned, to fit today's security environment.

As the debate stands, a consensus is emerging to the effect that the rules regulating the right to anticipation need to be revised along more permissive lines (though there is a significant body of resistance to such a move, too). This judgment is based on two factors: first, the fact that a greater number of theorists support Bush and Blair's challenge than oppose it, and second, this challenge has already been influential in terms of state practice and proposals for UNSC reform.

Predictably enough, a number of scholars have even sought to develop alternative criteria for a revised doctrine of anticipation, but none of these have managed so far to capture the field.[30] Nonetheless, they have contributed to a discursive environment in which new ideas and developments are being discussed. One of the most eye-catching developments in this respect is the wide advocacy of reserving an expansive right to anticipatory war for liberal-democratic states alone, or at least charging liberal democracies with a supranational managerial role in which they are responsible for permitting and legitimating anticipatory war. The field of scholars associated with such ideas have variously been labeled the "New Liberals"[31] or the "New Internationalists."[32] Whichever label one chooses, Buchanan and Keohane are perhaps the most high-profile members of this grouping. They argue against what they call the "just war blanket prohibition" on preventive force: "within an appropriate rule-governed, institutional framework that is designed to help protect vulnerable countries against unjustified interventions . . . decisions to employ preventive force can be justified."[33] The institutional framework they suggest entails a coalition of liberal-democratic states serving a jury role, determining whether a given use of preventive force should be deemed legitimate or not. They thus posit a two-tiered international system whereby liberal democracies stand in judgment over the actions of other states.

In this regard, Buchanan and Keohane share similar views to those expressed by Feinstein and Slaughter in an article published in *Foreign Affairs* in 2004. Drawing on the 2001 report issued by the International Commission on Intervention and State Sovereignty (ICISS), they argue that states must accept a "responsibility to prevent" much as they might a "responsibility to protect."[34] That is, just as states possess a right to intervene in the affairs of other states that are not fulfilling their responsibilities vis-à-vis their own citizens, states should wield a right to take anticipatory action in those cases where other states are not discharging their obligation to prosecute global terrorism and WMD proliferation.[35]

This idea is also echoed by Jean Bethke Elshtain in *Just War against Terror*. She claims that the United States, as a liberal polity founded on the principle of equal regard and the world's only superpower, should assume the lion's share of responsibility for "preventing or interdicting violence in other countries."[36]

Thus one of the developments seemingly precipitated by the Iraq debate is the emergence of a cluster of academics who, aligning themselves with just war thinking, argue in favor of the "formal re-hierarchisation of international society, whereby democratic states would gain special governance rights—particularly with regard to the proper use of force—and other states would have their categorical rights to self-determination and non-intervention qualified."[37]

It is possible to see, then, on the basis of this brief survey, how Bush and Blair's proposal regarding a broader right to anticipation prompted a vigorous response from the just war community. The outcome of this exchange, though somewhat obscure to us at the present moment, appears to be a shift in the direction of a more permissive right to anticipation.

Anticipation and the Just War Tradition Today

Three main points present themselves for discussion here. The first is the observation that the possibility of a broader, more far-reaching right to anticipatory war than hitherto available is on the table. It seems likely that the Caroline standard will be modified in some manner or other to reflect the nature of today's threats. Not surprisingly, where modification has been recommended by scholars, it has been directed toward lowering the threshold for the use of force. More specifically, much of the literature has suggested redefining what counts as an attack received in much more permissive terms. Jeff McMahan and Buchanan and Keohane, for example, submit that a conspiracy to harm should, in today's world, qualify as an attack received and thereby trigger a right to defensive action.[38] Gregory Reichberg has noted how such developments may have the rather dramatic effect of reversing one central and traditional aspect of just war thinking. Whereas traditional thinking demands, after Aquinas, that the burden of justification lies with those who wish to use force, the developments precipitated by the Iraq debate indicate that it may shift in the near future to those who would abstain from the early use of force.[39] Indeed, Blair's 2003 declaration (noted in Chapter 4) that the burden of proof rests with the antiwar lobby—he argued that they should articulate a case for inaction that outweighs the case for war—suggests that we are almost there. Of course, voices have been raised in protest at this general development: Crawford and Chris Brown have both argued strenuously that such a move is both uncalled for, as it presumes a more dangerous world than actually exists, and destabilizing, as it leads the international system closer toward a state of nature.[40] Yet, where Iraq was concerned, Brown was prepared to indulge in precisely the style of reasoning that Blair advocated, challenging the antiwar lobby to refute the view that the case for war outweighed the case for inaction.[41] At any rate, the general tenor of the debate currently taking place within the just war community suggests that it is likely to result in a more permissive right to anticipatory war than has hitherto been available.

The second point is more difficult, perhaps. It relates to the possibility that the concept of imminence might be jettisoned from the requirements of self-defense; this would signal, as Taylor puts it, "the end of imminence."[42] Such an event would be consequential not only in terms of how we understand the *right to* anticipatory war but also in terms of how we conceive of the very *idea of* anticipatory war. This is because the idea of anticipatory war acquires its meaning from the place it occupies within the particular conceptual scheme—constituted by the categories of preemption and preventive war and the requirement of imminence—within which it is traditionally located. Thus to remove the requirement of imminence from the equation is to alter the conceptual makeup of anticipatory war in a rather significant way. Once the requirement of imminence is abandoned, the whole constellation of ideas in orbit around it, including preemption, preventive war, and indeed the broader notion of anticipatory war, must be affected.[43] How is this so? Two observations suffice to make this apparent.

In the first place, as previously noted, such a move essentially renders the distinction between preemption and preventive war void—as the distinction rests upon the requirement of imminent threat—thereby calling into question the continued utility of this categorization. Once the requirement of imminence is jettisoned, the terms "preemption" and "preventive war" come to resemble anachronisms, or what MacIntyre terms "survivals."[44] They persist only as "fragments" detached from their own past and recall a fractured conceptual scheme that lacks the context from which its coherence previously derived.[45] So while Bush and Blair or any number of just war theorists may still opt to use the terms "preemption" and "preventive war," they no longer mean what they once did; these terms, having been blurred and conflated, no longer refer to differentiated practices. Interestingly, Walzer recognizes this development: he argues that "the line between pre-emption and prevention is harder to draw today, in an age of rapid delivery systems and weapons of mass destruction."[46] Given these technological innovations, threats are more immediate in the current security environment as they allow states "no time for arguments about how to respond." Consequently, the "gulf between pre-emption and prevention has now narrowed so that there is little strategic (and therefore little moral) difference between them."[47]

This leads us to our next observation: the very idea of anticipatory war comes to mean something very different in light of this conceptual shift. When disaggregated from the conventional framework of rules within which it resides, the term "anticipatory war" no longer functions as an umbrella category for the differentiated practices of preemption and preventive war. Instead, it has acquired a broader, more amorphous meaning. It has become a much more porous or open-ended concept. Subsequently, it is more amenable to manipulation and casuistry (as, critics have charged, has occurred with respect to the invasion of Iraq).[48] This, then, is a very clear example of an occasion where some modicum of change has been affected upon the just war tradition. As is typical, this change is circumscribed by a degree of continuity as the terminology of preemption and prevention, despite being hollowed out, remains in place.

Our third and final point for discussion in relation to anticipation in the just war tradition today pertains to the vision of world order that accompanies it. A swing to a more far-reaching and permissive articulation of anticipatory war such as we are witnessing at the moment is evidence of a loss of faith in the idea of an international rule of law. As Whitley Kaufman explains, the just war tradition typically rejects anticipatory war (of a far-reaching variety) as a defensive measure suitable only under a certain set of conditions—those belonging to a "state of nature."[49] Where a state of nature reigns, there is no higher authority to ensure international peace and security, and every state may do whatever they must, up to and including preventive war, to ensure its security. We might recall at this stage that this was precisely the claim made by Bush and Blair in the run-up to the invasion of Iraq: America and Britain promised to act against Iraq only if the UN and the international community failed in its responsibility to guarantee their security (see Chapter 3).

The advocacy of a more far-reaching right to anticipatory war than has hitherto been permitted therefore suggests that at least some commentators perceive the international system to resemble a state of nature, absent any rule of law. Johnson and Michael Glennon, for example, argue this position. Both theorists argue that the UN is not up to the task of ensuring international peace and security; consequently, states must be empowered with a right to do whatever is necessary to ensure their own survival where it is threatened.[50] Elshtain also asserts that it is the "burden of American power" to take charge of an unruly world and act so as to interdict and prevent future evils, as well as promote an ethic of equal regard.[51] Kaufman, on the other hand, claims that the UN is sufficient to meet the security challenges of the twenty-first century and therefore rejects the idea that states (including the United States) have a license to anticipatory war of the preventive variety.[52] Rather predictably perhaps, the UNHLP comes to a similar conclusion.

This issue is not specific to the debate on anticipatory war, as we will see in subsequent sections. It also figured in different and not always consistent ways in the debates on punitive and humanitarian war. The ubiquity of this particular issue and the vigor of these debates suggest that this is currently a contentious matter. This is interesting indeed, for it keys into one of the great debates that resounds throughout the history of the just war tradition. Are we to understand the just war as Hugo Grotius and Hans Kelsen did—that is, as a war of collective law enforcement, a war undertaken on behalf of the community for the common good? In which case, we may perceive every just war as comprising a struggle between a malefactor, guilty of breaking the rules, and a party, standing with justice well and truly on its side, who acts to vindicate the common values of international society. On this view, the flip side of every just war is a criminal delict. This account of the just war is grounded in the conviction that a rule of law underpins and orders international affairs. This is the perspective from which the UNHLP and Kaufman argue. Alternatively, we might understand the just war as Vattel and Westlake did. Accordingly, states possess a *competence de guerre*, a free right to war by virtue of their sovereign status. There is no notion of a fight on behalf of the community for the common good here; rather, contending states stand before the world as plaintiffs acting to further their own cause. The notion of justice does not really figure here; instead, war is conceived as a legal relation between states, and both parties are deemed to possess equal rights within its framework. Consequently, the idea that a state might go to war to vindicate international law is a misnomer. Rather, the law exists only to regulate states' recourse to, and conduct in, war. States are, however, in the final analysis, the ultimate judges of their own cause. This view is discernible in many of Bush and Blair's statements regarding Iraq and also in much of the just war literature emerging today. Consider, for example, Bush's claim that the United States would act preventively against Iraq because the peace and security of the American people was ultimately the responsibility of the U.S. government, which may act as it sees fit in this cause. There are, then, some interesting depths to the debates animating the just war community today. These depths will be further explored in the following sections on punitive war and humanitarian war, respectively.

Punishment

This section, dealing with the matter of punitive war in the just war tradition since the invasion of Iraq, follows a similar format to the previous section. That is, it will first outline the challenge posed to the just war tradition by Bush and Blair's arguments pertaining to punitive war against Iraq. In so doing, it will draw on the material covered in Chapter 3. Following this, it will survey the response these arguments have provoked from the just war community. Chapter 3 has already provided a brief overview of the response of one particular theorist, Jean Elshtain. This section, by contrast, will cast its net more widely and take in the broad range of reactions Bush and Blair's ideas on punishment generated in the just war community. Finally, it will draw some conclusions regarding the place of punitive war in the just war tradition today. Again, these conclusions lead us to important questions regarding how we conceive of the idea of just war and even the international order today.

The Challenge to the Just War Community

As Chapter 3 noted, the very idea of punitive war is regarded by many contemporary just war theorists as outdated, even archaic.[53] While most, if not all, theorists accept that the classical just war tradition contained a strong emphasis on punishment, many seem keen to argue that its relevance has withered over the past century or so. It has, in Oliver O'Donovan's words, suffered from a "loss of intelligibility" in the modern era.[54] Joseph Boyle, for instance, acknowledges the punitive elements of the just war as conceived by both Aquinas and Augustine but refuses to countenance that it might have continued validity in the twenty-first century. Although, he writes, punishment was central to the just war as envisioned by Augustine and Aquinas, "one of the major developments in twentieth century just war thinking [was] the rejection of the legitimacy of this punitive conception of just cause."[55] Bradley adopts a similar viewpoint. He recognizes that punishment enjoyed a prominent place in classic just war tradition but denies its continued authority in the twenty-first century.[56] Robert Jackson also notes its absence from the twentieth century jus ad bellum, while Richard Miller comments that, at the very least, it has "less currency" in the present age than it once had.[57]

In a very interesting paper on the International Law Commission, Anthony F. Lang contends that this widespread rejection of punitive war is not only confined to just war commentary but is also reflected in state practice. He observes that states and international organizations have affected a "move away from punishing states" in recent years.[58] Instead, they have tended to institute war-crime tribunals and to punish state leaders on an individual basis. This trend is evident in the recent establishment of war-crime tribunals in the former Yugoslavia and Rwanda. It was also reflected in the calls for, and indeed eventual establishment of, a tribunal to try Saddam Hussein for his various crimes.[59] In Lang's judgment, this trend is likely the result of the institutional architecture of international society today. It has evolved in such a way as to preclude the practice of punitive war and is much more amenable to the trial of individuals in leadership positions.[60] The establishment of the International Criminal Court is likely to lend further momentum to this trend.

If the idea of punitive war was one that had little traction in the just war tradition immediately prior to the 2003 invasion of Iraq, the rhetoric of good and evil occupied a more ambivalent position. It was still common parlance for some of the more theologically inclined just war theorists such as Johnson and the NCCB/USCCB, but others disdained it as an unhelpful relic of more religious times.[61] Yet even Johnson cedes that modern just war theorists have tended to shy away from any discussion of evil.[62] There are good grounds for this observation. Walzer notably denies the significance of the concept of evil in modern just war thought. He states quite categorically that it is "wrong to say . . . that the word 'evil'—as in 'axis of evil' or 'evil empire'—is a concept allied to or implied by Just War Theory . . . that is not the language of Just War Theory . . . There is a vast philosophical literature about evil, and it doesn't overlap at all with Just War Theory."[63] Crawford argues along much the same lines, although she acknowledges that the punishment of evil once figured in the mainstream of just war tradition:

> Although it historically included punishment . . . just cause has more recently been limited to self-defense, raising the question of whether causes once considered just are legitimate. Specifically, is it just to wage war to punish evil? Despite earlier just war theorizing, the answer is now no, perhaps because we now recognize that evil is in the eye of the beholder, that the aim of punishing 'evil' may be abused, and that international legal institutions (e.g., the ICC) may be used to punish specific evildoers. And although reparations are legal under international law, the punishment of *states* is not allowed.[64]

Skidelsky goes further: he actually describes just war thinking as "an antidote to the 'neo-con' division of the world into good and evil."[65] This refusal to engage with the idea of evil is not unique to the just war community, however. It is in fact common to modern Western society. The *Oxford English Dictionary* (2nd ed.) notes that evil is a term that lacks resonance in the modern world, and Roy Baumeister comments that the term carries an air of anachronism today, especially as belief in the devil fades in Western culture.[66]

In lieu of the just war community's lack of general support for both punitive war and the rhetoric of good and evil, Bush and Blair's espousal of war as law enforcement against Iraq, with the added aim of eradicating evil, stood as quite the challenge. Indeed, it prompted a new bout of reflection on the question of punitive war and the rhetoric of good and evil and their place within the contemporary just war tradition. Despite the fact that the number of theorists contributing to this reconsideration of punitive war and the question of good and evil is significantly less than the numbers partaking in discussions about anticipatory war, the exchange has still been rich and lively. Of particular interest is the claim made by a number of scholars that the revival of both punitive war and the rhetoric of good and evil should be welcomed as a recovery of the classical understanding of just war.

The Response from the Just War Community

There is a lack of consensus in the field as to whether punitive war is something that the just war community should welcome. It is, however, very much on the agenda following the invasion of Iraq. While it is true that a number of prominent theorists have rejected the idea that punitive war serves a valid purpose today, a number of scholars have welcomed its revival as a recovery of the proper spirit of just war. This section will survey both sets of arguments, beginning with the case against punitive war.

Bradley, Boyle, and Galston have all presented arguments rejecting the idea of punitive war. Bradley's statements are, however, too pithy to dwell on: he rejects out of hand the legitimacy of punitive war today, but offers no explanation why.[67] Boyle is more sophisticated in his approach. He contends, as previously noted, that punitive war withered in the twentieth century, replaced by a focus on defensive war. This is a good thing, according to Boyle: the eclipse of the idea of punitive war is, he argues, a "proper development of just war doctrine."[68] Boyle reaches this conclusion by adopting an Aristotelian approach to the just war tradition. He argues that the notion of just war is anchored in the concept of political authority, such that the right to war must always be related to the good of the community from which that authority derives. Accordingly, the just war is properly understood as an exercise of political authority directed toward the well-being of the community, on whose behalf the sovereign exercises authority in the first place. This framing allows no scope for punitive war; state leaders do not and cannot possess the authority, or the relevant jurisdiction, for waging punitive wars against external actors.[69] As Boyle puts it, the "relationship between punishment, the common good of a polity, and the authority of leaders who serve it are such that the punitive conception of just cause is not justifiable; in a word, leaders lack the authority to punish outsiders."[70] The only kind of war a state leader can wage against outsiders, or external malefactors, is a war of self-defense.[71]

Galston's approach is different. He rejects punitive war (and indeed condemns the invasion of Iraq) on the basis that it is not for states to punish other states. Rather, this is the business of the supranational authority, the

UN. One of the traditional principles of just war theory, he writes, is competent authority, "and it is clear that if we're talking about the war of law enforcement it is the United Nations that is the competent authority to enforce UN resolutions and not any individual member of the UN acting on its own. And to understand why, consider a domestic analogy: A government, a sovereign state, passes a law and then in some respects fails to enforce that law. Does that failure of enforcement give individual citizens within that sovereign state the moral right to enforce that law on their own? I think not."[72] Galston, then, rejects the idea of punitive war on the grounds that it approximates to vigilante action in the international sphere. As such, it undermines the rule of law. We might note here how Galston's argument assumes a Grotian view of just war, but this is something we will return to later.

The arguments for punitive war convey a more unified front. Those who have argued in favor of the practice of punitive war have generally taken the line that it constitutes the paradigmatic model of the just war. Among those who have made this claim are Elshtain, Johnson, and Oliver O'Donovan. Elshtain's thoughts on punitive war have already been discussed in Chapter 3, so perhaps it will suffice here to mention her only briefly. In short, she relates punitive war to the Augustinian call to judgment, thus associating it with what she perceives as the central thrust of the tradition.[73]

Johnson similarly aligns himself with the case for punitive war, specifically offering an argument for punitive war against Iraq. He makes two statements in his most recent book, *The War to Oust Saddam Hussein*, which are interesting in this regard. The first one suggests that Johnson believes a punitive war of law enforcement was justified against Iraq in March 2003. In Johnson's words, "the UNSC resolutions on disarmament and weapons inspections in Iraq, passed in 1991, have been flagrantly, and so far with impunity, violated by the Iraqi regime. The US and its allies should have been willing to fight a just war over this issue years ago."[74] The second statement stands as a categorical affirmation that the punishment of evil provides a just cause for war, and is relevant to Iraq. It expresses Johnson's certainty that "the traditional just war idea of just cause allows the use of force to punish evil, and this surely applied in the case of Saddam Hussein and his regime."[75] Of course, these statements tie in neatly with Johnson's long-held views that the idea of punitive war, which he associates with vindicative justice, is central to the just war tradition. As he puts it, "What Christian just-war doctrine is about, as classically defined, is the use of the authority and force of the rightly ordered political community (and its sovereign authority as Minister of God) to prevent, *punish*, and rectify injustice."[76]

Perhaps, however, it is O'Donovan who provides the boldest expression of the idea that punitive war is the paradigmatic model of just war. O'Donovan spells out this idea in his latest book, *The Just War Revisited*, where once again the trope of judgment figures prominently. According to O'Donovan, the just war tradition is best understood as a "praxis of judgment" wherein "armed conflict can and must be re-conceived as an extraordinary extension of ordinary acts of judgment."[77] Following this template, just war becomes a means of upholding the right in international affairs.[78] As such, it must serve a "law-generating" and law-enforcing role in international society and, more generally, the cause of justice in world politics.[79] The idea of punitive war is central to this conception of just war.[80] Indeed, O'Donovan specifically identifies the "penal attitude" with the purpose of just war thinking.[81] Such a view of the right to war is a world away from the legalist paradigm that O'Donovan laments as an emaciated reading of justice and war. The attempt to privilege the cause of self-defense within the jus ad bellum is, he writes, a misguided move. It favors a base concern with state survival ahead of the question of international justice.[82] Against this, O'Donovan suggests that by focusing on the imperatives of punishment, we are more likely to serve the proper end of just war thinking. In this way, he equates the revival of the idea of punitive war with the recovery of the proper understanding of the just war tradition.

The revival of the rhetoric of good and evil has also met with a mixed response from the just war community. As previously noted, Walzer and Crawford both denied its relevance to contemporary just war thought. Jutta Brunnee and Stephen Toope also weigh in against this emotive discourse. They argue that it renders clear thinking difficult as it introduces a crusading tone to the just war.[83] Johnson, on the other hand, explicitly spoke of the invasion of Iraq as a just war to punish evil, as we have just seen. Elshtain also utilizes the rhetoric of good and evil in her recent work. She presses the argument that there is evil in this world and claims that it would be an act of self-delusion to deny this. Indeed, she cautions those just war theorists who shirk from the consideration of evil that they must leave the "nursery" and face up to facts. Like the humanists scolded by Albert Camus in *The Plague*, they must steel themselves to the reality of evil.[84] Subsequently, she reaffirms the classical idea that the punishment of evildoers is a just cause. Indeed, as Chapter 3 noted, Elshtain draws quite heavily on Pauline thought—which is, of course, laden with a theological concern with evil—in her just war reasoning.

Other commentators have echoed Elshtain's message that there is evil in this world and this is something to be accepted and faced up to. The high-profile American theologian Michael Novak, for example, feigned surprise in the *Wall Street Journal* in February 2002 that Bush would use the term "evil" in his foreign policy speeches: "Evil? Isn't this supposed to be a non-judgmental country, in a non-judgmental time? What gives?"[85] He is, however, very supportive of this unexpected recognition of evil in our world. He writes,

> There is evil in the world. Our forebears knew that. Reinhold Niebuhr taught the generation of the 1940s that the problem of history is the persistent power of evil over good, even though corrupting the good. Our founders, taught by the dour Saint Augustine, who saw in all worldly systems the inner conflicts of injustice, never expected a pure triumph of the good . . . President Bush, like President Reagan before him, has returned us to the moral framework of good and evil, where our founders began all thinking. There is evil in the world and it coagulates, it gathers force, and if it bursts its bounds endangers everybody. Axis of evil? Yes, there can be such things. How could we have ever doubted it? What dream were we living in, what sort of mist, what fog?[86]

Approval of the revived rhetoric of good and evil has also been sounded by neoconservative supporters of the Bush administration. Kaplan and Kristol submit that Bush's use of the term evil elicited howls of derision but was nonetheless correct. "As the events of 9/11 remind us, evil exists in this world, and it has consequences."[87] The charge today, they argue, is to rid this evil from the world.

It is difficult to say whether the concept of evil is something that is likely to figure in future just war thinking to any great extent. However, we can at least conclude that it is squarely back on the agenda, along with the idea of punitive war. We might also observe that their return to the agenda has been trumpeted by some as an indicator of the recovery of the classical spirit of the just war tradition. This is an interesting move. It calls to mind, once again, Armstrong and Farrell's observation that the just war tradition is a site of competing claims. More exactly, it prompts us to consider how the site itself—that is, the just war tradition—is subject to different claims. These claims are often, as in this case, of a certain nature: they presume to fix the historical meaning of the just war tradition so as to stake some kind of claim over its future development. We will return to this matter in the closing sections of this chapter. Next, however, we will look to draw some conclusions regarding the place of punitive war in the just war tradition today.

Punishment and the Just War Tradition Today

The revival of punitive war may well signal a shift in the just war tradition whereby the first use of force is granted some consideration in certain circumstances. Where the legalist paradigm is concerned, the first use of force is

strictly prohibited. It requires that any recourse to military means is undertaken only in response to an act of aggression. The revival of punitive war
would suggest, however, that war may now be initiated absent the receipt of
an act of aggression.[88] The recourse to force may be deemed acceptable where
it is employed to enforce international law or, indeed, persecute rogue (evil)
regimes. While this conditional acceptance of the first use of force is nothing
new where the broad historical sweep of the just war tradition is concerned,
it does indicate a sharp departure from the conception of the right to war that
has dominated international society for the better part of the past century.
What, then, are the possible implications of such a development?

The most startling possibility, perhaps, is that such a development might
lead to more war. Adam Roberts notes that when we perceive war as a means
of responding to violations of international law, a temptation may arise to
treat every minor infraction of the law as a casus belli.[89] After all, every violation of the law, no matter how petty, may be perceived as a challenge the
authority of the international order. Pressure to respond naturally follows.
This argument is one that has been rehearsed by critics of the just war tradition before. Among others, Ken Booth and David Welsh have warned that
treating war as a means for upholding the law is a recipe for more war.[90] The
revival of the rhetoric of good and evil is likely to exacerbate this trend. The
idea that certain states are evil, or even just rogue, creates a standing justification for war whereby license is granted to tackle and punish these states.
Consequently, states that do not exhibit liberal-democratic credentials may
find their right to sovereignty and nonintervention severely qualified. This
development lends further credence to Reus-Smit's thesis, mentioned already
in the first section, that there is a move afoot toward the rehierarchization of
international society. The willingness to resort to the rhetoric of good and evil
in relation to international affairs indicates an inclination to disaggregate the
society of states into two camps, and tailor the rules regulating their interactions accordingly.

This leads to a subsidiary point that we might associate quite generally
with Carl Schmitt, but which has been reiterated by Gabriella Slomp in relation to the current War on Terror. Drawing on Schmitt, Slomp cautions that
any wars prompted by the rhetoric of good and evil are likely to be fought
with less restraint.[91] As she explains, the jus in bello imperatives of proportionality and discrimination tend to be eclipsed when jus ad bellum arguments are framed as strongly as this. This is evocative of the traditional
argument against crusading moralism, and it is in this light that it is referred
to by Brunnee and Toope.[92] Interestingly, some of those who have advocated
the idea of punitive war, and indeed utilized the rhetoric of good and evil,

have countered that punitive war is not inimical to restraint, nor is it a slippery slope to a crusading mentality. O'Donovan, for example, submits that "common prejudice is inclined to suppose that punitive objectives make for unbridled war, but the truth is more or less the opposite: they impose the tightest of reins, since punishment is measured strictly by desert."[93] Elshtain is also keen to confirm that punishment is a measured endeavor, and relates it to an equity-based notion of justice.[94]

Returning to the realm of jus ad bellum, the second development to note is that the revival of punitive war is premised on a different attitude toward the use of force than animated the legalist paradigm. The horror of war that underpins the legalist paradigm—the product, of course, of two world wars and the fear of nuclear apocalypse—is not evident in the arguments put forward by Elshtain, Johnson, and O'Donovan. All three present a more ambivalent attitude with respect to the use of force. Citing Augustine's influence, Elshtain argues that an aversion to war is not always a helpful predisposition. We must, she continues, be willing to consider war as a means of achieving positive change in the world. War sometimes offers the only means of correcting the many "horrors and injustices that traffic under the cover of' the status quo which masquerades as 'peace.'"[95] Likewise, Johnson follows J. S. Mill in arguing that although war is an ugly thing, it is not the ugliest of things.[96] As Chapter 4 demonstrated, he is prepared to countenance the use of force in the service of justice, and believes that war can serve a positive end in international society. O'Donovan, as we have just seen, conceives of war as an extraordinary act of judgment taken in the service of the right. What, then, are we to make of this more permissive attitude to the use of force?

Two conclusions may be drawn. The first relates to the elision of the traditional distinction between war and peace, and the subsequent willingness to consider the use of force as an instrument of foreign policy. The legalist paradigm posits a sharp distinction between war and peace. It represents war as a failure of normal power relations, and restricts its justification to cases of aggression received. This view is implicit in Walzer's assertions that there is a radical difference between war and other means of discharging policy goals.[97] By contrast, the argument for punitive war presume an almost Clausewitzian view that war may serve as the continuation of politics by other means—or, as Anthony Burke suggests, the continuation of morality by other means.[98] It suggests that war provides an effective mechanism for managing the international realm. This is certainly the message O'Donovan conveys. He argues that there is a strong parallel between "ordinary acts of judgment internal to government" and the idea of just war.[99] All that divides them is context: "What distinguishes the justified resort to armed conflict is the unavailability of ordinary means of judgment. Justice in war stood in relation to the exercise of domestic justice as an emergency operation, performed in a remote mountain hut with a pen-knife, stands to the same surgery performed under clinical conditions in a hospital. The reason for carrying the practice outside the ordinary institutions is simply the emergency: it was 'indispensable to mankind.'"[100] Put simply, because war and peace embody related modes of judgment and forms of justice, they should not be understood to comprise entirely distinct realms.

O'Donovan's refusal to attempt to establish any meaningful distinction between the realm of war and the realm of everyday politics stands in sharp contrast to Walzer's position, which supposes that the moral reality of war is different from moral reality elsewhere.[101] For Walzer, war forms its own moral realm, distinct and bounded from peacetime politics. O'Donovan, on the other hand, looks to extend into the realm of war the normal practices of moral judgment.[102] War is understood not as constituting its own realm, but as a practice residing within the general human moral realm, albeit at the more extreme end of it. This approach, which O'Donovan shares with Elshtain and Johnson, blurs the line between war and peace. It problematizes the moral utility of attempting to draw a distinction between war and peace, and establishes some kind of "normative harmony" between them.[103] It is Elshtain who provides the most succinct expression of this approach. She cites Augustine's famous line to the effect that peace and war had a contest in cruelty, which peace duly won, before adding that "peace should not be universally lauded even as war is universally condemned."[104]

Our second conclusion regarding the move toward a more liberal attitude to the use of force is more straightforward. It refers back to the discussion regarding the international rule of law that closed the first section of this chapter, relating it specifically to the case made for waging a punitive war against Iraq. The argument for punitive war against Iraq assumed a Grotian form in its more mature articulations. It presupposed an international rule of law that some state or group of states—in the case of Iraq, the U.S./UK-led coalition—sought to vindicate by bringing force to bear on Iraq. Viewed in this light, the justification for punitive war against Iraq reflected a different starting point than the argument for anticipatory war. Where the argument for anticipatory war was premised upon the conception of the international realm as a state of nature, the justification for punitive war assumed that the international realm approximated a rule of law. Yet the argument was not quite as simple as this, at least as it applied to Iraq. True enough, the grievance with Saddam Hussein's regime related to Iraq's violation of UNSC resolutions and so assumed a civil condition in international affairs. Iraq, Bush and Blair claimed on numerous occasions, was being punished for its failure to respect the authority of the UNSC. However, the burden of executing that punishment fell to America and Britain, Bush and Blair added, because the UNSC abdicated its responsibilities in this regard. Thus Bush and Blair pressed the circular and (apparently) self-defeating argument that their right to act on behalf of the authority of the UNSC flowed precisely from the dissolution of the UNSC's authority. Their just war, then, lay somewhere between the competing visions of Vattel and Grotius. Once again, it is possible to perceive a tangle of competing visions of the just war, and indeed international order, at play in the various justifications offered for the invasion of Iraq. The next section will focus on the third and final justification offered—that of humanitarian war.

Humanitarianism

The third justification offered by Bush and Blair for the invasion of Iraq focused on humanitarian imperatives. This justification was the subject matter of Chapter 4, which related how Bush and Blair pressed a far-reaching justification for humanitarian war against Saddam Hussein's regime that resonated quite strongly with the classical idea of the just war—at least as it is presented by Johnson. It also made the point that this justification cuts against the grain of most twentieth-century just war thinking on humanitarian war. This section will examine how Bush and Blair's humanitarian arguments have been received by the just war community since the outbreak of hostilities with Iraq. Have contemporary just war theorists been receptive to the expansive humanitarianism advocated by Bush and Blair, or have they refused its validity, preferring instead to reassert a more conventional twentieth-century approach? The aim of this section, then, is to ascertain whether or not Bush and Blair's arguments have impacted upon how humanitarian war is approached from a just war perspective. To this end, it will be divided into three subsections, as with the first two sections. The first subsection will outline the nature of the challenge posed to the just war tradition by Bush and Blair's arguments. The second will survey the response that these arguments generated from the just war community. The third will look to draw some conclusions regarding the place of humanitarian war in the just war tradition today. The principal argument that will be articulated here is that there is currently an influential and broad body of scholars who wish to expand the just war tradition to encompass a greater humanitarian impulse. Interestingly, the strategy adopted by these theorists has not included any attempt to argue that the current security environment presents a set of circumstances that justifies a greater emphasis on humanitarian concerns in the jus ad bellum than has hitherto been the case. Rather, their prime strategy has been to stress that the just war tradition has *historically* fostered humanitarianism in international affairs. Thus the call for a greater element of humanitarianism in the contemporary just war tradition takes on the semblance of a call for a return to roots for just war thinking. Such a move reflects a claim to fix the historical meaning of the just war tradition so as to stake some kind of claim over its future development.

The Challenge to the Just War Community

Bush and Blair's justifications for humanitarian war against Iraq "re-ignited" important jus ad bellum debates according to Alex Bellamy.[105] They did so mainly because they challenged extant understandings of the right to war today, particularly with respect to the license to use force for humanitarian ends. But how exactly did Bush and Blair's justifications for humanitarian war against Iraq frame a challenge to the just war tradition? As Chapter 4 indicated, they rejected the conventional twentieth-century understanding that humanitarian war is only acceptable as a response to cases of massive human suffering, or what Nicholas Wheeler terms "supreme humanitarian emergencies."[106] This view was given its clearest expression by R. J. Vincent who wrote, in his 1986 book *Human Rights and International Relations*, that "humanitarian intervention is . . . reserved for extraordinary oppression, not the day-to-day."[107] Walzer's writings, as noted in Chapter 4, reflect a similar position. *Just and Unjust Wars* set out the view that intervention is only justifiable in response to acts such as genocide and massacre, acts that "shock the conscience of mankind."[108] He reaffirmed and developed this view in subsequent papers.[109] In one piece published in 2002, he specifically makes the case that humanitarian war is only justified in the most horrendous of cases; put simply, routine oppression will not suffice as a cause for humanitarian war. In his own words,

> The occasions have to be extreme if they are to justify, perhaps even require, the use of force across an international boundary. Every violation of human rights isn't a justification. The common brutalities of authoritarian politics, the daily oppressiveness of traditional social practices—these are not occasions for intervention . . . But when what is going on is the "ethnic cleansing" of a province or country or the systematic massacre of a religious or national community, it doesn't seem possible to wait for a local response. Now we are on the other side of the chasm. The stakes are too high, the suffering already too great. Perhaps there is no capacity to respond among the people directly at risk and no will to respond among their fellow citizens. The victims are weak and vulnerable; their

enemies are cruel; their neighbors indifferent. The rest of us watch and are shocked. This is the occasion for intervention.[110]

Bush and Blair's justifications for humanitarian war against Iraq confront this conviction that only the worst cases of human rights abuse warrant intervention head-on.

Where Iraq was concerned, Bush and Blair articulated an argument that proclaimed their willingness to use force to bring democracy and human rights to what would have previously been considered a nasty but tolerable regime. Following Fernando Teson's analysis, it makes sense to break their arguments down into two rationales.[111] Teson characterizes the first rationale as a "narrow humanitarian justification"; this refers to the case for deposing Saddam Hussein on the grounds that he was culpable of inflicting harsh misrule upon his own people.[112] Although he may not have been engaged in an ongoing commission of large-scale and systematic atrocities, Saddam, the argument went, was guilty of "severe tyranny," and this was grounds enough for intervention.[113] The second rationale, which Teson labels the "grand humanitarian motive," was more expansive still. It supposes a broad reform program for international society such that democracy and a respect for human rights should be implanted wherever possible, and by force if necessary.

In pressing such strong arguments Bush and Blair (and their fellow travellers) "strained" the conventional understanding of humanitarian war.[114] Firstly, the narrow humanitarian justification constituted, according to both Gareth Evans and Terry Nardin, an attempt to "re-write" the right to humanitarian war.[115] It attempted to lower the bar for the use of force in order that humanitarian war may be undertaken even absent any supreme humanitarian emergency. This was quite clear from Blair's 2004 Sedgefield address, where he told constituents that he had been searching, since the events of September 2001, for a new approach to international relations that would allow greater scope for the humanitarian use of force:

> So, for me, before September 11th, I was already reaching for a different philosophy in international relations from a traditional one that has held sway since the treaty of Westphalia in 1648; namely that a country's internal affairs are for it and you don't interfere unless it threatens you, or breaches a treaty, or triggers an obligation of alliance. I did not consider Iraq fitted into this philosophy, though I could see the horrible injustice done to its people by Saddam . . . It may well be that under international law as presently constituted, a regime can systematically brutalize and oppress its people and there is nothing anyone can do, when dialogue, diplomacy and even sanctions fail, unless it comes within the definition of a humanitarian catastrophe (though

the 300,000 remains in mass graves already found in Iraq might be thought by some to be something of a catastrophe). This may be the law, but should it be? . . . We have obligations in relation to each other. If we are threatened we have a right to act. And we do not accept in a community that others have a right to oppress and brutalize their people.[116]

The proposal here is that humanitarian war should not just be reserved for the most egregious cases of genocide and ethnic cleansing, but should be permissible in certain cases as a response to instances of daily oppression.

Were this proposal to succeed, Nicholas Wheeler and Justin Morris comment, it would significantly depress the threshold for the recourse to humanitarian war. It would, they submit, ultimately render humanitarian war "coterminous with the spread of liberal values" and the export of democracy.[117] Such an approach deviates from the conventional idea of humanitarianism by focusing on the nature of the regime to be overthrown, rather than on thwarting the crimes they commit and rescuing the victims they create. It looks to challenge the status quo, by toppling rogue state dictators and imposing new forms of governance in their stead, rather than restore it in the face of violations. It produces a view of the use of force as a valid instrument of policy that can serve as a force for good in the world by remaking it along more liberal lines. The grand humanitarian motive also contributes to this end, emphasizing even further the potential of war to "reform" international society.[118] Bush clearly expressed such intentions in his second inaugural address. There he announced that it was "the policy of the [United States] to seek and support the growth of democratic movements and institutions in every nation and culture, with the ultimate goal of ending tyranny in the world."[119] As Nardin writes, this approximates a program of democracy promotion, or even informal empire. Considered together, both rationales amount to a provocative program of reform. Not surprisingly, this program of reform has reignited a "passionate humanitarian intervention debate," placing it once again on "the forefront of world politics."[120] In particular, it has stimulated a lively debate among contemporary just war theorists.

The Response from the Just War Community

There have been many voices in the just war community raised in objection to Bush and Blair's arguments. We will review these in brief before turning to the arguments made in support of Bush and Blair's proposal. Nardin, whom we have already encountered, opposed Bush and Blair's proposal for a broader right to humanitarian war and stated his allegiance to the conventional threshold requirements. He argues that the bar has traditionally been set high, and that this is where it should stay. It should only be an option in extreme circumstances—that is, cases such as genocide and enslavement.[121] Humanitarian war, he writes, should be "concerned with rescuing particular victims of violence here and now, not with achieving universal liberty in the long run. It is remedial, not revolutionary."[122] He rejects the focus on regime change, arguing that the emphasis of any intervention must be squarely on halting or alleviating ongoing atrocities rather than spreading the ideals of democratic governance.[123] Wheeler and Morris argue along much the same lines as Nardin. They display particular concern that the threshold for intervention should remain where it stood pre-Iraq. They write,

> There are two compelling reasons why the bar justifying the use of force in humanitarian emergencies should be kept high: the first is that resort to armed action as a means of halting or stopping slaughter must always be a last resort, and it should be taken in the full knowledge that using force inevitably imposes harm on some of the civilian population whom the intervention has come to rescue. Such interventions should only be launched where policy makers are reasonably confident that the moral costs of inaction far outweigh the moral consequences of using force, and this inevitably means restricting military intervention to extreme cases of humanitarian emergency . . . The second objection to lowering the threshold is that this opens the door to a range of interventions that can claim, with varying degrees of plausibility, to be humanitarian.[124]

Others—including Walzer, Bellamy, Evans, and Kenneth Roth—have articulated similar arguments specifically in relation to Iraq.

Walzer's arguments are especially clear on this subject. The Bush and Blair governments were correct, he concedes, to depict Saddam Hussein's regime as vile, but they were wrong to argue that it warranted humanitarian war. "Saddam's regime," he claims, "was brutal and repressive, but at the time of our invasion it was not engaged in mass murder . . . It is only massacre or ethnic cleansing or mass enslavement in progress that justifies marching an army into someone else's country. That is what humanitarian war is, and that is not what the Iraq war was."[125] He reiterated these views on other occasions, suggesting also that although the Iraqi government was a bastion of oppression, this by itself did not qualify it for regime change.[126] Evans made a similar case in an article published in 2003 in the *Financial Times*. Quite simply, he writes, the human rights situation in Iraq was not urgent or exceptional enough to justify humanitarian war. Humanitarian war should only be reserved for the "worst cases," and Iraq did not reach this level in 2003.[127] Likewise, Roth argues that "despite the horrors of Saddam Hussein's rule, the invasion of Iraq cannot be justified as a humanitarian intervention . . . Brutal as Saddam Hussein's reign had been, the scope of the Iraqi government's killing in March 2003 was not of the exceptional and dire magnitude that would justify humanitarian intervention."[128] In making this case, Roth reasserts the traditional threshold requirement that "only mass slaughter might permit the deliberate taking of life involved in using military force for humanitarian purposes."[129] Other forms of tyranny, as in Iraq, may be deplorable, but they do not rise to the level that justifies the use of force. Bellamy adopts the same position. There was "no supreme humanitarian emergency" in Iraq in March 2003, according to his judgment, and therefore no justification for humanitarian war.[130]

It is possible to see, then, that a substantial body of resistance has arisen to Bush and Blair's proposed extension of the right to humanitarian war. What is of particular interest is that all the scholars surveyed here attempt to prop up the traditional restraints on humanitarian war and reaffirm the threshold requirements. This response suggests an unconditional rejection of Bush and Blair's arguments. Yet this conclusion is hasty, and overlooks those theorists who have lent their support to the idea of a broader right to humanitarian war. Teson, for example, has notably supported Bush and Blair's arguments for an expanded right to humanitarian war and their proposed revision of the threshold requirements.

Teson is quite clear that Britain and America were justified in overthrowing the Iraqi regime on humanitarian grounds. Saddam's Iraq, he writes, satisfied all the requirements for intervention: "During his twenty-four year rule, Hussein presided over a state of terror. In addition to suppressing all civil and political liberties, Hussein murdered around 100,000 Kurds in 1998; killed about 300,000 Shi'ia after the 1991 war; buried about 30,000 in a single grave; murdered around 40,000 Marsh Arabs; caused millions of people to flee; and tortured many hundreds of thousands, perhaps millions, between 1998 and 2003."[131] In Teson's judgment, this record is sufficient to generate a right to humanitarian war against Iraq. He argues that although Saddam may not have been guilty of any major ongoing atrocities at the time of the invasion, his history of "severe tyranny" was enough to justify his overthrow.[132] There are two points to note here. The first is that Teson recognizes a state's historical human rights record as a relevant consideration in any deliberation about whether or not humanitarian war is justified in a given instance. This is in tune with Bush's emphasis on rogue states, and the relevant deliberations he has urged with respect to anticipatory war. It is also a direct rejection of orthodox thinking that only *ongoing* (and massive) human rights violations provide a license to use force for humanitarian purposes. The second point is that Teson moves away from the requirement of supreme humanitarian emergency more generally, and allows that humanitarian war may be justified in cases of "pervasive and serious" oppression.[133] This represents a significant departure from the oft-cited standard that intervention is only justified in the face of ongoing massive and systematic human rights violations that shock the conscience of mankind.

Johnson and Elshtain have also registered their support for the war against Iraq on humanitarian grounds. Their arguments are notable for their contention that a broad right to humanitarian war is in keeping with the historical development and proper spirit of the just war tradition. In their hands, the call for a more expansive right to humanitarian war takes on the semblance of a cry for a return to the roots of the just war tradition. Most recently, Johnson has registered disappointment that this justification for the war largely "fell flat" within the just war community.[134] This was unfortunate, according to Johnson, as the idea of humanitarian war has a strong foundation in just war thought and it should have applied to a regime as heinous as that of Saddam Hussein.[135] Elshtain's support of a broad right to humanitarian war is similarly reliant upon its historical foundations within the just war tradition. She refers in this regard to an ethic of "equal regard"; an idea that she presents as a foundational value for the conduct of politics and for just war theorizing.[136] The idea of equal regard functions, for Elshtain, as a reminder that there is always a presumptive case in favor of humanitarian war wherever human suffering is occurring.[137]

Interestingly, Elshtain traces the practice of humanitarian war back to Augustine. From Augustine on, she claims, "saving 'the innocent from certain harm' has been recognized as a justifiable cause: the innocent being those who are in no position to defend themselves . . . In our time, the saving of the innocent is usually referred to as humanitarian intervention."[138] This is by no means a standard history of humanitarian intervention, or indeed a standard reading of Augustine's just war thought. Most theorists would trace the notion of intervention back no further than Vitoria, while most specialists on Augustine would balk at identifying him so readily with humanitarianism. Indeed, the more accepted accounts of Augustine's political theory suggest that he placed great value on submission to governmental rule, even where it is blatantly unjust and tyrannical.[139] Indeed, Augustine cites the scriptures approvingly in *The City of God*, "The divine voice is clear on this matter, for the wisdom of God speaks as follows: 'By me, kings reign, and tyrants possess the land.'"[140] The proof of this is evident: God granted power to the cruel Nero no less than he gave it to the kindly Vespasii.[141] It is clear, then, that Augustine put no stock in humanitarian war. Rather, the proper response to tyranny is submission and prayerful endurance.[142]

We might account for Elshtain's idiosyncratic reading of Augustine by pointing to the context within which she is writing. Elshtain is reading Augustine in light of what Michael Ignatieff has referred to as the "rights revolution" in international affairs.[143] The rights revolution is significant in terms of how we should conceive of the just war tradition today, according to Elshtain. Taken seriously, it fortifies the tradition by extending its scope. According to Elshtain, the post–World War II universalization of human rights "deepens and enhances the importance and reach of the just war perspective rather than running counter to it. Just war argument and universal human rights are not only not incompatible, they can and should be placed within the single frame."[144] By treating universal human rights and just war argument within the same frame, Elshtain lends the just war tradition a strong juristic element that influences her reading of Augustine. The result is, as we have seen earlier, an account of the tradition that is less encumbered by modesty of purpose and more sure-footed than a traditional Augustinian would care for.[145] Elshtain essentially reads humanitarian war back into the very core of the tradition, suggesting that the rescue of innocents is a constitutive concern of the tradition since Augustine's time. She is joined in this approach by Johnson, as Chapter 4 has already demonstrated.

Humanitarianism and the Just War Tradition Today

It is difficult to assess what impact the Iraq debate will have (or even has had so far) upon the standing of humanitarian war in the just war tradition (though the conclusion to this chapter will attempt some remarks on this matter). What is clear is that there are a number of crucial issues in play at the present. These issues relate, respectively, to the esteem in which the status quo is held, the moral utility of the use of force as an instrument of foreign policy, and the (possible) demise of humanitarian war in the near future.

Johnson and Elshtain, along with Teson, appear very keen to put forward the case that the status quo as we know it today is a flawed peace. They argue that international society harbors many unsavory regimes that should, ideally, be eradicated. In this regard, they are on the same wavelength as Blair who has stated his preference for using force to overthrow tyranny wherever possible. In the early days of the Iraq war, with British opinion still lodged firmly in the antiwar camp, Blair remarked to Peter Stothard, "What amazes me is how many people are happy for Saddam to stay. They ask why don't we get rid of Mugabe, why not the Burmese lot? Yes, let's get rid of them all. I don't because I can't, but when you can, you should."[146] This view, which Blair shares with Elshtain and Johnson, rests upon the understanding that the status quo is a problematic state of affairs. It is represented as providing cover for harsh and repressive regimes and, on this basis, should have its privilege revoked. Instead, then, of advising a ban on the first use of force, and supporting a jus ad bellum that recognizes defense-against-aggression as the only just cause for war, these figures advocate a right to war that allows for the use of force to help create a better, more just "peace." This is the message of the NSS, which promises a more just and peaceful world and a balance of power favoring freedom. It is also the message of the just war tradition, as Elshtain understands it: the historical just war tradition constitutes an extended meditation upon the question of how it is that "war may be resorted to in order to preserve or to achieve peace—and not just any peace, but a just peace that leaves the world better off than it was prior to the resort to force."[147] This is a far cry from the legalist paradigm: the legalist paradigm, as Chapter 1 explained, presupposes a state of affairs such that the status quo is institutionally protected by the promulgation of a narrow right to war that only allowed the use of force for defensive purposes.

The second issue arises from the increased willingness on the part of contemporary just war theorists and key actors in the international arena to question the status quo and to amend it via the use of force. It refers to the emergent trend toward perceiving war as a valid instrument of foreign policy, and a possible force for the good in world politics. Teson is perhaps the boldest exponent of this view. He even goes so far as to accept the label "humanitarian imperialist" for himself, and to argue that the hegemon (the United States) should sometimes use force to advance "freedom, human rights, and democracy."[148] It is in a similar vein that Elshtain alludes to *The Man Who Shot Liberty Valance* as a parable for the just war tradition. She writes that the famous John Ford western serves as a reminder that force can sometimes serve justice in this quotidian world of ours.[149] In her own words, "the presupposition of just war thinking is that war can sometimes be an instrument of justice; that, indeed, war can help to put right a massive injustice or restore a right order where there is disorder, including those disorders that sometimes call themselves 'peace.'"[150] Johnson has also repeatedly argued that the just war tradition approaches the question of the use of force with an open mind; there is a recognition that war may be good or bad depending on the ends that it is made to serve. Blair, of course, famously argued that we must be prepared in the wake of September 11 to reorder the world around us, by force if necessary. In his 2001 Labour Party address at Brighton, which came just days after the terrorist attacks upon New York and Washington, Blair declared that this is a moment to seize: "The kaleidoscope has been shaken. The pieces are in flux. Soon they will settle again. Before they do, let us reorder the world around us."[151] It was time, he argued, to make the oppressed from all over the world "our cause."

This idea that war can serve as midwife to a bright new future is strongly contested by those with more conservative inclinations. There are those, like Rengger, Nardin, Boyle, and George Lopez, who stress the modesty of the just war tradition, and who look skeptically upon any scheme to remake the world over by declaring war upon it.[152] The debate that has developed on the basis of this disagreement invokes the historical divide between those just war theorists who perceive a presumption against war at the core of the tradition, and those who see instead a presumption against injustice. As these well-rehearsed debates assume their standard form, different conceptions of the just war are contested against one another. It is probably not the case, how-ever, that this debate will be won—now or ever. It is more likely that these two competing discourses will continue to exist side-by-side, as two different approaches to the idea of the just war.

Neither is it entirely clear yet what impact the Iraq war has had on human-itarian war. Theorists such as Bellamy, Johnson, and Thomas Weiss have expressed concern that the Iraq debate may have contributed to the prema-ture demise of humanitarian war.[153] Each theorist has offered his or her own reasons for this gloomy prognosis; they range from the idea that the debacle of postwar Iraq has irreparably damaged the reputation of humanitarian action to the view that there is no enthusiasm for the humanitarian agenda in a security environment conditioned by the War on Terror. These anxieties seem, however, a little premature. State leaders and just war theorists still pay lip service to humanitarian concerns when publicly contemplating the use of force. In the final analysis, it is hard to speculate either way as to what the future holds for humanitarian war, but it is unlikely that the humanitarian discourse will fade from the just war tradition any time soon. Questions such as this are difficult, as they lead us to confront the matter of how the just war tradition negotiates change, continuity, and contestation in its diurnal development.

Conclusion

This chapter has submitted that the moral debates precipitated by the inva-sion of Iraq bear witness to a current willingness to debate the right to war in broader terms than was previously acceptable. The legalist paradigm mold, it appears, has been cracked as state leaders and just war theorists debate the merits of a far-reaching right to anticipatory war, the utility of punitive war, and the possibility that war might be considered a valid instrument of foreign policy today. The rhetoric of good and evil has been revived and fear has acquired a certain prominence in debates pertaining to anticipatory war. Of course, all of these moves have been contested, but the fact that they are even on the agenda indicates that a significant shift in just war thinking has occurred. Prior to the end of the cold war, and even into the mid-1990s, the practice of punitive war, and the idea that war may serve a humanitarian (or even democratizing) end, would not have even been acknowledged by many just war theorists.[154] Indeed, the fact that Bush and Blair saw fit (and perceived it as good politics) to issue these justifications tells its own story. It indicates that some shift has occurred within the jus ad bellum. By way of concluding this chapter, I propose to offer some tentative conclusions regarding the form this shift has so far assumed, and suggest that this might be taken as an indicator of future trends and developments.

The area where the most marked shift is evident is the right to anticipation. There is almost unanimous agreement that the rules that currently define the parameters of self-defense are inadequate to cope with today's security climate. Even those, like Crawford, who are skeptical of Bush and Blair's proposals for a broader right to anticipation, have conceded this point. Furthermore, international organizations (including the UN and the European Union), state leaders, political commentators, and numerous just war theorists have openly subscribed to this view. It has, one might fairly say, established itself as the new baseline of the discussion pertaining to the right to defense. The manner in which UN reform has been undertaken reflects this shift: the UNHLP report acknowledges that the UN must respond to the clamor for a new approach to the right of national defense, otherwise it would condemn itself to irrelevance. Contained in this statement is an admission that some shift has already taken place.

There is less concord regarding actual proposals for what the new right to anticipation should look like. There appears to be a willingness to accept Bush and Blair's arguments that the old rules are no longer relevant today, but a lack of certainty about how to proceed beyond this. Many influential scholars have, however, converged upon a number of points. First, there is a greater willingness to conceive of force as a means of managing the global order. Thus war is treated as a legitimate means of forestalling emerging threats and dealing with the peril posed by rogue states, terrorist organizations, and WMD. Second, there is an almost unanimous acknowledgment that there is no proper peace in international affairs today; rather, international politics currently approximates a state of war. Bush's comment that we have currently moved into a "world of terror, missiles, and madmen" captures this prevailing sentiment quite nicely. When such a view prevails, the idea of war is normalized and accepted as a legitimate instrument of foreign policy. These areas of agreement constitute the presuppositions that govern the ongoing debate regarding the right to anticipation.

The issue of punitive war is tougher to call. If anything, however, it appears likely that the practice of punishment will not be successfully (re-) established within the contemporary jus ad bellum. While most commentators warm to the ideal of law enforcement, many appear reticent to grant that war may serve this purpose. The experience of Iraq does not aid the case of those who argue that war can indeed serve this end. Despite the support of influential scholars such as Elshtain, O'Donovan, and Johnson, the notion of punitive war has not gained traction within the just war community. Scholars have expressed unease that a general acceptance of punitive war would in fact lead to a proliferation of wars. In general, those who have contested the idea of punitive war have rejected it quite sharply. Scholars such as Galston, Boyle, and Burke have decried the very notion as an anachronism—drawn from an earlier time when princes believed themselves entitled to stand in judgment of other kingdoms—misapplied to the contemporary society of states. This conclusion is supported by the fact that the legal-political architecture of international society is not equipped to undertake punitive wars. Instead, it is tailored toward a judicial approach to international law enforcement, with war-crime tribunals the preferred modus operandi. In summary, it is the sharpness of their response that suggests that, even though punitive war may have its backers, it is never likely to command widespread consensus. Put simply, it is too contentious.

Likewise, efforts to lower the bar for the recourse to humanitarian war are likely to fail. The general response to Bush and Blair's arguments with respect to humanitarian war has been outright rejection. Indeed, the only change Bush and Blair's arguments regarding humanitarian war have achieved is a further retrenchment of the twentieth century position. Scholars such as Wheeler, Bellamy, Roth, Nardin, and Walzer have reaffirmed the conventional "humanitarian exception" as the proper approach to humanitarian war. The reasons they cite are straightforward: order must be balanced against any preference for spreading democracy or challenging everyday oppression across the world. Accordingly, humanitarian war is a legitimate option in worst-case scenarios, where massive and systematic atrocities are taking place and the moral conscience of mankind is shocked; in any other instance, however, it represents a step too far.

Overall, then, we might conclude that the most discernible shift is taking place with respect to the right to anticipation. It is currently in the process of being renegotiated but it is clear, at least, that the traditional parameters of self-defense have been superseded. On the other hand, neither the idea of punitive war nor the notion of a broader right to humanitarian war has achieved significant momentum in the years since the invasion of Iraq. While they have not quite stalled, it is fair to say that they have generated a substantial amount of resistance that will probably suffice to ensure that the jus ad bellum remains relatively unaltered in both these respects. On a more general level, however, the jus ad bellum is betraying signs of change and development. Scholars currently debate the rights and wrongs of punitive war and humanitarian war in a way that was not imaginable twenty years ago. The rhetoric of good and evil, as well as that of fear, human rights, and law enforcement, is now common currency within current jus ad bellum debates, suggesting a broader, more moralistic approach to debates over the right to war.

Conclusion
The Negotiation and Renegotiation
of the Just War Tradition

Introduction

This book opened with an observation. This observation was simply that the jus ad bellum debate attending the invasion of Iraq seemed to mark a distinct turn away from the legalist paradigm, the dominant just war discourse since the conclusion of the First World War. Rather than referring to a restrictive right to war equated solely with defense-against-aggression, the Iraq debate was couched in much broader terms. Prompted by Bush and Blair's unorthodox justifications for the invasion, the imperatives of anticipation, punishment, and humanitarianism provided the main focus of the debate. This book has submitted that these justifications resonated with certain classical articulations of the right to war and traced these justifications to their roots in medieval just war thought.

The invocation of these justifications in the context of the Iraq debate suggests a significant development is taking place within the contemporary just war tradition. It indicates a willingness on the part of today's just war theorists to consider a more expansive jus ad bellum than the legalist paradigm provided for. Indeed, it reflects an eye-catching shift of direction where the historical development of the just war tradition is concerned. The history of the tradition over the past two hundred years reflects a progressive tightening and restriction of the right to war; the terms in which the Iraq debate has been conducted suggests that this process has been halted, and maybe even reversed. This book has provided grounds for thinking that such a reversal is indeed taking place. It has drawn our attention to the recent proclivity on the part of state leaders and political theorists alike to address the question of the right to war in moralistic terms.

More generally, this book has provided an account of the Iraq debate that is sensitive to the terms in which it has been conducted, and also to the implications it might have for the future development of the just war tradition. At its core, it addresses the stories of change, continuity, and contestation that animate the ongoing development of the tradition. These stories, and the modalities of development they give rise to within the just war tradition, may be summed up in terms of a motif that has been confined to the margins of this thesis thus far. This motif is *negotiation*.

What does the word negotiation mean? The Oxford English Dictionary offers three definitions of negotiation, each capturing a different possible meaning of the word. The first definition of negotiation treats it as a structured conversation between two opposing parties about how best to resolve a common problem. The definition reads, "[A negotiation is] a discussion or process of treaty with another (or others) aimed at reaching an agreement about a particular issue, problem, et cetera, especially in affairs of state." A negotiation in this sense is an occurrence, a *historical event*—it is something that takes place. In contrast to this, the second definition of negotiation stresses the *processual* element of negotiation; negotiation here is a verb. It is the "action, activity, or process of negotiating with another or others." It is, in other words, the *mode of engagement* that animates those instances where parties come together to discuss some common problem. The third definition of negotiation is different again. It refers to those cases where a given problematic is *worked through*: negotiation in this sense stands for the "action of crossing or getting over, round, or through some obstacle by skilful maneuvering; manipulation." The plurality of meanings attached to negotiation is relevant for our purposes because each of these different definitions of negotiation captures a certain aspect of the dynamics of change, continuity, and contestation that animate the evolution of the just war tradition (as considered here against the backdrop of the jus ad bellum debate over Iraq). By way of concluding this book, I propose to draw on each of these meanings in turn in order to tease out some of the implications of the arguments presented thus far.

Negotiation I

The first definition of negotiation refers to it as "a discussion or process of treaty with another (or others) aimed at reaching an agreement about a particular issue, problem, et cetera, especially in affairs of state." This understanding of negotiation refers to a set of dealings actors may engage in with the express purpose of confronting and resolving a common problematic or dilemma. The jus ad bellum debate over Iraq can certainly be viewed through this lens. Doing so requires an appreciation of four particular aspects of the debate. I am referring here to the problematic of the debate, the participants to the debate, the terms of the debate, and the conclusion of the debate. This book has offered some novel insights into each of these matters.

The problematic of the debate was determined by Bush and Blair in the course of their public statements on Iraq and the post-9/11 security environment. They initiated the debate and established as its primary subject matter the legitimacy of the invasion of Iraq. This issue provided the catalyst for a reexamination of the right to war in the contemporary security environment. Crucially, Bush and Blair succeeded in prompting an extended discussion on both of these matters. Numerous theorists and commentators sought to engage with Bush and Blair, and indeed one another, on the need (or lack thereof) both to invade Iraq and to revise the jus ad bellum. Thus, contemporary just war theorists found themselves debating the matter of whether the ends of punishment, humanitarianism, and anticipation provide any justification for war today as well as addressing questions pertaining to the legality and justice of the invasion of Iraq. While these two lines of discussion cannot be entirely separated, they do constitute different, albeit related, issues.

This leads to the second aspect of the debate that we must explore here: that is, who are the participants to this debate? This is a crucial question, for only when we have an answer to it can we account for what counts as an engagement in the context of this debate. The present work has submitted a response to this question which draws on Michael Walzer's work on interpretative communities, and that stands as an original and potentially consequential contribution to the just war tradition. The participants to this debate comprise those members of the just war community who choose to address the invasion of Iraq. But what, then, is the just war community, and who might qualify as a member? The phrase "just war community" is borrowed from Brian Orend, but it reflects Walzer's notion of the interpretative community. For Walzer, an interpretative community is a body of people bound to a certain tradition by the fact that they look to find meaning and a vocabulary through which to express themselves within it.[1] This book has extended this idea to those people who look to find meaning and a mode of expression within the just war tradition. Consequently, the just war community comprises that body of people who engage the tradition by arguing through (and about) the historically loaded terminology and vocabulary that is associated with it. This is a broad understanding of the just war community that allows that membership is open to anyone, be they an academic, a politician, or a member of the general public, who speaks its language. This approach recognizes the potential for those outside academia, most obviously state leaders, to make a contribution to the tradition; in this sense it breaks down some of the divides between the business of politics and the working out of the just war tradition. This is, so far as I am aware, the first such attempt to theorize the deliberations that might guide us when considering who might count as a potential contributor to the just war tradition. Accordingly, any members of the just war community who chose to discuss the invasion of Iraq whilst utilizing the language and reasoning of the just war tradition might be considered to have participated in the jus ad bellum debate over Iraq.

The terms of the debate were, as I have previously noted, set by Bush and Blair. They revolved around the imperatives of anticipation, punishment, and humanitarianism, but were anchored in the terminology of the legalist paradigm. Thus, for example, Bush chose to speak of preemption when referring to an expansive right to anticipatory war, claiming that this was a doctrine of self-defense that was long acknowledged in international law. In a similar manner, Blair presented his arguments for a broader right to humanitarian war as a modification of, rather than departure from, the dominant discourse that treats humanitarianism as an exception to a general ban on the first use of force. The decision to pay tribute to the legalist paradigm by (superficially) couching a series of far-reaching arguments in its terms was a pragmatic one. The idiom of the legalist paradigm provided a Trojan horse within which to smuggle a rather more expansive vision of the right to war. This is particularly apparent with respect to the reconfiguration of preemption and humanitarian war. Interestingly, the terms chosen by Bush and Blair have continued to structure the debate about Iraq and the expansion of the jus ad bellum. Even where certain theorists and commentators have questioned the use of certain terms—Freedman's determination to point out that preemption is an inaccurate label for what Bush and Blair were proposing stands out as an example here—their analysis still assumes the same starting point. Only a small minority has attempted to shift the terms of the debate away from the discursive terrain selected by Bush and Blair. These efforts have been largely ignored by most participants to the debate.

This leads us to the matter of the conclusion of the debate. It is, of course, too soon to tell what if any agreement or consensus has been reached. At any rate, any conclusions reached are always provisional, with the debate liable to be reopened or reassessed further down the road. Still, it is possible to point to some interesting and potentially very consequential developments, and these developments suggest a modicum of consensus has been achieved with respect to some issue areas. Most theorists, for example, accept the idea that the rules governing the right to self-defense need to be adjusted to fit the nature of today's threats. There is a certain well of support for the view that a threat may give rise to a right to self-defense even before it registers as imminent. There is, however, less consensus regarding the right to punitive war and the more permissive articulations of humanitarian war. These issue areas are still being contested and have not yet yielded any significant developments one way or the other, suggesting that any change they undergo will be modest and piecemeal at best.

Moving away from the areas of anticipation, punishment, and humanitarianism for a moment, it is possible to see indications of consensus in other respects. I will make three brief points in this respect. First, and most obviously, a more permissive attitude vis-a-vis the use of force has been revealed by the Iraq debate. Although not all commentators and theorists agree that a broader right to war would be a good thing, or is even emerging, the fact that they are discussing this at all suggests that it is at least on the table. This is a rather interesting development. The fact that this exchange calls to mind competing visions of the just war—sometimes Grotian, sometimes Vattelian—is also interesting. It suggests that there is contestation and dispute even among those theorists who would argue for an expansion of the jus ad bellum. Second, the idea that war may serve as an instrument of foreign policy, and indeed of justice, has emerged as one of the dominant tropes in the jus ad bellum debate over Iraq. Force, it is argued, can not only rescue people from oppression, it can also export democracy and good governance to the darkest corners of the globe and project the will of the international community into those areas where diplomacy has failed. This represents an interesting counterpoint to the pessimistic attitude regarding the use of force that dominated the latter years of the twentieth century, when war was equated with nuclear apocalypse and deemed unusable. This relates closely to the third and final point, which is that the Iraq debate signaled a greater willingness among the just war community to challenge the value of the status quo, or the peace as it is sometimes known. Again, this is in stark contrast to the twentieth century position that placed enormous stock in the status quo, so much so that any disruption of the peace—that is, any first use of force—came ultimately to be equated with aggression.

This, however, is just one way of characterizing the jus ad bellum debate over Iraq. A second definition of *negotiation* captures another aspect of it. This definition describes negotiation as "the action, activity, or process of negotiating with another or others." This definition stresses the intersubjective element of negotiation; it supposes some form of dialectical engagement with others. This understanding of negotiation draws attention to the function the just war tradition may play as a *site* of engagement. It played this role in the Iraq debate.

Negotiation II

Very little attention has been paid in the literature on the just war tradition to the tradition as a site through which argumentation and debate can be enjoined.[2] This book has stepped into the breach in this respect, and cast some light on the tradition as a site of contestation in the context of the Iraq debate. In this respect, it presented the tradition as a medium through which the parties to the Iraq debate could engage one another. The aim in doing so was to examine the tradition as a shared framework of meaning that has conditioned the possibility for debate in the context of the Iraq war. Two related issues emerged in lieu of this enquiry. The first issue refers to the vocabulary of the just war tradition and the manner in which it has been employed and deployed in this particular debate, while the second refers to the way in which a certain representation of the tradition itself has been invoked in order to discipline the terms of the debate.

Turning firstly to the vocabulary of the just war tradition, this book has demonstrated that this particular idiom framed the debate over Iraq. As Chapters 2 through 6 have illustrated, this debate has been conducted through certain words, phrases, and modes of reasoning that are historically connected to the just war tradition. We can think here of the common usage of terms such as "preemption," "preventive war," "humanitarian war," "punitive war," or even Bush's confident declaration that the war in Iraq was fought with a "just cause," as clear-cut examples of this tendency. Indeed, it was Bush and Blair who cast the debate in the idiom of the just war. This idiom was then taken up by those who wished to engage with Bush and Blair's arguments, either to endorse or to contest them. Interestingly, the choice of idiom itself was rarely challenged, though its application often was. Nobody questioned, or at least very few did, that it was appropriate to discuss the invasion of Iraq in terms that are generally associated with the jus ad bellum. Even, for example, those critics who rejected the idea that the Bush doctrine satisfies the legal requirements associated with preemption still accept that the idea of "preemption" provided the best template for questioning just what it was that the NSS did propose. For the most part, where there was disagreement about the use of a particular phrase or word, this disagreement referred more to the way in which that word was employed, and the scope that was attributed to it, than to its general relevance or utility. Thus we might recall Walzer's rejoinder to the Bush administration that humanitarian war is what occurs when a state intervenes in a foreign country to halt an ongoing case of mass murder, and this "is not what the Iraq war was."[3] Instances such as this implicitly accept, and indeed reaffirm, the just war tradition as the idiom through which to enjoin debate. This suggests that the tradition provides a medium—perhaps not the only one, but certainly a prominent one—through which the Iraq debate has been conducted. Of course, every argument conducted through the just war tradition must also be, to some extent, about the just war tradition. We will return to this issue in the next section. More immediately, we must ask how the tradition itself has sometimes been invoked as a means of disciplining the debate over Iraq.

Over the course of the Iraq debate, certain scholars have deployed the just war tradition to validate, or shore up, their own contentions regarding the justice (or lack thereof) of the invasion of Iraq. Jean Bethke Elshtain, for instance, writes that the just war tradition provides support for the view that the war in Iraq was justified.[4] The just war tradition thus functions in her argument as the object of an "authority citation," and is posited as a source of legitimation with respect to moral claims in international affairs.[5] We can see this dynamic at work when scholars such as Lawrence Kaplan and William Kristol cite Hugo Grotius, Thomas More, and Richard Regan in order to make the case that a broad right to anticipatory war may be justified. Indeed, Condoleezza Rice referred to the Caroline standard in a similar manner in order to shore up the broad interpretation of the right to anticipatory war offered by the NSS. In all of these cases, the tradition is deployed in order to endorse the author's point of view rather than to interrogate it.

In other cases, scholars have referred to the just war tradition in a manner designed to discipline the terms of the debate. These scholars seek to control the debate by securing a particular reading (*their* reading) of the just war tradition as the bedrock of any discussion. They understand that by doing so they can marginalize those views and arguments they disagree with merely by indicating that they have no place in the tradition, as it has been articulated. This technique is most apparent where scholars have attempted to fix some historical meaning to the tradition, which then operates to dictate the parameters of any future argument. Consider, for example, James Turner Johnson's assertions that the just war tradition is properly inspired by a presumption against injustice rather than a presumption against war. Such an argument pronounces on the meaning of the just war tradition in a manner designed to discipline future just war thinking. It directs future just war thinking down a particular path, determined (in this instance) by Johnson, and closes down the possibility of alternative conceptions of the tradition. In particular, it promulgates a vision of the tradition that is favorable to the policies Johnson, a self-professed "liberal hawk," supports, while simultaneously delegitimizing a more "dovish" approach to international affairs. Of course, Johnson is not the only scholar guilty of such gatekeeping practices, but he is one of the most influential just war theorists today and consequently his utterances have ramifications for the wider just war community.

The long-term danger with such an approach is that theorists may occasionally be led by their own momentum to forget that their perspective is partial. Thus, what is initially a point of departure may easily turn into a powerful myth of origin such that other possible starting points are rendered unthinkable. Succumbing to this temptation contributes to the reification of the tradition, and may lead to its ossification by directing it down a rigidly predetermined path. There are good grounds, then, to exercise caution when confronted with a claim that is ostensibly derived from a "proper," "faithful," or "historical" reading of the just war tradition. The more immediate danger, however, is that the discussion of substantive issues such as, for example, the right to punitive war tend to be overwhelmed and subtly undercut by the grander preoccupation with accounting for how the tradition should properly be understood. Consequently, the substantive issues that ignited the debate tend to be under-examined and/or displaced as the just war tradition itself is thrust forward as the subject as well as the medium of debate. Where this occurs, we must always be mindful that the tradition is itself reconstituted and rewritten by this very process.

Negotiation III

This mention of the possible reconstitution of the just war tradition leads us to the third definition of *negotiation*. This definition suggests that negotiation may be understood as "the action of crossing or getting over, round, or through some obstacle by skilful maneuvering; manipulation." Negotiation is presented here as a process by which a given resource is navigated and/or exploited. This book has suggested that we might view the practice of engagement with the just war tradition as a negotiation of this type. This is a route suggested by the work of James Boyd White, among others. White writes, "For while a person acts both within and upon the language that he uses, at once employing and reconstituting its resources, his language at the same time acts upon him."[6] The dialectic identified by White begs the question of how malleable the tradition is, and directs our attention to the possibility that the tradition is an entirely mutable commodity. In doing so, it highlights the stories of change, continuity, and contestation as they animate the historical development of the tradition. These will be dealt with in turn.

Change

Mutability is indeed a feature of the just war tradition. This study has called attention to the capacity of the tradition to adapt to meet changing historical circumstances. In the first place, it suggested that there have been certain cases in the context of the Iraq debate where there was a conscious endeavor on the part of those who engaged the tradition to revise it so that it may better fit today's world. The attempts of the Bush and Blair governments (and their fellow travellers) to revise the parameters of self-defense speak to this scenario. This was a purposive effort to adapt the limits of self-defense to meet the current security environment, conditioned as it is by American hegemony and the fear of WMD-terrorism. More specifically, it constituted an attempt to break free of traditional restraints on anticipatory action.[7]

As Chapter 6 demonstrated, the conceptual schema within which the idea of anticipatory war is rooted has been disturbed by the excise of the requirement of imminence (prompted by Bush and Blair's arguments and seemingly endorsed by the just war community). Consequently, the terms "preemption," "preventive war," and "anticipatory war" have been denuded of their traditional point of reference and meaning. They have been, as Chapter 6 noted, hollowed out. In this case, however, various actors (including the Bush and Blair governments) have moved into this void to impose or project a meaning of their own choosing upon these terms. Such efforts seek to take advantage of a particular moment where the conventional just war idiom appears especially vulnerable to manipulation and revision.

In other cases, change may take another form, quite different from that outlined earlier in the chapter. In these instances, change does not resemble a purposive innovation; rather, it reflects a structural phenomenon. We might think of contemporary understandings of punitive war in this regard. The idea of punitive war has undergone profound changes not because it has been the subject of deliberate revision or manipulation, but because the world around it has changed. The current understanding of punitive war deviates from its traditional expression largely because the normative structure of international affairs (within which it is embedded) has been transformed. International society no longer comprises an institutional framework favorable to the notion that states can stand in judgment of one another; instead, it more closely resembles a juristic community that favors war-crime tribunals aimed mainly at state leaders.[8] Punitive war must, it follows, come to mean something different in this context than it did for Augustine, the scholastics, or Grotius.

This belies a broader point that the international society never stands still; change is a continual process that must somehow be accounted for. To quote Heraclitus, "Everything flows and nothing abides; everything gives way and nothing stays fixed."[9] On this view, every attempt to interpret the just war tradition and apply it the world around us must also serve in some respect to extend it to a new reality and thereby reconstitute it. As Nardin writes, to engage with a tradition is to "move back and forth between the general and the particular—to draw upon general principles in reaching particular judgments and decisions, and, at the same time, to revise those principles in light of the particular circumstances in which they are used."[10] Such a view empha-sizes the mutability of the just war tradition by locating it in an ever-shifting frame. What, then, of continuity? Is there no such thing with respect to the just war tradition? Does the just war tradition reflect flux rather than histori-cal coherence?

Continuity

This book has argued against this view, and has presented a case that the mutability of the just war tradition is conditioned by a certain element of continuity. It has called attention to the fact that those new meanings that have been projected upon the idiom of the just war tradition over the course of the Iraq debate are still tied to a very conventional discourse. Thus, the Bush and Blair governments have confined themselves to arguing about what "preemption" or "preventive war" or "humanitarian war" must mean today, rather than seeking to construct an entirely new moral vocabulary. Indeed, the legalist paradigm continues to structure the Iraq debate even as those engaging the debate attempt to engineer a departure from the paradigm.

Consider, for example, how the case put forward by the NSS for a broader right to anticipatory war pays lip service to the paradigm even as it subverts it. This should not be surprising. Change is most effectively induced by fil-tering it through extant conventions, and is rarely achieved by rewriting the rulebook *de novo*. As Quentin Skinner advises, innovation or manipulation always relies (at least in part) on the existing discourse; ideological innovation is always organic in this sense.[11] The result is that this conventional discourse continues to inform the way Bush and Blair argue and the moves they can make. Again, this is not surprising, for it is this conventional discourse that provides the terms through which parties to the debate can communicate with one another and convey their points to a wider audience. If the legalist paradigm does not entirely resemble a prison house from which the theorist or state leader wishes to escape, it is still restrictive enough to say that its con-ventions must be negotiated by anybody who does wish to break free from it.

Moreover, it is still possible to say, contra those historians who would refuse to accept the notion of political theory outside of historical time, that the just war tradition provides a moral language that displays a strong ele-ment of continuity over many generations. The fact that we can acquire a firmer grasp on the ideas of the present by comparing them with those of the past—consider here how our understanding of the contemporary under-standing of punitive war was sharpened by contrasting it with more classical understandings—suggests that there is a degree of continuity between them. They are not, it would seem, worlds apart; instead, they reflect a common frame of reference. The point here is that the idiom, and indeed the just war tradition more generally, provides a common framework of understanding that allows us to connect the past to the present in some form of critical enquiry. They have retained enough connection with their past to facilitate some form of dialogue with it. Of course, this is not equally true of all terms; some have had more tortuous histories than others, but it is fair to suppose that very few have been entirely rent asunder from their own etymology. Thus it is possible to speak, as Walzer does, of the tradition possessing a certain timelessness (even if it is historical, sociological, and contingent). Perhaps, however, it is as far as we can go at the present to indicate that change and continuity circumscribe or condition one another in respect to the historical development of the just war tradition. Even so, this is a consequential point, for it suggests that an element of contestation is also at play here.

Contestation

As Alasdair MacIntyre writes, traditions may be conceived as continuities of conflict.[12] This book has presented the just war tradition as a site of contestation where innovation and change is constantly being set against elements of continuity, and competing parties maneuver against one another to sway this process. Consider, for example, the efforts by various parties to fix some new meaning to the idea of "preemption." Bush and Blair (and their fellow travellers) were not of course the only parties attempting to project a meaning of their choice upon the terminology of preemption, et cetera. A number of parties, all seeking different ends, have actually attempted to act upon the just war tradition in a similar manner. As a result the idiom of the just war tradition resembles a site of contestation, a site where rival voices compete with one another to determine the meaning of these terms. In these instances, there are no secondary rules to regulate such contestation, and the just war tradition itself becomes an arena within which a *realpolitik* of sorts plays itself out. That is, there is no predetermined means for arbitrating between competing claims over the meaning of a particular word or term; rather, there is only open contestation. As White puts it, "No conventions of argument exist, and no authoritative agencies, by which a settled meaning for the term might be established and the dispute be brought to a close; more than that there does not even seem to be an impulse to solve the case in general rather than specific terms. The question is always particular, and the central issue is always this: Who shall dominate, and who shall submit."[13]

Yet this is not to say that the development of the just war tradition is reducible to the will of the stronger. Although will alone is enough in most cases to ensure a hearing for a particular argument or claim, it is not sufficient to ensure its acceptance by the just war community. Contestation therefore often takes the form of negotiation—understood in a holistic way that encompasses all three definitions discussed here. Accordingly, the range of innovation or change that an actor or group of actors can induce is conditioned by the language that is available to them and the collective will of the just war community. The ability to affect change is a matter of manipulating the existing terminology in such a way as to produce new meanings that meet with the approval of the just war community that is, of course, partially constituted by the existing discourse.

Renegotiation?

Yet even where change is (apparently) successfully induced, it is important to note that this is only a provisional or contingent achievement. As J. G. A. Pocock writes, "Even when an author has succeeded in innovating, that is, in uttering speech in such a way as to compel others to respond to it in some sense not hitherto conventional, it does not follow that he will succeed in ruling the response of others."[14] It is always possible that others actors may intervene at a later time to reverse the innovation or take it in a different direction and it would be foolish to think that any change is ever permanent. The just war tradition is, after all, a protean body of thought that evolves to meet its historical circumstances. Still, it is possible to see, in the context of the Iraq debate, that certain innovations have been enacted upon the just war tradition that appear to have some momentum behind them. They contribute to those developments listed earlier: the broadening of the jus ad bellum, the acceptance that force may serve as an instrument of foreign policy, and a greater willingness to challenge the value of the status quo.

Conclusion

This book has presented an account of the negotiation of the just war tradition in the context of the debate over Iraq. In this respect, it has provided an account of the "transformations, complexities, and continuing resonance of just war as a mode of discourse and a language of justification."[15] In doing so, it has drawn our attention to the stories of change, continuity, and contestation that animate the historical development of the tradition, and questioned what they might tell us about (a) the modalities of the tradition, and (b) the direction in which it is moving today. The modalities of the tradition may be summed up by the three definitions of negotiation just presented, and the tradition may be fairly depicted as moving toward a broader jus ad bellum than was typical throughout the latter half of the twentieth century. This, we ought to recall, is a rather significant development: it reverses the progressive narrowing of the jus ad bellum that has been evident in just war literature since as early as the nineteenth century. These conclusions raise a number of possibilities for future avenues of research.

In the first place, there is interesting work to be done tracking the course of the debates initiated by the invasion of Iraq. The next few years will no doubt witness the publication of a number of texts on the invasion of Iraq and the just war tradition. It will be interesting to see how the debates that have been sketched here develop over the coming years when this greater wealth of material becomes available. Will the broadening or loosening of the jus ad bellum continue apace, will it be consolidated in its present form, or will it be checked and maybe even reversed? Presumably, the answer to this question lies, at least in part, in the contingencies of international politics: if the postwar reconstruction of Iraq continues to go badly, this will presumably impact upon future assessments of the justifications offered for the invasion of Iraq. If, on the other hand, future months are marked by an upsurge in peace and prosperity in the Middle East, efforts to expand the jus ad bellum are likely to be perceived as having received some post hoc vindication, with the result that they might enjoy further endorsement. It will be interesting to observe whether the idea of punitive war and a more permissive right to anticipatory war come eventually to be seen as credible just causes for war and, indeed, as peremptory norms in international society.

In the second place, this book has prompted us to reflect upon how we think about the just war tradition, and especially what we consider its conditions of possibility. There is much scope to develop this line of analysis, and to expand upon the ideas it leads us to. This book has laid the grounds for approaching the tradition as an ongoing project that is made and remade by those who engage it, while still allowing for the possibility that it respects certain parameters and boundaries. Future research might take the route of exploring these parameters and boundaries in greater depth, with the aim of fostering a more self-reflexive just war tradition. Such an agenda might involve applying the questions raised by political theorists who explore the idea of traditions—theorists such as J. G. A. Gunnell, Alasdair MacIntyre, and Terry Nardin—to the just war. A fresh perspective on the just war tradition may thus be revealed that would surely go some way toward developing an account of the just war as a critical tradition. This would serve as a counter to those facile critiques of the just war tradition that denigrate it as a static (and anachronistic) set of rules or checklists. It would contribute toward developing the tradition as a "source of critical opportunity," rather than a "legitimation of reification and closure."[16]

This book has taken some modest steps toward laying the foundations for such research, but must leave any further engagement with this material to another time. It stakes its claim to originality and significance on its treatment of the modalities of the just war tradition—those stories of change, continuity, and contestation that animate its historical development—against the context of the debate precipitated by the invasion of Iraq.

Notes

Introduction

1. Ian Clark, *Legitimacy in International Society* (Oxford: Oxford University Press, 2005), 224–28. Also see Andrew Hurrell, "'There are no Rules': International Order After September the 11th," *International Relations* 16, no. 2 (2002): 185–204.

2. Jean Bethke Elshtain, *Just War Against Terror: The Burden of American Power in a Violent World* (New York: Basic Books, 2004), 151.

3. Prime Minister Tony Blair, "Statement in Response to Terrorist Attacks in the United States," September 11, 2001, http://www.number-10.gov.uk/output/Page1596.asp (accessed February 3, 2006).

4. President George W. Bush, "President Bush Delivers Graduation Speech at West Point," June 1, 2002, http://www.whitehouse.gov/news/releases/2002/06/2002 0601-3.html (accessed October 29, 2007).

5. Susan Neiman, *Evil in Modern Thought* (Princeton, NJ: Princeton University Press, 2002), 3.

6. Prime Minister Tony Blair, "Address to the Labour Party Conference at Brighton, 2 October 2001," http://politics.guardian.co.uk/labour2001/story/0,,562006,00.html (accessed October 29, 2007). Also see Prime Minister Tony Blair, "The Sedgefield Speech," March 5, 2004, http://politics.guardian.co.uk/iraq/story/0,12956,1162991,00.html (accessed April 12, 2004).

7. Michael Walzer, *Just and Unjust Wars: A Moral Argument with Historical Illustrations*, 2nd ed. (New York: Basic Books, 1992), 62.

8. Robert Tucker, *The Just War* (Baltimore: Johns Hopkins University Press, 1960), 11.

9. Michael Hunt, *Ideology and US Foreign Policy* (New Haven, CT: Yale University Press, 1987), 15.

10. Quentin Skinner, *Visions of Politics, Volume I: Regarding Method* (Cambridge: Cambridge University Press, 2002), 174.

11. I would like to thank Chris Brown for pointing this out to me.

12. Terry Nardin, "Ethical Traditions in International Affairs," in *Traditions of International Ethics*, ed. Terry Nardin and David R. Mapel (Cambridge: Cambridge University Press, 1992), 3.

13. Nardin, "Ethical Traditions," 3.

Chapter 1

1. I take the term "loosening" from Richard Haas, quoted in Ian Clark, *The Post–Cold War Order: The Spoils of Peace* (Oxford: Oxford University Press, 2001), 37.

2. William V. O'Brien, *The Conduct of Just and Limited Wars* (New York: Praeger, 1981), 13–14.

3. James Turner Johnson, *Can Modern War Be Just?* (New Haven, CT: Yale University Press, 1984), 15.

4. Michael Walzer, *Just and Unjust Wars: A Moral Argument with Historical Illustrations*, 2nd ed. (New York: Basic Books, 1992).

5. Michael Ignatieff, *The Warrior's Honour* (New York: Metropolitan Books, 1997), 112.

6. James Turner Johnson, *Morality and Contemporary Warfare* (New Haven, CT: Yale University Press, 1999), 11.

7. National Conference of Catholic Bishops, "The Challenge of Peace: God's Promise and Our Response—the Pastoral Letter on War and Peace," in *Just War Theory*, ed. Jean Bethke Elshtain (Oxford: Blackwell, 1992), 77–168. In 2001, the NCCB merged with the United States Catholic Conference to form the United States Conference of Catholic Bishops (USCCB).

8. Johnson, *Morality and Contemporary Warfare*, 13.

9. Walzer introduces the legalist paradigm in *Just and Unjust Wars*, 51–59. Walzer seeks to revise the paradigm in his book, but I concentrate here on the unrevised paradigm as he sets it out. Chris Brown writes that Walzer's legalist paradigm is a "reasonably accurate account of the legal regime on war" in the twentieth century. See Chris Brown, *Sovereignty, Rights and Justice: International Political Theory Today* (Cambridge: Polity, 2002), 103.

10. Walzer, *Just and Unjust Wars*, 21.

11. William V. O'Brien, "The Challenge of War: A Christian Realist Perspective," in *Just War Theory*, ed. Jean Bethke Elshtain (Oxford: Blackwell, 1992), 172.

12. Walzer, *Just and Unjust Wars*, 51.

13. Ibid., 31, 51.

14. Ibid., 62.

15. "The victim of aggression fights in self-defense, but he isn't only defending himself, for aggression is a crime against humanity as a whole. He fights in its name and not only in his own. Other states can rightfully join the victim's resistance; their war has the same character as his own, which is to say, they are entitled not only to repel the attack but to punish it. All resistance is also law enforcement." Walzer, *Just and Unjust Wars*, 59.

16. Walzer, *Just and Unjust Wars*, 62.

17. Walzer quotes Vitoria approvingly, "'There is a single and only just cause for commencing a war, namely, a wrong received.'" Walzer suggests that the legalist paradigm equates the idea of wrongs received with the crime of aggression. Walzer, *Just and Unjust Wars*, 62.

18. Walzer, *Just and Unjust Wars*, 72.

19. Ibid., 268.

20. Robert H. Jackson, *The Global Covenant* (Oxford: Oxford University Press, 2000), 18.

21. National Conference of Catholic Bishops, "The Challenge of Peace," 252.

22. Pope Paul VI, "Gaudium Et Spes: The Pastoral Constitution: On the Church in the Modern World," 1965, http://www.rc.net/rcchurch/vatican2/gaudium.ets (accessed January 24, 2005).

23. William V. O'Brien, *War and/or Survival* (New York: Doubleday, 1969), 22; Robert W. Tucker, *The Just War* (Baltimore: Johns Hopkins University Press, 1960), 11.

24. Walzer, *Just and Unjust Wars*, 34.

25. Ibid., 124.

26. Ibid., 36.

27. Ibid., 21.

28. Ibid., 127.

29. Walzer, *Just and Unjust Wars*, 39. Walzer's views on this issue are not very different from those of Jean-Jacques Rousseau. For comparison, see Jean-Jacques Rousseau, *The Social Contract*, trans. H. J. Tozer (Ware, Hertfordshire: Wordsworth, 1998), 11–12.

30. Mary Kaldor, *New and Old Wars: Organized Violence in a Global Era* (Cambridge: Polity, 2001), 28.

31. Quoted in National Conference of Catholic Bishops, "The Challenge of Peace," 93.

32. As Johnson writes, "We live today in an era in which the destructive capabilities of weapons . . . are so great as to threaten civilization itself in the case of an all-out war. At the same time, strong ideological differences divide East from West, and hatred and distrust rooted in the colonial period divide North from South. While the expectation of general destruction in the case of all-out war tends to call into question whether any war can be morally justified in our time, the existence of strong ideological and cultural differences among peoples and nations promotes the expectation that, if war is begun, it cannot be restrained." James Turner Johnson, *Just War Tradition and the Restraint of War* (Princeton, NJ: Princeton University Press, 1981), xxxii.

33. James Turner Johnson, "Threats, Values, and Defence: Does the Defence of Values by Force Remain a Moral Possibility?" in *Just War Theory*, ed. Jean Bethke Elshtain (Oxford: Blackwell, 1992), 63. Also see Geoffrey Best, *Humanity and Warfare* (New York: Columbia University Press, 1980), 223.

34. Seyom Brown, *The Illusion of Control: Force and Foreign Policy in the 21st Century* (Washington, D.C.: Brookings Institution, 2003), 32–34.

35. William Shawcross, *Deliver Us from Evil: Warlords and Peacekeepers in a World of Endless Conflict* (London: Bloomsbury, 2000); Nicholas J. Wheeler, *Saving Strangers: Humanitarian Intervention in International Society* (Oxford: Oxford University Press, 2000).

36. Johnson, *Morality and Contemporary Warfare*, 65. An example of such a delegated use of force for reasons other than national defense was the UN's post-facto approval of the ECOWAS intervention in Liberia; also its approval of France's dubiously motivated Operation Turquoise in Rwanda.

37. This is the message Tony Blair delivered in his Chicago Club speech; Prime Minister Tony Blair, "Doctrine of the International Community: Remarks at the Economics Club of Chicago," April 22, 1999, http://www.ndol.org/print.cfm?contentid=829 (accessed April 12, 2004).

38. George Robertson, "This is a Just War," *Sunday Business*, April 11, 1999, http://www.fco.gov.uk/news/speechtext.asp?2316 (accessed March 2001); Quoted in: Mohammad Taghi Karoubi, *Just or Unjust War: International Law and Unilateral Use of Armed Force by States at the Turn of the Twentieth Century* (Dartmouth: Ashgate, 2004), 3.

39. Melanie McDonagh, "Can There Be Such a Thing as a Just War?" in *The Kosovo Tragedy*, ed. Ken Booth (London: Frank Cass, 2001), 289.

40. See the series of essays on Walzer and intervention published in Charles R. Beitz et al., eds., *International Ethics: A Philosophy and Public Affairs Reader* (Oxford: Princeton University Press, 1985).

41. Michael Walzer, *Arguing About War* (New Haven, CT: Yale University Press, 2004), xiii.

42. For a discussion of this letter, see Johnson, *Morality and Contemporary Warfare*, 92–94.

43. Quoted in Johnson, *Morality and Contemporary Warfare*, 94.

44. Brown, *The Illusion of Control*, 124.

45. Mona Fixdal and Dan Smith, "Humanitarian Intervention and Just War," *Mershon International Studies Review* 42 (1998): 283–312; Jean Bethke Elshtain, "Just War and Humanitarian Intervention," *Ideas* 8, no. 2 (2001): 1–21; Anthony F. Lang, ed., *Just Intervention* (Washington, D.C.: Georgetown University Press, 2003). George R. Lucas, "From Jus ad Bellum to Jus ad Pacem: Re-Thinking Just War Criteria for the Use of Military Force for Humanitarian Ends," in *Ethics and Foreign Intervention*, ed. Dean K. Chatterjee and Don E. Scheid (Cambridge: Cambridge University Press, 2003), 72–97; Gregory Reichberg and Henrik Syse, "Humanitarian Intervention: A Case of Offensive Force?," *Security Dialogue* 33, no. 3 (2003): 309–22; George R. Lucas, "The Role of the International Community in International Community in Just War Tradition—Confronting the Challenges of Humanitarian Intervention and Preemptive War," *Journal of Military Ethics* 2, no. 2 (2003): 122–44; Duane L. Cady and Robert L. Phillips, *Humanitarian Intervention: Just War Versus Pacifism* (London: Rowman and Littlefield, 1996).

46. For a review of the literature on humanitarian intervention, see Penelope C. Simons, "Humanitarian Intervention: A Review of Literature," Project Ploughshares Working Papers, http://www.ploughshares.ca/content/working%20papers/wp012.html (accessed July 30, 2004).

47. Stanley Hoffmann, "Intervention: Should It Go On, Can It Go On?" in *Ethics and Foreign Intervention*, ed. Dean K. Chatterjee and Don E. Scheid (Cambridge: Cambridge University Press, 2003), 21. For analysis, see Adam Roberts, "Humanitarian War: Military Intervention and Human Rights," *International Affairs* 69, no. 3 (1993): 436.

48. Brown, *The Illusion of Control*, 49.

49. Johnson, *Morality and Contemporary Warfare*, 71.

50. Clark, *The Post-Cold War Order*, 248.

51. Brown, *The Illusion of Control*, 3, 48; Chris Coker, *Humane Warfare* (London: Routledge, 2001).

52. This argument is put forward in question form by Michael Ignatieff in *Virtual War* (Toronto: Viking Books, 2000); see also Eric Hobsbawm, *The New Century* (London: Abacus, 2000), 11. Hobsbawm writes that the RMA "makes possible an increasingly frequent and frivolous recourse to destruction. If you believe yourself to be so powerful that you can choose exactly what you want to destroy, it becomes easier to be tempted to resolve your problems by bombing, as occurred in Iraq [1991]."

53. That is not to say that these arguments were invoked concurrently. Greater emphasis was placed on the humanitarian argument later in the buildup to war. Some critics suggest that this focus on the humanitarian argument only developed after it had become apparent that the British and American governments would be unable to pilot a second resolution (following 1441) through the Security Council and so secure UN authorization for the use of force against Iraq. See Alex J. Bellamy, "Ethics and Intervention: The 'Humanitarian Exception' and the Problem of Abuse in the Case of Iraq," *Journal of Peace Research* 41, no. 2 (2004): 136; Stefan Halper and Jonathan Clarke, *America Alone: The Neo-Conservatives and the Global Order* (Cambridge: Cambridge University Press, 2004), 218–19.

54. President George W. Bush, "State of the Union Address," January 29, 2002, http://www.whitehouse.gov/news/releases/2002/01/20020129–11.html (accessed May 18, 2004).

55. For an argument that runs along these lines, see James P. Rubin, "Stumbling into War," *Foreign Affairs* 82, no. 5 (2003): 46–65. Even if this were the case, it would not vitiate the value of this work. As W. L. Lacroix writes, "In their public pronouncements, leaders employ appeals to those moral terms that . . . are significant for the international milieu: 'assisting friends,' 'stopping aggression,' 'territorial security,' 'protecting the freedom of individuals,' and the like . . . Because leaders make such appeals to justify state actions, we know that certain standards are morally operative, whether the particular actions are truly instances of them or not. It is with this kind of evidence that we properly begin an ethical study." See W. L. Lacroix, *War and International Ethics: Tradition and Today* (Lanham, MD: University Press of America, 1988), 1–2.

56. Jutta Brunnee and Stephen J. Toope, "Slouching Towards New 'Just' Wars: The Hegemon after September 11," *International Relations* 18, no. 4 (2004): 405.

Adam Roberts makes a similar point in "Law and the Use of Force after Iraq," *Survival* 45, no. 2 (2003): 34.

57. Geoffrey Best, *War and Law Since 1945* (Oxford: Clarendon, 1994), 20.

58. Arthur Nussbaum, *A Concise History of the Law of Nations* (New York: Macmillan, 1954), 126; Best, *Humanity and Warfare*, 87.

59. Francis Lieber, "Instructions for the Government of Armies of the United States in the Field, General Orders No. 100," in *The Ethics of War: Classic and Contemporary Readings*, ed. Gregory M. Reichberg, Henrik Syse, and Endre Begby (Malden, MA: Blackwell, 2006), 566–72.

60. Best, *Humanity and Warfare*, 155.

61. Best, *War and Law Since 1945*, 42.

62. Nicholas J. Rengger, "The Just War Tradition in the Twenty First Century," *International Affairs* 78, no. 2 (2002): 356. Karoubi makes a similar point: "International jurists," he writes, tended to "concentrate more on the legality of methods of conduct of war, *jus in bello*, rather than on the legality of war, *jus ad bellum*." Karoubi, *Just or Unjust Wars*, 6.

63. Best, *Humanity and Warfare*, 159.

64. Ibid.

65. Ibid.

66. Stephen E. Lammers, "Approaches to Limits on War in Western Just War Discourse," in *Cross, Crescent and Sword*, ed. James Turner Johnson and John Kelsay (Westport, CT: Greenwood, 1990), 56.

67. Lammers, "Limits on War," 56.

68. Ibid., 64.

69. Best, *War and Law Since 1945*, 235.

70. Best, *Humanity and Warfare*, 7.

71. Hedley Bull, "The Importance of Grotius in the Study of International Relations," in *Hugo Grotius and International Relations*, ed. Hedley Bull, Benedict Kingsbury, and Adam Roberts (Oxford: Clarendon, 1990), 89.

72. W. E. Hall, *International Law*, 8th ed. (Oxford: Clarendon, 1924), 82. Quoted in Karoubi, *Just or Unjust Wars*, 92.

73. G. I. A. D. Draper, "Grotius' Place in the Development of Legal Ideas About War," in *Hugo Grotius and International Relations*, ed. Hedley Bull, Benedict Kingsbury, and Adam Roberts (Oxford: Clarendon, 1990), 201–2.

74. Best, *Humanity and Warfare*, 305–8.

75. Ibid., 308.

76. Rengger, "Just War Tradition in the Twenty First Century," 359. Mary Kaldor makes a similar point. She writes, "State interests became the legitimate justification for war [in the 18th century], supplanting concepts of justice, jus ad bellum, drawn from theology." See Kaldor, *New and Old Wars*, 17.

77. Nicholas Politis, *Neutrality and Peace* (New York: Carnegie Endowment For International Peace, 1935), 6. Rosalyn Higgins traces this development back to the work of Hugo Grotius. Rosalyn Higgins, "Grotius and the Development of International Law in the UN. Period," in *Hugo Grotius and International*

Relations, ed. Hedley Bull, Adam Roberts, and Benedict Kingsbury (Oxford: Clarendon, 1990), 268.

78. Politis, *Neutrality and Peace*, 8.
79. Best, *War and Law Since 1945*, 54.
80. Draper, "Grotius's Place," 204.
81. Following decades of debate about what constitutes aggression and whether the first use of force might ever be lawful, it is fairly obvious that these categories failed to live up to these hopes.
82. Johnson, *Can Modern War Be Just?*, 21; Oliver O' Donovan, *The Just War Revisited* (Cambridge: Cambridge University Press, 2003), 54.
83. Karoubi, *Just or Unjust Wars*, 96.
84. Quoted in ibid., 93.
85. Ibid., 101.
86. Quoted in ibid., 102.
87. Quoted in ibid., 103.
88. Quoted in Tucker, *The Just War*, 78.
89. O'Brien, *The Conduct of Just and Limited Wars*, 22–3.
90. Richard Falk, *Law, Morality and War in the Contemporary World* (New York: Praeger, 1963), 74.
91. Karoubi, *Just or Unjust Wars*, 124.
92. A. J. Coates, *The Ethics of War* (Manchester: Manchester University Press, 1997), 156.
93. Douglas P. Lackey, *The Ethics of War and Peace* (Englewood Cliffs, NJ: Prentice Hall, 1989), 33.

Chapter 2

1. On Thucydides, see Francis Bacon, "Considerations Touching a Warre with Spain," in *Certaine Miscellany Works*, ed. W. Rawley (London: Da Capo, 1629), 13; Niccolo Machiavelli, *The Prince*, ed. and trans. David Wootton (Indianapolis and Cambridge: Hacket, 1995), 11; W. L. Lacroix, *War and International Ethics: Tradition and Today* (Lanham, MD: University Press of America, 1988), 151.
2. In his own words: "The idea of undertaking a war because it might be inevitable later on and might then have to be fought under more unfavorable conditions has always remained foreign to me, and I have always fought against it . . . For I cannot always look into Providence's cards in such a manner that I would know things beforehand." Cited in Brian Crisher, "Altering Jus ad Bellum: Just War Theory in the 21st Century and the 2002 National Security Strategy of the United States," *Critique: A Worldwide Journal of Politics*, 2005: 1.
3. President George W. Bush, *The National Security Strategy of the USA*, http://www.whitehouse.gov/nsc/nss.html (accessed September 6, 2006).
4. Michael Walzer, *Just and Unjust Wars: A Moral Argument with Historical Illustrations*, 2nd ed. (New York: Basic Books, 1992), chap. 5.

5. Thomas M. Franck, *Recourse to Force: State Action against Threats and Armed Attacks* (Cambridge: Cambridge University Press, 2002), chaps. 1, 7; Anthony Clark Arend, "International Law and the Preemptive Use of Military Force," *Washington Quarterly* 26, no. 2 (2003): 89–103.

6. Daniel Webster, "Letter to British Ambassador Henry Fox, Dated 24 April 1841," in *The Ethics of War: Classic and Contemporary Readings*, ed. Gregory Reichberg, Henrik Syse, and Endre Begby (Malden, MA, and Oxford: Blackwell, 2006), 563–64.

7. Walzer, *Just and Unjust Wars*, 74.

8. Ibid., 75.

9. In Walzer's words, "Imagine a spectrum of anticipation: at one end is Webster's reflex, necessary and determined; at the other end is preventive war, an attack that responds to a distant danger, a matter of foresight and free choice." Ibid.

10. Ibid.

11. Thucydides, *History of the Peloponnesian War*, trans. Rex Warner (Harmondsworth: Penguin, 1972), 49. For an analysis of Thucydides' views on fear, see David Boucher, *Political Theories of International Relations* (Oxford: Oxford University Press, 1998), 72–74.

12. Cicero, *On Duties* (Cambridge: Cambridge University Press, 1991), 10.

13. Richard Tuck, *The Rights of War and Peace: Political Thought and the International Order from Grotius to Kant* (Oxford: Oxford University Press, 1999), 16; Coleman Phillipson's introduction to *De Iure Belli Libri Tres*, by Alberico Gentili (Oxford: Clarendon, 1933), 18.

14. Francisco de Vitoria, "On the Law of War," in *Vitoria: Political Writings*, ed. Anthony Pagden and Jeremy Lawrance (Cambridge: Cambridge University Press, 1991), 303.

15. Vitoria, "On the Law of War," 316.

16. Gentili, *De Iure Belli*, book 1, chap. 2.

17. "Let the Theologians keep silent about a matter which is outside of their province." Gentili, *De Iure Belli*, 57.

18. Ibid., 61–62.

19. Ibid.

20. Interestingly, it is couched in just war terms. For example, by way of introduction, Bacon announces, "To a warre are required; A just quarrel; sufficient forces and provisions; and a prudent choice of designs." Francis Bacon, "Considerations Touching a Warre with Spaine," in *Francis Bacon: Certaine Miscellany Works*, ed. W. Rawley (London: De Capo, 1629), 3. In addition to this, he cites Thomas Aquinas and Augustine in the course of his discussions, as on p. 23.

21. Bacon, "Considerations," 21.

22. Ibid.

23. Ibid.

24. Ibid., 17.

25. Francis Bacon, "Of Delays," in *The Essays*, ed. John Pitcher (London: Penguin Books, 1985), 125.

26. On fears, see Bacon, "Considerations," 23. On suspicions, see Francis Bacon, "Of Suspicion," in *The Essays*, ed. John Pitcher (London: Penguin Books, 1985), 159; Gentili, *De Iure Belli*, 63.

27. Bacon, "Considerations," 12–13.

28. Ibid., 16. Bacon quotes Antiochus, "'That the Romans came to pull down all kingdoms, and to make the state of Rome an universal monarchy . . . So that as every state lay next to the other that was oppressed, so the fire perpetually grazed.'"

29. Ibid.

30. Ibid., 19.

31. Ibid., 24–25.

32. D. D. Raphael, *Hobbes: Morals and Politics* (London and New York: Routledge, 1996), 9.

33. Tuck, *The Rights of War and Peace*, 127; Raphael, *Hobbes*, 11; Noel Malcolm, *Aspects of Hobbes* (Oxford and New York: Oxford University Press, 2002), 6–7; A. P. Martinich, *A Hobbes Dictionary* (Oxford: Blackwell, 1995), 7.

34. I am influenced here by Richard Tuck's reading of Hobbes's philosophy and its relation to the work of Hugo Grotius. See Richard Tuck, *Hobbes* (Oxford and New York: Oxford University Press, 1989), 58. Tuck's work has been the source of much critical debate. For example, see R. Shaver, "Grotius on Scepticism and Self-Interest," in *Grotius, Pufendorf, and Modern Natural Law*, ed. Knud Haakonnsen (Dartmouth: Ashgate, 1999), 63–83.

35. Hugo Grotius, *The Rights of War and Peace*, ed. Richard Tuck (Indianapolis: Liberty Fund, 2005), 398.

36. Thomas Hobbes, *Leviathan* (Cambridge: Cambridge University Press, 1996), 91. On Grotius, see Grotius, *The Rights of War and Peace*, Book 1, chap. 2.

37. Thomas Hobbes, *De Cive*, ed. and trans. Richard Tuck and Michael Silverthorne (Cambridge: Cambridge University Press, 1998), 29. Richard Tuck explains the consequences of this sticking point: "Despite our initial agreement about the right of self-preservation, there will in practice still be a radical instability in the state of nature. There is not much point in my saying that I agree with you in principle about your right to preserve yourself, if I disagree with you about whether this is the moment for you to implement that right. Suppose I see you walking peacefully through the primitive savannah, whistling, and swinging your club: are you a danger to me? You may well think not: you have an entirely pacific disposition. But I may think you are, and the exercise of my natural right of self-preservation depends only on my assessment of the situation. So if I attack you, I must be justified in so doing." Tuck, *Hobbes*, 59.

38. Hobbes, *De Cive*, 145.

39. Ibid., 29.

40. Ibid., 30.

41. Hobbes, *Leviathan*, 89.

42. Ibid., 89–90.

43. Ibid., 88.

44. Ibid.

45. Hobbes, *De Cive*, 145.

46. Michael C. Williams, *The Realist Tradition and the Limits of International Relations* (Cambridge: Cambridge University Press, 2005), 24. Williams quotes Jans Blits on the same topic, "'Fear is pain, and men naturally avoid pain. Men therefore seek to avoid not only the object of fear, but fear itself. But an objectless fear is an unresolvable fear. No one can fight or flee what he cannot identify or know . . . Thus when an object is lacking, men will find an imaginary one. They will invent an identifiable object they can fear.'"

47. Donald H. Rumsfeld, "Secretary Rumsfeld Press Conference at NATO Headquarters, Brussels," June 6, 2002, http://www.defenselink.mil/transcripts/2002/t06062002_t0606sd.html (accessed November 30, 2005). In context, "The message is that there are no 'knowns.' There are thing we know that we know. There are known unknowns. That is to say there are things that we now know we don't know. But there are also unknown unknowns. There are things we don't know we don't know. So when we do the best we can and we pull all this information together, and we then say well that's basically what we see as the situation, that is really only the known knowns and the known unknowns. And each year, we discover a few more of those unknown unknowns."

48. Williams, *The Realist Tradition*, 27.

49. Ibid., 25.

50. Walzer, *Just and Unjust Wars*, 77–80.

51. "We move along the spectrum of anticipation," Walzer gestures, "in search of enemies; not possible or potential enemies, not merely present ill-wishers, but states and nations that are already harming us (and who have already harmed us, by their threats, even if they have not yet inflicted any physical injury)." Ibid., 81.

52. Samuel Pufendorf, "Of the Law of Nature and of Nations," in *The Political Writings of Samuel Pufendorf*, ed. Craig L. Carr (Oxford: Oxford University Press, 1994), 258.

53. Pufendorf, "Of the Law of Nature," 258.

54. Emmerich de Vattel, *The Law of Nations or the Principles of Natural Law*, ed. James Brown Scott, trans. Charles G. Fenwick (New York and London: Oceana Publications and Wildy and Sons, 1902), 248.

55. Grotius, *The Rights of War and Peace*, 1102.

56. Vattel, *The Law of Nations*, 14.

57. Ibid., 250.

58. Grotius, *Rights of War and Peace*, 1102. Italics added.

59. Vattel, *The Law of Nations*, 252.

60. Ibid.

61. Ibid.

62. Ibid., 130.

63. Ibid., 250.

64. Ibid.

65. Ibid.

66. Walzer, *Just and Unjust Wars*, 79.

67. Ibid., 80.

68. Ibid., 78–80.

69. Ibid., 81. Italics added.

70. Ibid.

71. Ibid.

72. Compare to Vattel, *The Law of Nations*, 250.

73. Walzer, *Just and Unjust Wars*, 85.

74. President George W. Bush, "President Discusses Growing Danger Posed by Saddam Hussein's Regime," September 14, 2002, http://www.whitehouse.gov/news/releases/2002/09/print/20020914.html (accessed May 18, 2004). George Lucas has written on the role played by the notion of international peace and security and the international community in these arguments. George R. Lucas, "The Role of the International Community in International Community in Just War Tradition—Confronting the Challenges of Humanitarian Intervention and Preemptive War," *Journal of Military Ethics* 2, no. 2 (2003): 122–44.

75. President George W. Bush, "President Bush Outlines Iraqi Threat," October 7, 2002, http://www.whitehouse.gov/news/releases/2002/10/print/20021007–8.html (accessed May 18, 2004).

76. For a discussion of these two reasons, see Dieter Janssen, "Preventive Defense and Forcible Regime Change: A Normative Assessment," *Journal of Military Ethics* 3, no. 2 (2004): 109.

77. Bush, "President Bush Outlines Iraqi Threat."

78. Ibid.

79. President George W. Bush, "President Delivers State of the Union," January 28, 2003, http://www.whitehouse.gov/news/releases/2003/01/print/20030128–19.html (accessed May 18, 2004).

80. President George W. Bush, "President's Remarks at the United Nations General Assembly," September 12, 2002, http://www.whitehouse.gov/news/releases/2002/09/print/20020912–1.html (accessed May 18, 2004).

81. President George W. Bush, "President Bush Discusses Iraq with Congressional Leaders," September 26, 2002, http://www.whitehouse.gov/news/releases/2002/09/print/20020926–7.html (accessed May 18, 2004).

82. Prime Minister Tony Blair, "P.M.'s Speech Opening Commons Debate on Iraq," March 18, 2003, http://www.politics.guardian.co.uk/iraq/story/0,12956,916790,00.html (accessed April 12, 2004).

83. Bush, "President's Remarks at the United Nations General Assembly."

84. Prime Minister Tony Blair, "Prime Minister's Speech to TUC Conference in Blackpool," September 10, 2002, http://www.number-10.gov.uk/output/page1725.asp (accessed May 18, 2004).

85. Bush, "President Bush Discusses Iraq with Congressional Leaders."

86. Bush, "President Outlines Iraqi Threat." Quoted in Ivo H. Daalder and James M. Lindsay, *America Unbound: The Bush Revolution in Foreign Policy* (Washington D.C.: Brookings Institute, 2003), 157; Michael E. O'Hanlon, "Saddam's Bomb: How Close Is Iraq to Having a Nuclear Weapon?" http://www.brookings.edu/views/op-ed/ohanlon/20020918.htm (accessed August 1, 2004).

87. On this matter, see Michael Byers, "Preemptive Self-Defense: Hegemony, Equality and Strategies of Legal Change," *Journal of Political Philosophy* 11, no. 2 (2003): 171–90.

88. Neta C. Crawford, "The Best Defense," *Boston Review*, February/March 2003, http://www.bostonreview.net/br28.1/crawford.html (accessed August 15, 2006).

89. Richard Haass, "Sovereignty: Existing Rights, Evolving Responsibilities— Remarks to the Mortara Center for International Studies at Georgetown," http://usinfo.state.gov/topical/pol/terror/03011501.htm (accessed December 5, 2003).

90. Bush, *The National Security Strategy*, chap. 5.

91. Quoted in Whitley Kaufman, "What's Wrong with Preventive War? The Moral and Legal Basis for the Preventive Use of Force," *Ethics & International Affairs* 19, no. 3 (2005): 23.

92. President George W. Bush, "President Says Saddam Hussein Must Leave Iraq within 48 Hours," March 17, 2003, http://www.whitehouse.gov/news/releases/2003/03/print/20030317-7.html (accessed May 18, 2004).

93. Prime Minister Tony Blair, "The Sedgefield Speech," March 5, 2004, http://politics.guardian.co.uk/iraq/story/0,12956,1162991,00.html (accessed April 12, 2004).

94. Bush, *The National Security Strategy*, chap. 5.

95. Blair, "The Sedgefield Speech."

96. There were occasions where representatives of the Bush and Blair governments attempted (but failed by most counts) to offer solid evidence linking Iraq to al Qaeda, notably Powell's address to the United Nations Security Council (UNSC); Colin Powell, "U.S. Secretary of State Colin Powell Addresses the UN Security Council," February 5, 2003, http://www.whitehouse.gov/news/releases/2003/02/print/20030205-1.html (accessed May 18, 2004).

97. David Coates and Joel Krieger, *Blair's War* (Cambridge: Polity, 2004), 58.

98. Blair, "The Sedgefield Speech."

99. Ibid.

100. Neta C. Crawford, "Just War Theory and the U.S. Counter-terror War," *Perspectives on Politics* 1, no. 1 (2003): 15.

101. President George W. Bush, "President Calls for Quick Passage of Defence Bill," March 15, 2002, http://www.whitehouse.gov/news/releases/2002/03/print/20020315.html (accessed May 17, 2004).

102. Toni Erskine, "'As Rays of Light to the Human Soul'? Moral Agents and Intelligence Gathering," *Intelligence and National Security* 19, no. 2 (2004): 365.

103. Condoleezza Rice, "Dr. Condoleezza Rice Discusses President's National Security Strategy," October 1, 2002, http://www.whitehouse.gov/news/releases/2002/10/print/20021001–6.html (accessed May 18, 2005).

104. Gentili, *De Iure Belli*, 61.

105. The Bush administration provided for a definition of the term "rogue state" in the NSS. According to the NSS, rogue states are states that "brutalize their own people and squander their natural resources for the personal gain of the rulers; Display no regard for international law, threaten their neighbors, and callously violate international treaties to which they are party; Are determined to acquire weapons of mass destruction, along with other advanced military technology, to be used as threats or offensively to achieve the aggressive designs of these regimes; Sponsor terrorism around the globe; Reject basic human values and hate the United States and everything for which it stands." Bush, *The National Security Strategy*.

106. This argument also finds expression in the NSS; it proclaims that deterrence is not likely to work vis-à-vis a state like Iraq. Deterrence, it claims, might have worked during the Cold War against an adversary such as the Soviet Union, but "it is less likely to work against leaders of rogue states more willing to take risks, gambling with the lives of their people, and the wealth of their nations." See Bush, *The National Security Strategy*.

107. Bush, "President Bush Outlines Iraqi Threat."

108. Ibid. "Some ask why Iraq is different from other countries or regimes that also have terrible weapons. While there are many dangers in the world, the threat from Iraq stands alone—because it gathers the most serious dangers of our age in one place. Iraq's weapons of mass destruction are controlled by a murderous tyrant who has already used chemical weapons to kill thousands of people."

109. Ibid.

110. Coates and Krieger, *Blair's War*, 128.

111. See also Prime Minister Tony Blair, "PM Interviewed on Iraq, WMD, Europe and the Euro," http://www.number-10.gov.uk/output/page3797.asp (accessed May 18, 2005).

112. Coates and Krieger, *Blair's War*, 71.

113. Prime Minister Tony Blair, "Opening Speech at the House of Commons Debate on the Iraq Crisis," March 18, 2003, http://politics.guardian.co.uk/iraq/story/0,12956,916790,00.html (accessed April 12, 2004); Blair, "Prime Minister's Speech to TUC Conference"; Prime Minister Tony Blair, "Prime Minister's Iraq Statement to Parliament," September 24, 2002, http://www.number-10.gov.uk/output/page1727.asp (accessed May 18, 2004); Prime Minister Tony Blair, "Speech to the Labour Party's Glasgow Conference," February 15, 2003, http://www.iraqcrisis.co.uk/resources.php?idtag=R3E50FD 20EDCFA (accessed October 4, 2004); President George W. Bush, "President, House Leadership Agree on Iraq Resolution," October 2, 2002, http://www.whitehouse.gov/news/releases/2002/10/print/20021002–7.html (accessed May 18, 2004); President George W. Bush, "Remarks by the President at

Massachusetts Victory 2002 Reception," October 4, 2002, http://www
.whitehouse.gov/news/releases/2002/10/print/20021004–3.html (accessed May
18, 2004); Bush, "President Bush Outlines Iraqi Threat." President George W.
Bush, "President Signs Iraq Resolution," October 16, 2002, http://www
.whitehouse.gov/news/releases/2002/10/print/20021016–1.html (accessed May
18, 2004).

114. Blair, "Prime Minister's Speech to TUC Conference."

115. Bush, "President, House Leadership Agree on Iraq Resolution."

116. Robert S. Litwak, "The New Calculus of Preemption," *Survival* 44, no. 4
(2002–3): 67.

117. Vice President Dick Cheney, "Vice President Speaks at VFW 103rd National
Convention," August 26, 2002, http://www.whitehouse.gov/news/releases/
2002/08/print/20020826.html (accessed May 17, 2004).

118. Powell, "U.S. Secretary of State Colin Powell Addresses the UN Security
Council."

119. Walzer, *Just and Unjust Wars*, 81.

Chapter 3

1. Elements of this chapter have appeared in Cian O'Driscoll, "Renegotiating the
Just War: The Invasion of Iraq and Punitive War," *Cambridge Review of
International Affairs* 19, no. 3 (2006): 405–20; Cian O'Driscoll, "New Thinking
in the Just War Tradition: Theorizing the War on Terror," in *Security and the War
on Terror: Civil-Military Cooperation in a New Age*, ed. Alex J. Bellamy, Roland
Bleiker, Sara Davies, and Richard Devetak (London: Routledge, 2007).

2. Robert H. Jackson, *The Global Covenant* (Oxford: Oxford University Press,
2000), 19; Richard B. Miller, *Interpretations of Conflict: Ethics, Pacifism and the
Just War Tradition* (Chicago: University of Chicago Press, 1991), 13.

3. Michael Walzer, *Just and Unjust Wars: A Moral Argument with Historical
Illustrations*, 2nd ed. (New York: Basic Books, 1992), 51–59.

4. Jeff McMahan, "Just Cause for War," *Ethics & International Affairs* 19, no. 3
(2005): 1. The point is not that punishment has no place in the just war tradition, rather it is that many (if not most) contemporary just war theorists have
chosen to ignore or even disregard it in their writings. Johnson makes a similar
point, "Just cause in the middle ages could be construed in terms of punishing
evildoers in the stead of God, while today it tends to be put, especially in international law, in terms of outlawing aggression and defining a limited right of
self-defense." See James Turner Johnson, *Just War Tradition and the Restraint of
War* (Princeton, NJ: Princeton University Press, 1981), xxii.

5. Indeed, on the same day that the NSS, containing within it the Bush administration's case for anticipatory war against Iraq, was published, the White House
press office was more concerned to trumpet a document calling for the punishment of Iraq in response to its violation of international law.

6. Oliver O'Donovan, *The Just War Revisited* (Cambridge: Cambridge University Press, 2003), 13.

7. O'Donovan, *Just War Revisited*, 16.

8. Ibid., 14.

9. Ibid., 23–28.

10. Ibid., 131–34.

11. Jean Bethke Elshtain, *Just War against Terror: The Burden of American Power in a Violent World* (New York: Basic Books, 2004), 46. This book has generated much comment. For a discussion of the response it provoked within the academy, see the collection of essays by O'Driscoll, Walzer, Elshtain, and Zehfuss gathered in *International Relations* 21, no. 4 (2007).

12. See Elshtain's contribution to "Just War Tradition and the New War on Terrorism," Pew Forum on Religion and Public Life, http://pewforum.org/events/?EventID=15 (accessed October 30, 2007).

13. Elshtain, *Just War against Terror*, 52.

14. Jean Bethke Elshtain, "How to Fight a Just War," in *Worlds in Collision: Terror and the Future of Global Order*, ed. Ken Booth and Tim Dunne (Basingstoke and New York: Palgrave Macmillan, 2002), 264.

15. This discussion draws on a number of sources, primarily H. L. A. Hart, *Punishment and Responsibility—Essays in the Philosophy of Law* (Oxford: Clarendon, 1968). This was helpful with regards to what I term the lower-order goals of punishment (what Hart labels its "general justifying aims"). Discussions of the various lower-order goals are provided in the following texts: Nigel Walker, *Why Punish?* (Oxford and New York: Oxford University Press, 1991); C. L. Ten, *Crime, Guilt, and Punishment: A Philosophical Introduction* (Oxford: Clarendon, 1987); R. A. Duff and D. Garland, "Introduction: Thinking About Punishment," in *A Reader on Punishment*, ed. Antony Duff and David Garland (Oxford and New York: Oxford University Press, 1994). On the higher-order goals of punishment, see P. Hirst, "The Concept of Punishment," in *A Reader on Punishment*, ed. Antony Duff and D. Garland (Oxford and New York: Oxford University Press, 1994); Hyman Gross, *A Theory of Criminal Justice* (New York: Oxford University Press, 1979); Joel Feinberg, *Doing and Deserving: Essays in the Theory of Responsibility* (Princeton, NJ: Princeton University Press, 1970); Michel Foucault, *Discipline and Punish: The Birth of the Prison* (London: Penguin Books, 1977).

16. Lori Fisler Damrosch and Bernard H. Oxman, "Editors' Introduction to Agora: Future Implications of the Iraq Conflict," *American Journal of International Law* 97, no. 3 (2003): 554. This view is echoed by Ruth Wedgwood, "The Fall of Saddam Hussein: Security Council Mandates and Preemptive Self-Defense," *American Journal of International Law* 97, no. 3 (2003): 578; Adam Roberts, "Law and the Use of Force after Iraq," *Survival* 45, no. 2 (2003): 48.

17. President George W. Bush, "President Discusses the Future of Iraq," February 26, 2003, http://www.whitehouse.gov/news/releases/2003/02/print/20030226–11.html (accessed May 18, 2004); President George W. Bush,

"President Salutes Sailors at Naval Station Mayport in Jacksonville," February 13, 2003, http://www.whitehouse.gov/news/releases/2003/02/print/20020213 –3.html (accessed May 18, 2004).

18. President George W. Bush, "President Says Saddam Hussein Must Leave Iraq within 48 Hours," March 17, 2003, http://www.whitehouse.gov/news/releases/ 2003/03/print/20030317–7.html (accessed May 18, 2004).

19. Prime Minister Tony Blair, "PM's Speech Opening Commons Debate on Iraq," March 18, 2003, http://www.politics.guardian.co.uk/iraq/story/0,12956 ,916790,00.html (accessed April 12, 2004).

20. Prime Minister Tony Blair, "The Sedgefield Speech," March 5, 2004, http:// politics.guardian.co.uk/iraq/story/0,12956,1162991,00.html (accessed April 12, 2004); Prime Minister Tony Blair, "PM Interviewed on Iraq, WMD, Europe and the Euro," http://www.number-10.gov.uk/output/page3797.asp (accessed May 18, 2004).

21. President George W. Bush, "President Bush Discusses Iraq with Congressional Leaders," September 26, 2002, http://www.whitehouse.gov/news/releases/2002/ 09/print/20020926–7.html (accessed May 18, 2004).

22. Condoleezza Rice, "Dr. Condoleezza Rice Discusses President's National Security Strategy," October 1, 2002, http://www.whitehouse.gov/news/releases/ 2002/10/print/20021001–6.html (accessed May 18, 2004).

23. Blair, "PM's Speech Opening Commons Debate on Iraq."

24. Ibid.

25. President George W. Bush, "President's Remarks at the United Nations General Assembly," September 12, 2002, http://www.whitehouse.gov/news/releases/ 2002/09/print/20020912–1.html (accessed May 18, 2004).

26. Prime Minister Tony Blair, "Prime Minister's Iraq Statement to Parliament," September 24, 2002, http://www.number-10.gov.uk/output/page1727.asp (accessed May 18, 2004).

27. Hannah Arendt, *Eichmann in Jerusalem: A Report on the Banality of Evil*, revised and enlarged ed. (New York: Penguin Books, 1994), 277.

28. Dorothy V. Jones, *Code of Peace: Ethics and Security in the World of States* (Chicago and London: University of Chicago Press, 1991), 10.

29. David Frum and Richard Perle, *An End to Evil* (New York: Random House, 2004).

30. This is not surprising really, as David Frum was President Bush's chief speechwriter and was responsible for composing Bush's 2001 State of the Union address where he introduced the notion of there being an "axis of evil" in the world today.

31. Peter Singer, *The President of Good and Evil* (London: Granta Books, 2004).

32. Prime Minister Tony Blair, "Address to the Labour Party Conference at Brighton," October 2, 2001, http://politics.guardian.co.uk/labour2001/story/ 0,,562006,00.html (accessed October 29, 2007); President George W. Bush, "Statement by the President in His Address to the Nation," September 11, 2001,

http://www.whitehouse.gov/news/releases/2001/09/20010911–16.html (accessed September 6, 2006).

33. Prime Minister Tony Blair, "Statement in Response to Terrorist Attacks in the United States," September 11, 2001, http://www.number-10.gov.uk/output/Page1596.asp (accessed February 3, 2006). For analysis of Blair's response, see David Coates and Joel Krieger, *Blair's War* (Cambridge: Polity, 2004), 44; Bush, "Statement September 11, 2001"; President George W. Bush, "President's Remarks at National Day of Prayer and Remembrance, the National Cathedral, Washington D.C.," September 14, 2001, http://www.whitehouse.gov/news/releases/2001/09/20010914–2.html (accessed May 16, 2004).

34. Bush, "Remarks at National Day of Prayer and Remembrance."

35. Blair, "Statement in Response to Terrorist Attacks, September 11, 2001."

36. Singer, *The President of Good and Evil*, 2.

37. President George W. Bush, "President Bush Delivers Graduation Speech at West Point," June 1, 2002, http://www.whitehouse.gov/news/releases/2002/06/20020601–1.html (accessed December 5, 2003).

38. President George W. Bush, "President Bush Delivers State of the Union Address," January 29, 2002, http://www.whitehouse.gov/news/releases/2002/01/20020129–11.html (accessed December 5, 2003). This was the occasion on which Bush labeled Iraq, Iran, and North Korea an axis of evil. Bush subsequently referred to Iraq as evil in the following speeches: President George W. Bush, "President Delivers State of the Union Address," January 28, 2003, http://www.whitehouse.gov/news/releases/2003/01/print/20030128–19.html (accessed May 18, 2004). President George W. Bush, "President Rallies Troops at Macdill Air Force Base in Tampa," March 26, 2003, http://www.whitehouse.gov/news/releases/2003/03/print/20030326–4.html (accessed May 18, 2004).

39. President George W. Bush, "President Bush Addresses the Nation," March 19, 2003, http://www.whitehouse.gov/news/releases/2003/03/print/20030319–17.html (accessed May 18, 2004).

40. Bush, "Bush Addresses the Nation."

41. President George W. Bush, "President Bush Announces Major Combat Operations in Iraq Have Ended," May 1, 2003, http://www.whitehouse.gov/news/releases/2003/05/iraq/20030501–15.html (accessed May 18, 2004).

42. Bush, "Bush Announces Major Combat Operations Have Ended."

43. Michael J. Mazarr, "George W. Bush, Idealist," *International Affairs* 79, no. 3 (2003): 515.

44. Blair, "PM's Speech Opening Commons Debate on Iraq"; Prime Minister Tony Blair, "Prime Minister's Address to the Nation," March 20, 2003, http://www.number-10.gov.uk/output/page3327.asp (accessed May 18, 2004). Prime Minister Tony Blair, "Speech to the Labour Party's Glasgow Conference," February 15, 2003, http://www.iraqcrisis.co.uk/resources.php?idtag=R3E50FD20EDCFA (accessed October 2, 2004). Blair, "Address to the Labour Party Conference."

45. Blair, "Address to the Labour Party Conference."

46. Prime Minister Tony Blair, "P.M. Message to Iraqi People," April 8, 2003, http://www.number-10.gov.uk/output/page3449.asp (accessed May 18, 2004).

47. Roy F. Baumeister, *Evil: Inside Human Violence and Cruelty* (New York: W. H. Freeman and Company, 1997), 67.

48. Terry Eagleton, *After Theory* (London: Allen Lane, 2003), 216–17.

49. Tony Blair, "Foreword," in *Reclaiming the Ground: Christianity and Socialism*, ed. Christopher Bryant (London: Spire and Christian Socialist Movement, 1993), 12.

50. John Rentoul, *Tony Blair: Prime Minister* (London: Little, Brown, and Company, 2001), 351–57; Philip Stephens, *Tony Blair: The Price of Leadership* (London: Politico's, 2004), 32; Paul Hoggett, "Iraq: Blair's Mission Impossible," *British Journal of Politics and International Relations* 7, no. 3 (2005): 418–29.

51. Peter Stothard, *30 Days: A Month at the Heart of Blair's War* (London: HarperCollins, 2003).

52. Bob Woodward, *Plan of Attack* (London: Simon and Schuster, 2004), 279.

53. George W. Bush, *A Charge to Keep* (New York: William Morrow and Company, 1999).

54. Michael Sherry, "Dead or Alive: American Vengeance Goes Global," *Review of International Studies* 31 (2005): 259.

55. For more on the influence Bush's religious beliefs have upon his foreign policy, see Ron Suskind, "Without a Doubt," *New York Times*, October 17, 2004; Raymond Tanter, *Classifying Evil: Bush Administration Rhetoric and Policy toward Rogue Regimes, Research Memorandum 44* (Washington, D.C.: Washington Institute for Near East Policy, 2003).

56. Anthony F. Lang, "Punitive Intervention: Enforcing Justice or Generating Conflict?" in *Just War Theory: A Reappraisal*, ed. Mark Evans (New York: Palgrave Macmillan, 2005), 50–70.

57. For a good account of Grotius's remarkable life and career, see C. G. Roelofsen, "Grotius and the International Politics of the Seventeenth Century," in *Hugo Grotius and International Relations*, ed. Hedley Bull, Benedict Kingsbury, and Adam Roberts (Oxford: Clarendon, 1990), 93–131; Arthur Nussbaum, *A Concise History of the Law of Nations* (New York: Macmillan, 1954), 102–15.

58. Hugo Grotius, *The Rights of War and Peace*, ed. Richard Tuck (Indianapolis: Liberty Fund, 2005), 1752.

59. Grotius, *The Rights of War and Peace*, 949.

60. Ibid., 954.

61. Ibid., 955.

62. Bush, "President's Remarks at the United Nations General Assembly."

63. Grotius, *Rights of War and Peace*, 1021.

64. Ibid., 1161–62.

65. Vitoria and Molina did actually allow for intervention on behalf of third parties, but only to protect the innocent rather than to uphold natural law. Francisco de Vitoria, "On Dietary Laws, or Self-Restraint," in *Vitoria: Political Writings*, ed. Anthony Pagden and Jeremy Lawrance (Cambridge: Cambridge University

Press, 1991), 225. On Molina, see Bernice Hamilton, *Political Thought in Sixteenth Century Spain: A Study of the Political Ideas of Vitoria, De Soto, Suarez, and Molina* (Oxford: Clarendon, 1963), 129.

66. Grotius, *Rights of War and Peace*, 1024. It is likely that Grotius was influenced in regard of this argument by Alberico Gentili's earlier statement in favor of punitive war on the basis of natural law; Alberico Gentili, *De Iure Belli Libri Tres*, trans. John C. Rolfe (Oxford and London: Clarendon, 1933), 87–88. Interestingly, Pufendorf and Vattel would both later reject the assertion of a natural law jurisdiction for punitive war. Emmerich de Vattel, *The Law of Nations or the Principles of Natural Law*, ed. James Brown Scott, trans. Charles G. Fenwick, 1758 ed. (New York and London: Oceana Publications and Wildy and Sons, 1902), 8, 13; Samuel Pufendorf, "On the Law of Nature and of Nations," in *The Political Writings of Samuel Pufendorf*, ed. Craig Carr and Michael Seidler (Oxford: Oxford University Press, 1994), 134, 259.

67. Grotius, *Rights of War and Peace*, 1018.

68. Ibid., 1018.

69. Ibid., 1027.

70. Ibid., 1165.

71. Ibid., 1040.

72. Ibid., 963.

73. I borrow the idea and phrase that Bush and Blair *tap into* the just war tradition from Elshtain, *Just War against Terror*, 50.

74. Peter Brown, *Augustine of Hippo: A Biography* (London: Faber and Faber, 1967).

75. Herbert A. Deane, "The Political and Social Ideas of Saint Augustine," in *Essays in the History of Political Thought*, ed. Isaac Kramnick (Englewood Cliffs, NJ: Prentice Hall, 1969), 85.

76. Saint Augustine, "Letter 153: Augustine to Macedonius, AD413," in *Augustine: Political Writings*, ed. E. M. Atkins and R. J. Dodaro (Cambridge: Cambridge University Press, 2001), 80.

77. Augustine, "Letter 153," 80.

78. Saint Augustine, *The City of God against the Pagans*, trans. R. W. Dyson (Cambridge: Cambridge University Press, 1998), 938.

79. Saint Augustine, "Contra Faustum," in *The Political Writings of Saint Augustine*, ed. Henry Paolucci (Chicago: Regnorey Gateway, 1962), 70.

80. Augustine, "Letter 153," 83.

81. Saint Thomas Aquinas, "Summa Theologiae IIaIIae," in *Aquinas: Political Writings*, ed. R. W. Dyson (Cambridge: Cambridge University Press, 2002), 240.

82. Aquinas, "Summa Theologiae," 241.

83. Francisco de Vitoria, "On the Law of War," in *Vitoria: Political Writings*, ed. Anthony Pagden and Jeremy Lawrance (Cambridge: Cambridge University Press, 1991), 304–5.

84. Francisco Suarez, "On War," in *Selections from Three Works*, ed. Gwladys Williams (Oxford: Oxford University Press, 1944), 805.

85. Suarez, "On War," 817; Vitoria, "On Dietary Laws," 217–30.
86. Bush, "President Rallies Troops at Macdill Air Force Base."

Chapter 4

1. Prime Minister Tony Blair, "Speech to the Labour Party's Glasgow Conference," February 15, 2003, http://www.iraqcrisis.co.uk/resources.php?idtag=R3E50FD 20EDCFA (accessed October 2, 2004).

2. Prime Minister Tony Blair, "Speech to the Labour Party's Glasgow Conference," February 15, 2003, http://www.iraqcrisis.co.uk/resources.php?idtag=R3E50FD 20EDCFA (accessed October 2, 2004). Of course such a distinction is more illusory than real, but his choice to present the humanitarian justification for war in this manner is telling. It suggests a broader agenda than national security concerns and a willingness to trade in justice-charged discourse.

3. Quoted in Michael J. Mazarr, "George W. Bush, Idealist," *International Affairs* 79, no. 3 (2003): 511.

4. Melvyn P. Leffler, "9/11 and the Past and Future of American Foreign Policy," *International Affairs* 79, no. 5 (2003): 1055.

5. President George W. Bush, *The National Security Strategy of the United States of America*, (Washington D.C.: Whitehouse, 2002), chap. 2, http://www. whitehouse.gov/nsc/nss.html (accessed September 6, 2006).

6. Bush, *The National Security Strategy*, chap. 1.

7. Ibid., preface.

8. President George W. Bush, "President Bush Delivers Graduation Speech at West Point," June 1, 2002, http://www.whitehouse.gov/news/releases/2002/06/2002 0601–1.html (accessed December 5, 2003).

9. Ivo H. Daalder and James M. Lindsay, *America Unbound: The Bush Revolution in Foreign Policy* (Washington, D.C.: Brookings Institute, 2003), 13.

10. President George W. Bush, "President Bush Meets with Prime Minister Howard of Australia," February 10, 2003, http://www.whitehouse.gov/news/releases/ 2003/02/print/20030210–10.html (accessed May 18, 2004).

11. President George W. Bush, "President Delivers State of the Union Address," January 28, 2003, http://www.whitehouse.gov/news/releases/2003/01/print/ 20030128–19.html (accessed May 18, 2004).

12. President George W. Bush, "World Can Rise to This Moment," February 6, 2003, http://www.whitehouse.gov/news/releases/2003/02/print/20030206–17 .html (accessed May 18, 2004).

13. President George W. Bush, "President Discusses the Future of Iraq," February 26, 2003, http://www.whitehouse.gov/news/releases/2003/02/print/20030226 –11.html (accessed May 18, 2004).

14. President George W. Bush, "President Salutes Sailors at Naval Station Mayport in Jacksonville," February 13, 2003, http://www.whitehouse.gov/news/releases/ 2003/02/print/20020213–3.html (accessed May 18, 2004); Blair, "President Discusses Future of Iraq."

15. President George W. Bush, "President Rallies Troops at Macdill Air Force Base in Tampa," March 26, 2003, http://www.whitehouse.gov/news/releases/2003/03/print/20030326–4.html (accessed May 18, 2004).

16. Philip H. Gordon, "Bush's Middle East Vision," *Survival* 45, no. 1 (2003): 157.

17. Bush, "President Discusses Future of Iraq."

18. Prime Minister Tony Blair, "Prime Minister's Speech to TUC Conference in Blackpool," September 10, 2002, http://www.number-10.gov.uk/output/page 1725.asp (accessed May 18, 2004).

19. Chris Brown makes a similar argument. See Chris Brown, "Self-Defense in an Imperfect World," *Ethics & International Affairs* 17 (2003): 2–8.

20. Christopher Bluth, "The British Road to War: Blair, Bush and the Decision to Invade Iraq," *International Affairs* 80, no. 5 (2004): 890.

21. Blair, "Speech to the Labour Party's Glasgow Conference."

22. Prime Minister Tony Blair, "PM Statement on Iraq," February 25, 2003, http://www.number-10.gov.uk/output/page3088.asp (accessed May 18, 2004).

23. Prime Minister Tony Blair, "Address to the Labour Party Conference at Brighton," October 2, 2001, http://politics.guardian.co.uk/labour2001/story/0,,562006,00.html (accessed October 29, 2007).

24. Anthony Burke, "Against the New Internationalism," *Ethics & International Affairs* 19, no. 2 (2005): 82. In this regard, it has much in common with the position of the influential Washington lobby group, the Project For a New American Century (PNAC), whose membership included leading officials in the Bush administration such as Dick Cheney, Donald Rumsfeld, and Paul Wolfowitz; Project For a New American Century, "Statement of Principles," http://www.newamericancentury.org/statementofprinciples.htm (accessed October 16, 2004).

25. Burke, "Against the New Internationalism."

26. Prime Minister Tony Blair, "The Sedgefield Speech," March 5, 2004, http://politics.guardian.co.uk/iraq/story/0,12956,1162991,00.html (accessed April 12, 2004).

27. Blair, "The Sedgefield Speech."

28. Mona Fixdal and Dan Smith, "Humanitarian Intervention and Just War," *Mershon International Studies Review* 42 (1998): 299; Michael J. Smith, "Humanitarian Intervention: An Overview of the Ethical Issues," *Ethics & International Affairs* 12 (1998): 77; Adam Roberts, "Law and the Use of Force after Iraq," *Survival* 45, no. 2 (2003): 48–9; George R. Lucas, "The Role of the International Community in International Community in Just War Tradition— Confronting the Challenges of Humanitarian Intervention and Preemptive War," *Journal of Military Ethics* 2, no. 2 (2003): 132; Chris Brown, "A Qualified Defence of the Use of Force for Humanitarian Reasons," in *The Kosovo Tragedy*, ed. Ken Booth (London: Frank Cass, 2001), 283–84; Alex J. Bellamy, "Ethics and Intervention: The 'Humanitarian Exception' and the Problem of Abuse in the Case of Iraq," *Journal of Peace Research* 41, no. 2 (2004): 132; Alex J.

Bellamy, "Motives, Outcomes, Intent and the Legitimacy of Humanitarian Intervention," *Journal of Military Ethics* 3, no. 3 (2004): 217.

29. J. Bryan Hehir, "Intervention: From Theories to Cases," *Ethics & International Affairs* 9 (1995): 6–8.

30. Michael Walzer, *Just and Unjust Wars: A Moral Argument with Historical Illustrations*, 2nd ed. (New York: Basic Books, 1992), 86–108. Note that the position detailed here is presented by Walzer as his correction of the legalist paradigm. The legalist paradigm, Walzer argues before this, supposes a blanket ban on all forms of intervention and strictly upholds the principle of nonintervention.

31. Walzer, *Just and Unjust Wars*, 90. For more details on Mill's writings and Walzer's debt to him, see Georgios Varouxakis, "John Stuart Mill on Intervention and Non-Intervention," *Millenium* 26, no. 1 (1997): 57–76.

32. Walzer, *Just and Unjust Wars*, 90.

33. Ibid., 107. Walzer later adds ethic cleansing and all instances of state terrorism to this list. Michael Walzer, "The Politics of Rescue," in *Arguing About War*, ed. Michael Walzer (New Haven, CT: Yale University Press, 2004), 68.

34. Walzer, *Just and Unjust Wars*, 101.

35. Ibid., 90.

36. Ibid., 91.

37. Michael Walzer, "The Argument About Humanitarian Intervention," *Dissent* 49, no. 1 (2002), http://www.dissentmagazine.org/menutest/archives/2002/wi02/walzer_hum.shtml.

38. Walzer makes this point with reference to Cambodia. He writes, "Pol Pot's killing fields had to be shut down—and by a foreign army if necessary. The prisons of all the more ordinary dictators in the modern world should also be shut down. But this is properly the work of their own subjects." Walzer, "The Argument About Humanitarian Intervention."

39. Ibid.

40. Nicholas J. Wheeler, *Saving Strangers: Humanitarian Intervention in International Society* (Oxford: Oxford University Press, 2000), 34.

41. Wheeler, *Saving Strangers*, 34.

42. Bellamy, "Motives, Outcomes, Intent," 219.

43. Gregory Reichberg and Henrik Syse, "Humanitarian Intervention: A Case of Offensive Force?" *Security Dialogue* 33, no. 3 (2003): 309–22.

44. National Conference of Catholic Bishops, "The Challenge of Peace: God's Promise and Our Response—the Pastoral Letter on War and Peace," in *Just War Theory*, ed. Jean Bethke Elshtain (Oxford: Blackwell, 1992), 99.

45. National Conference Catholic Bishops, "The Challenge of Peace," 97.

46. Simon Chesterman, *Just War or Just Peace? Humanitarian Intervention and International Law* (Oxford: Oxford University Press, 2002), 53.

47. Interestingly, the 1993 pastoral letter changes direction and recognizes the justice of humanitarian war when undertaken in the proper circumstances. See Chapter 1 for more details.

48. It must be noted that Johnson is not alone in arguing this. He is joined by, among others, Jean Bethke Elshtain and George Weigel. I focus in this chapter on Johnson's work alone for the reason that he specifically relates the debate regarding the presumption against war to the invasion of Iraq. See George Weigel, *Tranquillitas Ordinis: The Present Failure and Future Promise of American Catholic Thought on War and Peace* (Oxford: Oxford University Press, 1987); Jean Bethke Elshtain, *Just War against Terror: The Burden of American Power in a Violent World* (New York: Basic Books, 2004).

49. James Turner Johnson, *Morality and Contemporary Warfare* (New Haven, CT: Yale University Press, 1999), 2.

50. For examples of these approaches, see Peter Dula, "The War in Iraq: How Catholic Conservatives Got It Wrong," *Commonweal*, December 3, 2004. Hehir, "Intervention: From Theories to Cases."

51. Johnson, *Morality and Contemporary Warfare*, 34.

52. Paul Ramsey, *The Just War: Force and Political Responsibility* (Maryland: Catholic University Press of America, 1986), 190–91.

53. James Turner Johnson, *The War to Oust Saddam Hussein: Just War and the New Face of Conflict* (Lanham, MD: Rowman and Littlefield, 2005), 35.

54. Johnson, *Morality and Contemporary Warfare*, 36. Additionally, this approach can be fairly accused of giving "pride of place to judgments about contingent conditions over obligations inherent in moral duty." See James Turner Johnson, "The Broken Tradition," *National Interest* 45 (1996): 34.

55. Johnson, *The War to Oust Saddam Hussein*, 28.

56. Ibid., 36.

57. Johnson, *Morality and Contemporary Warfare*, 36. Also see James Turner Johnson, "The Just War Tradition and the American Military," in *Just War and the Gulf War*, ed. James Turner Johnson and George Weigel (Lanham, MD: Ethics and Public Policy Centre, 1991), 6.

58. Johnson, "Broken Tradition," 30.

59. Johnson, *The War to Oust Saddam Hussein*, 124.

60. Johnson, *Morality and Contemporary Warfare*, 44.

61. Saint Thomas Aquinas, "Summa Theologiae IIaIIae," in *Aquinas: Political Writings*, ed. R. W. Dyson (Cambridge: Cambridge University Press, 2002), 241.

62. James Turner Johnson, "The Just War Idea: The State of the Question," *Social Philosophy and Policy* 23, no. 1 (2006): 177; James Turner Johnson, "Humanitarian Intervention after Iraq: Just War and International Law Perspectives," *Journal of Military Ethics* 5, no. 2 (2006): 119–20.

63. For example, see Johnson, *Morality and Contemporary Warfare*, 41–51.

64. Aquinas, "Summa Theologia," 240.

65. Joseph Boyle, "Just War Doctrine and the Military Response to Terrorism," *Journal of Political Philosophy* 11, no. 2 (2003): 158.

66. Chris Brown, Terry Nardin, and Nicholas Rengger, eds., *International Relations in Political Thought* (Cambridge: Cambridge University Press, 2002), 183; Saint

Thomas Aquinas, "De Regime Principum," in *Aquinas: Political Writings*, ed. R. W. Dyson (Cambridge: Cambridge University Press, 2002), 7–8.

67. Johnson, *The War to Oust Saddam Hussein*, 18.

68. James Turner Johnson, *Ideology, Reason and the Limitation of War* (Princeton, NJ: Princeton University Press, 1975), 28.

69. For more on this see Cian O'Driscoll, "New Thinking in the Just War Tradition: Theorizing the War on Terror," in *Security and the War on Terror: Civil-Military Cooperation in a New Age*, ed. Alex J. Bellamy, Roland Bleiker, Sara Davies, Richard Devetak (London: Routledge, 2007).

70. Johnson, *Morality and Contemporary Warfare*, 49.

71. Saint Augustine, *The City of God against the Pagans*, trans. R. W. Dyson (Cambridge: Cambridge University Press, 1998), 933–37; Saint Augustine, "Letter 189: Augustine to Boniface," in *Augustine: Political Writings*, ed. E. M. Atkins and R. J. Dodaro (Cambridge: Cambridge University Press, 2001), 214–18; Aquinas, "Summa Theologiae," 241. Francisco de Vitoria, "On the American Indians," in *Vitoria: Political Writings*, ed. Anthony Pagden and Jeremy Lawrance (Cambridge: Cambridge University Press, 1991), 283.

72. Aquinas, "Summa Theologiae," 241; Francisco Suarez, "On War," in *Selections from Three Works*, ed. Gwladys Williams (Oxford: Oxford University Press, 1944), 802.

73. Suarez, "On War," 819.

74. Vitoria, "On the American Indians," 288.

75. James Brown Scott, *The Spanish Origins of International Law: Francisco De Victoria and His Law of Nations* (Oxford: Clarendon, 1934), 211.

76. Suarez, "On War," 806.

77. Though Grotius had his disagreements with how Vitoria and Suarez addressed this matter. See Chapter 3 for more details.

78. Aquinas, "Summa Theologiae," 241.

79. Johnson, *Ideology*, 39–40.

80. Francisco de Vitoria, "On the Law of War," in *Vitoria: Political Writings*, ed. Anthony Pagden and Jeremy Lawrance (Cambridge: Cambridge University Press, 1991), 303–4.

81. Suarez, "On War," 816.

82. Ibid., 818.

83. John Finnis, *Aquinas: Moral, Political, and Legal Theory* (Oxford and New York: Oxford University Press, 1998), 285.

84. Finnis, *Aquinas*, 213.

85. Herbert A. Deane, *The Political and Social Ideas of Saint Augustine* (New York: Columbia University Press, 1963), 83.

86. Augustine, *The City of God*, 942.

87. Ibid.

88. Paul Ramsey, *War and the Christian Conscience* (Durham, NC: Duke University Press, 1961), xx.

89. Brown, Nardin, and Rengger, eds., *International Relations in Political Thought*, 98.
90. Ramsey, *War and the Christian Conscience*, xx.
91. Lisa Sowle Cahill, "Christian Just War Tradition: Tensions and Development," in *The Return of the Just War*, ed. Maria Pilar Aquino and Dieter Mieth (London: SCM, 2001), 75.
92. Saint Augustine, "Contra Faustum," in *The Political Writings of Saint Augustine*, ed. Henry Paolucci (Chicago: Regnorey Gateway, 1962).
93. Saint Augustine, "Sermon 13, At the Altar of Cyprian," in *Augustine: Political Writings*, ed. E. M. Atkins and R. J. Dodaro (Cambridge: Cambridge University Press, 2001), 126.
94. F. H. Russell, *The Just War in the Middle Ages* (Cambridge: Cambridge University Press, 1975), 17.
95. Saint Augustine, "Letter 138: Augustine to Marcellinus," in *Augustine: Political Writings*, ed. E. M. Atkins and R. J. Dodaro (Cambridge: Cambridge University Press, 2001), 38. Cited by Vitoria, "On the Law of War," 297.
96. Suarez, "On War," 802.
97. Saint Augustine, "Letter 104, Augustine to Nectarius," in *Augustine: Political Writings*, ed. E. M. Atkins and R. J. Dodaro (Cambridge: Cambridge University Press, 2001), 15.
98. Quoted in Deane, *The Political and Social Ideas of Saint Augustine*, 79.
99. Quoted in Bernice Hamilton, *Political Thought in Sixteenth Century Spain: A Study of the Political Ideas of Vitoria, De Soto, Suarez, and Molina* (Oxford: Clarendon, 1963), 109.
100. Ramsey, *The Just War*, 142.
101. James Turner Johnson, *Can Modern War Be Just?* (New Haven, CT: Yale University Press, 1984), 22.
102. Vitoria, "On the American Indians," 288.
103. Ibid.
104. Ibid.
105. Francisco de Vitoria, "On Dietary Laws, or Self-Restraint," in *Vitoria: Political Writings*, ed. Anthony Pagden and Jeremy Lawrance (Cambridge: Cambridge University Press, 1991), 225.
106. Suarez, "On War," 826. Molina is cited in Hamilton, *Political Thought in Sixteenth Century Spain*, 130.
107. Suarez, "On War," 826; Vitoria, "On Dietary Laws," 226.
108. Johnson presents Ramsey as a "benchmark" thinker on Christian love and the duty to protect the innocent where they suffer tyranny. See Johnson, "The Just War Idea," 172.
109. Johnson, *Morality and Contemporary Warfare*, 81.
110. Ramsey, *The Just War*, 36.
111. Johnson, *Morality and Contemporary Warfare*, 76.
112. Johnson, "Broken Tradition," 28.
113. Aquinas, "Summa Theologiae," 241.

114. Johnson, *The War to Oust Saddam Hussein*, 140; Johnson, "The Just War Idea,"
     192.
115. Aquinas, "Summa Theologiae," 241.
116. Cited in Johnson, *Morality and Contemporary Warfare*, 49.
117. Aquinas, "Summa Theologiae," 241.
118. Jonathan Barnes, "The Just War," in *The Cambridge History of Later Medieval
     Philosophy*, ed. Norman Kretzman, Anthony Kenny, and Jan Pinborg
     (Cambridge: Cambridge University Press, 1982), 782.
119. Barnes, "The Just War," 782. Also see Alexander of Hales, "Summa Theologica,
     III," in *The Ethics of War: Classic and Contemporary Readings*, ed. Gregory
     Reichberg, Henrik Syse, and Endre Begby (Malden, MA: Blackwell, 2006),
     156–61.
120. Russell, *Just War in the Middle Ages*, 220.
121. Johnson, *The War to Oust Saddam Hussein*, 22.
122. Ibid., 122.
123. James Turner Johnson, "Threats, Values, and Defence: Does the Defence of
     Values by Force Remain a Moral Possibility?" in *Just War Theory*, ed. Jean Bethke
     Elshtain (Oxford: Blackwell, 1992), 57.
124. Johnson, *The War to Oust Saddam Hussein*, 124.
125. Johnson, "Broken Tradition," 36.
126. Quentin Skinner, "Language and Political Change," in *Political Innovation and
     Conceptual Change*, ed. Terence Ball, James Farr, and Russell L. Hanson
     (Cambridge: Cambridge University Press, 1989), 22.
127. James Tulley, "The Pen Is a Mighty Sword: Quentin Skinner's Analysis of
     Politics," in *Meaning and Context: Quentin Skinner and His Critics*, ed. James
     Tulley (Cambridge: Polity, 1988), 13.
128. J. R. Searle, *Speech Acts* (Cambridge: Cambridge University Press, 1969), 25.
129. Mike Marqusee, "A Name That Lives in Infamy," *Guardian*, November 10,
     2005, 32.
130. Ibid.
131. Jutta Brunnee and Stephen J. Toope, "Slouching Towards New 'Just' Wars: The
     Hegemon after September 11," *International Relations* 18, no. 4 (2004): 405–23.
132. James Turner Johnson, *Just War Tradition and the Restraint of War* (Princeton, NJ:
     Princeton University Press, 1981), 328; Johnson, *Ideology*, 268; Johnson, "The
     Broken Tradition"; Johnson, *Can Modern War be Just?* 22.

Chapter 5

  1. For more on the notion of postulates, see Michael Oakeshott, *On Human
     Conduct* (Oxford: Oxford University Press, 1975), 9–12.
  2. Walzer has published six essays on Iraq; Johnson has devoted a book to it; and
     Elshtain has treated it in two journal articles and an afterword in her *Just War
     Against Terror: The Burden of American Power in a Violent World* (New York: Basic
     Books, 2004).

3. Oakeshott, *On Human Conduct*, 9.

4. R. B. J. Walker, *Inside/Outside: International Relations as Political Theory* (Cambridge: Cambridge University Press, 1993), 106.

5. Elements of this discussion appear in Cian O'Driscoll, "Learning the Language of Just War Theory: The Value of Engagement," *Journal of Military Ethics* 6, no. 2 (2007): 107–116.

6. James Turner Johnson, *Just War Tradition and the Restraint of War* (Princeton, NJ: Princeton University Press, 1981), 21; Brian Orend, *Michael Walzer on War and Justice* (Cardiff: University of Wales Press, 2000); Michael J. Smith, "Growing up with Just and Unjust Wars: An Appreciation," *Ethics & International Affairs* 11 (1997): 1–18. Also see Cian O'Driscoll, "Learning the Language of Just War Theory: The Value of Engagement," *Journal of Military Ethics* 6, no. 2 (2007): 107–116.

7. Michael Walzer, "Introduction" in *Arguing About War*, ed. Michael Walzer (New Haven, CT: Yale University Press, 2004), x.

8. Michael Walzer, "The Triumph of Just War Theory," in *Arguing About War*, ed. Michael Walzer (New Haven, CT: Yale University Press, 2004), 7–8.

9. Michael Walzer, *Just and Unjust Wars: A Moral Argument with Historical Illustrations*, 2nd ed. (New York: Basic Books, 1992), xxv.

10. Walzer, *Just and Unjust Wars*, xxv.

11. Walzer, "The Triumph of Just War Theory," 12.

12. Terence Ball, James Farr, and Russel L. Hanson, "Editors' Introduction," in *Political Innovation and Conceptual Change*, ed. Terence Ball, James Farr, and Russel L. Hanson (Cambridge: Cambridge University Press, 1989), 2. Ball, Farr, and Hansen are not writing specifically about the just war tradition here, but about the role that moral languages play in our everyday lives.

13. Walzer, *Just and Unjust Wars*, 14.

14. Terence Ball, *Transforming Political Discourse: Political Theory and Critical Conceptual History* (Oxford and New York: Basil Blackwell, 1988), 4. Ball is not referring to the just war tradition specifically, but to the role that moral languages generally play in shaping the arguments we make.

15. Walzer, *Just and Unjust Wars*, 15.

16. Ibid.

17. Hans-Georg Gadamer, *Truth and Method*, 2nd rev. ed., trans. Joel Weinsheimer and Donald Marshall (New York: Continuum, 1994), 389. Georgia Warnke has written an excellent piece exploring the possible connection between Walzer's political theory and Gadamer's hermeneutics. See Georgia Warnke, "Walzer, Rawls, and Gadamer: Hermeneutics and Political Theory," in *Festivals of Interpretation: Essays on Hans-Georg Gadamer*, ed. Kathleen Wright (Albany: SUNY, 1990), 136–161. For a helpful account of Gadamer's work as it relates to IR, see Richard Shapcott, *Justice, Community, and Dialogue in International Relations* (Cambridge: Cambridge University Press, 2001). I hope to explore Walzer's relation to hermeneutic theory in a project I am currently developing with Toni Erskine.

18. Oakeshott, *On Human Conduct*, 58.

19. Michael Walzer, *Interpretation and Social Criticism* (Cambridge, MA, and London: Harvard University Press, 1987), 24.

20. Toni Erskine, "Qualifying Cosmopolitanism? Solidarity, Criticism, and Michael Walzer's 'View from the Cave,'" *International Politics* 44, no. 1 (2007): 140.

21. James Boyd White, *When Words Lose Their Meaning: Constitutions and Reconstitutions of Language, Character, and Community* (Chicago and London: University of Chicago Press, 1984), 8.

22. Oakeshott, *On Human Conduct*, 64.

23. Walzer, *Interpretation and Social Criticism*, 23.

24. Michael Walzer, "Universalism, Equality, and Immigration," in *Constructions of Practical Reason: Interviews on Moral and Political Philosophy*, ed. Herlinde Pauer-Studer (Stanford, CA: Stanford University Press, 2003), 205.

25. Walzer, *Just and Unjust Wars*, 63.

26. Ibid., 75.

27. R. M. Dworkin, "To Each His Own," *New York Review of Books*, April 1983. I should point out that Dworkin does not extend this critique to Walzer's writings on the just war tradition, though it is fair to assume that the same reasoning applies.

28. Dworkin, "To Each His Own," 4.

29. Ibid., 5. Also see Walzer, *Interpretation and Social Criticism*, 22.

30. Dworkin, "To Each His Own," 4.

31. Chris Brown refers to Midgely's review in "IR Theory in Britain—The New Black?" *Review of International Studies* 32 (2006): 681.

32. Jean Bethke Elshtain, "Reflections on War and Political Discourse: Realism, Just War, and Feminism in a Nuclear Age," in *Just War Theory*, ed. Jean Bethke Elshtain (Oxford: Blackwell, 1992), 265–66.

33. Walzer, *Just and Unjust Wars*, xxix. Also see Walzer, *Interpretation and Social Criticism*, 39.

34. Michael Walzer, "Just and Unjust Occupations," in *Arguing About War*, ed. Michael Walzer (New Haven, CT: Yale University Press, 2004), 162–68.

35. Walzer, *Just and Unjust Wars*, 16.

36. Ibid. "Even fundamental social and political transformations within a particular culture may well leave the moral world intact or at least sufficiently whole so that we can still be said to share it with our ancestors. It is rare indeed that we do not share it with our contemporaries, and by and large we learn how to act among our contemporaries by studying the actions of those who have preceded us. The assumption of that study is that they saw the world much as we do. That is not always true, but it is true enough of the time to give stability and coherence to our moral lives (and to our military lives)."

37. Ibid., 19.

38. Johnson picks up on this tension between change and continuity evident in Walzer's work when he comments that Walzer's work could be summed up by

the motto, *plus ca change, plus c'est la meme guerre*. Johnson, *Just War Tradition*, 38.

39. Toni Erskine, *Embedded Cosmopolitanism* (Oxford: Oxford University Press, 2008).

40. Michael Walzer, "Spheres of Justice: An Exchange," *New York Review of Books*, July 21, 1983, 43.

41. Elements of this discussion appear in Cian O'Driscoll, "Jean Bethke Elshtain's Just War against Terror: A Tale of Two Cities," *International Relations* 21, no. 4 (2007).

42. See for example Nicholas J. Rengger, "Just a War against Terror? Jean Bethke Elshtain's Burden and American Power," *International Affairs* 80, no. 1 (2004): 107–16; Nicholas J. Rengger, "The Judgment of War," *Review of International Studies* 31 (2005): 143–63. Elshtain offered her thoughts regarding the reception her book received in "Response," *International Relations* 21, no. 4 (2007).

43. Consider Walzer's statement of intent in the preface to the first edition of *Just and Unjust Wars*. He states "I am not going to expound morality from the ground up. Were I to begin with the foundations, I would probably never get beyond them; in any case, I am by no means sure what the foundations are. The substructure of the ethical world is a matter of deep and apparently unending controversy. Meanwhile, however, we are living in the superstructure . . . For the moment, at least, practical morality is detached from its foundations, and we must act as if that separation were a possible (since it is an actual) condition of moral life." *Just and Unjust Wars*, xxix. Pocock's ideas on traditions of "usage" appear in a typology he offers of traditions. He does not apply this typology to the just war tradition specifically, but I have found it provides a useful tool for analyzing different approaches to this tradition. J. G. A. Pocock, *Politics, Language and Time: Essays on Political Thought and History* (London: Methuen, 1972), 244.

44. Walzer, *Just and Unjust Wars*, xiv.

45. Jean Bethke Elshtain, "Epilogue: Continuing Implications of the Just War Tradition," in *Just War Theory*, ed. Jean Bethke Elshtain (Oxford: Blackwell, 1992), 323–24.

46. Jean Bethke Elshtain, "Just War and Humanitarian Intervention," *Ideas* 8, no. 2 (2001): 3.

47. Elshtain, *Just War against Terror*, 50.

48. Elshtain, "Just War and Humanitarian Intervention," 18.

49. Ibid., 18–19.

50. Elshtain, *Just War against Terror*, 49.

51. Ibid., 50.

52. Elshtain, "Epilogue," 323–24. Also, see how Elshtain's latest contribution refers to Augustinian codes; Jean Bethke Elshtain, "International Justice as Equal Regard and the Use of Force," *Ethics & International Affairs* 17, no. 2 (2003): 63–75.

53. Pocock, *Politics, Language and Time*, 244. Again, this terminology is drawn from Pocock's typology of traditions, and extended by the author to Elshtain's conception of the just war tradition.

54. Incidentally, this view of authority as deriving from origins is actually quite in line with the etymology of the word: the root of the word "authority" is in the Latin word "*auctoritas*," which implies an originator in the sphere of opinion, counsel, and command. Richard Tuck, "Why Is Authority Such a Problem?" in *Philosophy, Politics and Society*, ed. Peter Laslett, W. G. Runciman, and Quentin Skinner (London: Blackwell, 1972), 197.

55. Elshtain, "Just War and Humanitarian Intervention," 18

56. Ibid.

57. Alasdair MacIntyre, *After Virtue: A Study in Moral Theory* (London: Duckworth, 1981), 137–38.

58. Alasdair MacIntyre, *Three Rival Versions of Moral Enquiry: Encyclopaedia, Genealogy and Tradition* (London: Duckworth, 1990), 25. Elsewhere, MacIntyre provides an interesting example of how a practice or tradition might be handed down from generation to generation, but done in such a manner as to separate the item handed down from its own past. For instance, he writes, "When the Catholic mass becomes a genre available for concert performance by Protestants, when we listen to the scripture because of what Bach wrote rather than because of what St. Matthew wrote, then sacred texts are being preserved in a form in which the traditional links with belief have been broken." MacIntyre, *After Virtue*, 36–37.

59. Gregory Reichberg, Henrik Syse, and Endre Begby, eds., *The Ethics of War: Classic and contemporary Readings* (Malden, MA: Blackwell, 2006); Paul Christopher, *The Ethics of War and Peace: An Introduction to Legal and Moral Issues*, 3rd ed. (Englewood Cliffs, NJ: Prentice Hall, 2004), chap. 1.

60. Augustine defines a just war "as those which avenge injuries, when the nation or city against which warlike action is to be directed has neglected either to punish wrongs committed by its own citizens or to restore what has been unjustly taken by it." See Saint Augustine, "Quaestionnes in Heptateuchum," in *The Catholic Tradition of the Law of Nations*, ed. John Eppstein (London: Burns, Oates, and Washburne, 1935), 74.

61. James Turner Johnson, *Ideology, Reason and the Limitation of War* (Princeton, NJ: Princeton University Press, 1975), 8.

62. Walker, *Inside/Outside*, 27.

63. Michael Oakeshott, "The Activity of Being an Historian," in *Rationalism in Politics and Other Essays*, ed. Michael Oakeshott (Indianapolis: Liberty Fund, 1991), 176.

64. Walker, *Inside/Outside*, 27.

65. R. B. J. Walker, "History and Structure in the Theory of International Relations," *International Theory: Critical Investigations*, ed. James Der Derian (London: Macmillan, 1995), 323.

66. Michael Oakeshott, "The Voice of Poetry in the Conversation of Mankind," in *Rationalism in Politics*, ed. Michael Oakeshott (Indianapolis: Liberty Fund, 1991), 494. For a more recent exposition of an Oakeshottian approach to traditions, see Renee Jeffery, "Tradition as Invention: The 'Traditions Tradition' and the History of Ideas in International Relations," *Millennium: Journal of International Studies* 34, no. 1 (2005): 57–84.

67. Walker, *Inside/Outside*, 31.

68. Elshtain, *Just War against Terror*, 107.

69. James Turner Johnson, "The Just War Idea: The State of the Question," *Social Philosophy and Policy* 23, no. 1 (2006): 179.

70. James Turner Johnson, *Morality and Contemporary Warfare* (New Haven, CT: Yale University Press, 1999), 25.

71. James Turner Johnson, *Can Modern War Be Just?* (New Haven, CT: Yale University Press, 1984), 15. Incidentally, Johnson presents these circumstances as being closely tied to the development of international society as it evolved beyond its basis in Christendom. See Johnson, *Ideology*, 13.

72. Johnson, "The Just War Idea," 194.

73. James Turner Johnson, *The War to Oust Saddam Hussein: Just War and the New Face of Conflict* (Lanham, MD: Rowman and Littlefield, 2005), 35.

74. Johnson, *The War to Oust Saddam Hussein*, 41.

75. Ibid.

76. For a discussion of this methodology, see John G. Gunnell, "The Myth of the Tradition," *American Political Science Review* 72 (1978): 131.

77. Johnson, "The Just War Idea," 168.

78. Quoted in Johnson, *Just War Tradition*, 5.

79. James Turner Johnson, "Humanitarian Intervention after Iraq: Just War and International Law Perspectives," *Journal of Military Ethics* 5, no. 2 (2006): 114–27.

80. Johnson, *The War to Oust Saddam Hussein*; Johnson, "The Just War Idea," 194.

81. Johnson, "The Just War Idea," 194.

82. Ibid., 168.

83. Johnson, *The War to Oust Saddam Hussein*, 21.

84. Ibid., 18.

85. Johnson, "The Just War Idea," 167.

86. Ibid., 195. Italics added.

87. Ibid., 194.

88. Ibid., 167.

89. Ibid., 195.

90. Ibid., 194.

91. On this idea, see Ian Clark, "Traditions of Thought and Classical Theories of International Relations," in *Classical Theories of International Relations*, ed. Ian Clark and Iver B. Neumann (London and New York: Macmillan and St. Martin's, 1996), 7.

92. Edmund Burke, *Reflections on The Revolution in France and on The Proceedings in Certain Societies in London Relative to that Event*, ed. Conor Cruise O'Brien (Baltimore: Penguin, 1969), 119–20.

93. Ibid., 192–93.

94. Ibid.

95. Iain Hampsher-Monk, *The Political Philosophy of Edmund Burke* (London and New York: Longman, 1987), 36.

96. United States Conference of Catholic Bishops, "Statement on Iraq 2003," http://www.usccb.or/bishops/iraq/htm (accessed July 15, 2006); Johnson, *Morality and Contemporary Warfare*, 35; Johnson, *The War to Oust Saddam Hussein*, 27; Johnson, "The Just War Idea," 180–82; James Turner Johnson, "The Broken Tradition," *National Interest* 45 (1996): 30.

97. Johnson, "The Just War Idea," 181.

98. J. Bryan Hehir, "In Defense of Justice," *Commonweal* 127, no. 5 (2000): 32–33.

99. Johnson, *The War to Oust Saddam Hussein*, 35. Italics added.

100. Johnson's thoughts on this matter are dealt with in more detail in Chapter 4.

101. Johnson, *The War to Oust Saddam Hussein*, 28.

102. Ibid., 27–28; Johnson, "The Just War Idea," 177–79.

103. On the idea of occupying the headwaters of a tradition, see Pocock's analysis of Mo Tzu's radical/reactionary "return to roots" strategy: "You are only following the Chou, not the Hsia dynasty. Your antiquity does not go back far enough." Pocock, *Politics, Language and Time*, 246–48.

104. "Contrary to Hehir's argument and the idea of the 'presumption against war', for just war tradition as a whole the mere existence of military power does not itself stand as an evil, for it remains within the compass of moral decision whether and how to use the power available. *That is where the focus of just war thinking traditionally has been, and in my view it is where it should properly remain.*" Johnson, "The Just War Idea," 182–83. Italics added.

105. Johnson, "The Just War Idea," 194.

106. Walker, *Inside/Outside*, 29.

107. Johnson, *The War to Oust Saddam Hussein*, chap. 2.

108. On the tyranny of presentism, see Ken Booth, "The Three Tyrannies," in *Human Rights in Global Politics*, ed. Tim Dunne and Nicholas J. Wheeler (Cambridge: Cambridge University Press, 1999), 31–70.

109. Still, it must be added, the writings of past greats figure indirectly in Walzer's thoughts, as they have surely contributed to the moral realities of international society and war, which Walzer takes as his starting point.

110. Johnson, *Just War Tradition*, xxii. Johnson's own writings follow through on this view; he has discussed Walzer's contribution to the just war tradition in a number of his publications. Indeed, he even discusses the contribution made by the NCCB/USCCB to the just war tradition. However, the manner by which Johnson discusses the writings of Walzer and the NCCB/USCCB is instructive: he looks to critique their contribution to the just war tradition by holding it up against a deeper, more classically oriented understanding of that same tradition.

See Johnson, *Just War Tradition*, chap. 1. Also Johnson, "The Just War Idea." Similarly, Elshtain has referred to both Johnson and Walzer in her work. Walzer is the odd one out here; his writings do not reference Johnson or Elshtain.

111. This view is echoed by Ian Clark, who describes the tradition as a "mosaic of thought fashioned by theologians, philosophers, jurists, statesmen and soldiers." Ian Clark, *Waging War: A Philosophical Introduction* (Oxford: Clarendon, 1990), 31.

112. Jean Bethke Elshtain, "Introduction," in *Just War Theory*, ed. Jean Bethke Elshtain (Oxford: Blackwell, 1992); Michael Walzer, "Arguing About War: Interview at the Carnegie Council on Ethics & International Affairs," 2004, http://www.carnegiecouncil.org/printerfriendlymedia.php/prmID/5024?PHPS ESSID= (accessed November 3, 2004).

113. Immanuel Kant, *Political Writings*, ed. Hans Reiss (Cambridge: Cambridge University Press, 1970/1991), 103. Kant specifically refers to "Grotius, Pufendorf, and the rest (sorry comforters as they are) are still dutifully quoted in *justification* of military aggression."

114. The idea of conversation is drawn from the work of Michael Oakeshott. Oakeshott, "The Voice of Poetry in the Conversation of Mankind" in *Rationalism in Politics and Other Essays*, ed. Michael Oakeshott (Indianapolis: Liberty Fund, 1991), 488–543.

115. K. R. Minogue, "Revolution, Tradition and Political Continuity," in *Politics and Experience: Essays Presented to Professor Michael Oakeshott on the Occasion of His Retirement*, ed. Preston King and B. C. Parekh (Cambridge: Cambridge University Press, 1968), 286–87.

116. See the story of the Tower of Babel: Saint Augustine, *The City of God against the Pagans*, trans. R. W. Dyson (Cambridge: Cambridge University Press, 1998), 928.

117. Walzer, *Interpretation and Social Criticism*, 29.

118. J. L. Austin, *Philosophical Papers*, 2nd ed., ed. J. O. Urmson and G. J. Warnock (Oxford: Clarendon, 1970), 201. This view that words contain or reflect their own history is also shared by, among others, Gadamer. See *Truth and Method*, 417.

119. Brian Orend, *The Morality of War* (Toronto: Broadview, 2006).

120. Walzer, *Interpretation and Social Criticism*, 20. Walzer's idea of the interpretative community may also be compared to Charles Taylor's notion of the "speech community." See Charles Taylor, *Human Agency and Language: Philosophical Papers 1* (Cambridge: Cambridge University Press, 1985), 237.

121. Walzer, *Interpretation and Social Criticism*, 29.

122. These debates, it should be noted, are never closed or final; they can always be revisited, reopened, or even revised at a later date by the same or a new interpretative community. Walzer, *Interpretation and Social Criticism*, 30.

123. Walzer, *Interpretation and Social Criticism*, 32.

Chapter 6

1. As Chapter 5 set out, the interpretative community working within the just war tradition—what we might term "the just war community"—comprises all of those actors who engage with and through the terms and tropes of the just war tradition in the course of moral argument; this might include state leaders, academics, journalists, lawyers, and public intellectuals (among others). The term "just war community" is borrowed from Brian Orend, though he uses it in a different way. Brian Orend, *The Morality of War* (Toronto: Broadview, 2006).

2. David Armstrong and Theo Farrell, "Introduction," *Review of International Studies* 31 (2005): 11.

3. Kofi Annan, "The Secretary-General's Address to the General Assembly," September 23, 2003, http://www.un.org/webcast/ga/58/statements/sg2eng030 923 (accessed August 8, 2006).

4. President George W. Bush, *The National Security Strategy of the USA* (Washington D.C.: Whitehouse, 2002), foreword, http://www.whitehouse.gov/nsc/nss.html (accessed September 6, 2006).

5. Michael Byers, "Preemptive Self-Defense: Hegemony, Equality and Strategies of Legal Change," *Journal of Political Philosophy* 11, no. 2 (2003): 181–82. Also see Michael Byers, *War Law: International Law and Armed Conflict* (London: Atlantic Books, 2005), 78.

6. Michael Byers, "Not Yet Havoc: Geopolitical Change and the International Rules on Military Force," *Review of International Studies* 31 (2005): 61. Walter Slocombe makes a similar point in "Force, Preemption and Legitimacy," *Survival* 45, no. 1 (2003): 124.

7. Quoted in Neta C. Crawford, "The Best Defense," *Boston Review*, February/March 2003, http://www.bostonreview.net/br28.1/crawford.html (accessed August 15, 2006).

8. Alex J. Bellamy, *Just Wars: From Cicero to Iraq* (Cambridge and Malden, MA: Polity, 2006), 164; Robert S. Litwak, "The New Calculus of Preemption," *Survival* 44, no. 4 (2002–3): 73; Dieter Janssen, "Preventive Defense and Forcible Regime Change: A Normative Assessment," *Journal of Military Ethics* 3, no. 2 (2004): 113; James Turner Johnson, *The War to Oust Saddam Hussein: Just War and the New Face of Conflict* (Lanham, MD: Rowman and Littlefield, 2005), 51, 115; Peter Dumbrowski and Rodger A. Payne, "The Emerging Consensus for Preventive War," *Survival* 48, no. 2 (2006): 115; Robert Skidelsky, "The Just War Tradition," *Prospect*, December 2004, 32; Miriam Sapiro, "Iraq: The Shifting Sands of Pre-Emptive Self-Defense," *American Journal of International Law* 97, no. 3 (2003): 600; Crawford, "The Best Defense"; Neta C. Crawford, "Just War Theory and the US Counterterror War," *Perspectives on Politics* 1, no. 1 (2003): 5–23; Neta C. Crawford, "The Slippery Slope to Preventive War," *Ethics & International Affairs* 17 (2003).

9. Sapiro, "Iraq: The Shifting Sands of Pre-Emptive Self-Defense," 600.

10. Bush, *The National Security Strategy*, chap. 5.

11. See Blair quoted in Lawrence Freedman, "War in Iraq: Selling the Threat," *Survival* 46, no. 2 (2004): 16; Powell quoted in Crawford "Just War Theory and the US Counterterror War"; President George W. Bush, "President Bush Delivers Graduation Speech at West Point," June 1, 2002, http://www.whitehouse.gov/news/releases/2002/06/20020601–1.html (accessed December 5, 2003).

12. Bush, *The National Security Strategy*, chap. 5.

13. Richard Falk, "What Future for the UN Charter System of War Prevention?" *American Journal of International Law* 97, no. 3 (2003): 590–98; Gareth Evans, "When Is It Right to Fight?" *Survival* 46, no. 3 (2004): 59–82.

14. Janssen, "Preventive Defense and Forcible Regime Change," 113; James Steinberg, "Preventive Force in U.S. National Security Strategy," *Survival* 47, no. 4 (2005): 56.

15. Crawford, "Just War Theory and the US Counterterror War"; Crawford, "The Best Defense."

16. Terence Taylor, "The End of Imminence?" *Washington Quarterly* 27, no. 4 (2004): 65.

17. John Yoo, "International Law and the War in Iraq," *American Journal of International Law* 97, no. 3 (2003): 563–76; Ruth Wedgwood, "The Fall of Saddam Hussein: Security Council Mandates and Preemptive Self-Defense," *American Journal of International Law* 97, no. 3 (2003): 576–85; Gerald Bradley, "Iraq and Just War: A Symposium," Pew Forum, http://pewforum.org/events/print.php?EventID=15 (accessed May 18, 2004); Litwak, "The New Calculus of Preemption"; Lee Feinstein and Anne-Marie Slaughter, "A Duty to Prevent," *Foreign Affairs* 83, no. 1 (2004): 136–50; Whitley Kaufman, "What's Wrong with Preventive War? The Moral and Legal Basis for the Preventive Use of Force," *Ethics & International Affairs* 19, no. 3 (2005): 23–38; Allen Buchanan and Robert O. Keohane, "The Preventive Use of Force: A Cosmopolitan Institutional Approach," *Ethics & International Affairs* 17, no. 1 (2004): 1–18; Michael N. Schmitt, "The Legality of Operation Iraqi Freedom under International Law," *Journal of Military Ethics* 3, no. 2 (2004): 82–104; Michael Walzer, "Arguing About War: Interview at the Carnegie Council on Ethics & International Affairs," 2004, http://www.carnegiecouncil.org/printerfriendly media.php/prmID/5024?PHPSESSID= (accessed November 3, 2004); Michael Walzer, *Arguing About War* (New Haven, CT: Yale University Press, 2004); Michael Ignatieff, *The Lesser Evil—Political Ethics in an Age of Terror* (Edinburgh: Edinburgh University Press, 2004); Johnson, *The War to Oust Saddam Hussein*.

18. Johnson, *The War to Oust Saddam Hussein*, 120.

19. Ibid., 53.

20. See United Nations, *A More Secure World: Our Shared Responsibility. Report of the High-Level Panel on Threats, Challenges and Change* (Geneva: United Nations, 2004), 13.

21. A number of commentators have noted how the UNHLP report adopts the language of the just war tradition. Steinberg, "Preventive Force," 56; Dumbrowski and Payne, "Emerging Consensus for Preventive War," 124; Dumbrowski and Payne also draw attention to the fact that many state leaders have also supported this logic.
22. Bellamy, *Just Wars*, 163.
23. Orend, *The Morality of War*, 78–82.
24. Ibid., 78.
25. Skidelsky, "The Just War," 32.
26. Sapiro, "Iraq: The Shifting Sands of Pre-Emptive Self-Defense," 600.
27. Alan M. Dershowitz, *Pre-Emption: A Knife That Cuts Both Ways* (New York: W. W. Norton, 2006), 156–60; Lawrence Freedman, "Prevention, Not Preemption," *Washington Quarterly* 26, no. 2 (2003): 105–14; Francois Heisbourg, "A Work in Progress: The Bush Doctrine and Its Consequences," *Washington Quarterly* 26, no. 2 (2003): 75.
28. Bradley, "Iraq and Just War."
29. Schmitt, "The Legality of Operation Iraqi Freedom," 92.
30. See Yoo, "International Law and the War in Iraq," 575–76; Jeff McMahan, "Preventive War and the Killing of the Innocent," in *The Ethics of War: Shared Problems in Different Traditions*, ed. David Rodin and Richard Sorabji (Aldershot: Ashgate, 2006), 69–91; Ignatieff, *The Lesser Evil*, 164; Evans, "When Is It Right to Fight?"; Chris Brown, "Self-Defense in an Imperfect World," *Ethics & International Affairs* 17 (2003).
31. Bellamy, *Just Wars*.
32. Anthony Burke, "Against the New Internationalism," *Ethics & International Affairs* 19, no. 2 (2005): 73–89.
33. Buchanan and Keohane, "The Preventive Use of Force," 1.
34. Feinstein and Slaughter, "A Duty to Prevent," 137. Also see International Commission on Intervention and State Sovereignty, *The Responsibility to Protect: The Report of the ICISS* (Toronto: International Commission on Intervention and State Sovereignty, 2001).
35. Like Buchanan and Keohane, Feinstein and Slaughter anchor this argument in the experience of dealing with Iraq. They write, "The world cannot afford to look the other way when faced with the prospect, as in Iraq, of a brutal ruler acquiring nuclear weapons or other WMD." Feinstein and Slaughter, "A Duty to Prevent," 136.
36. Jean Bethke Elshtain, *Just War against Terror: The Burden of American Power in a Violent World* (New York: Basic Books, 2004), 151, 168; Johnson makes a similar argument: Johnson, *The War to Oust Saddam Hussein*, 131.
37. Christian Reus-Smit, "Liberal Hierarchy and the Liberal License to Use Force," *Review of International Studies* 31 (2005): 72.
38. Jeff McMahan, "Just Cause for War," *Ethics & International Affairs* 19, no. 3 (2005): 15; Buchanan and Keohane, "The Preventive Use of Force," 6.

39. Gregory Reichberg, "Pre-Emptive War: What Would Aquinas Say?" *Commonweal* 121, no. 2 (January 30, 2004). There are similar developments afoot with respect to humanitarian war, as we will see.

40. Brown, "Self-Defense in an Imperfect World"; Crawford, "The Slippery Slope to Preventive War."

41. Brown, "Self-Defense in an Imperfect World."

42. Taylor, "The End of Imminence?"

43. Language, as Charles Taylor writes, is holistic: words are always part of a greater whole. He demonstrates this point by reference to the word "triangle." He writes, "It appears that a word like 'triangle' could not figure in our lexicon alone. It has to be surrounded by a skein of other terms, some of which contrast with it, and some which situate it, as it were, give its property dimension, not to speak of the wider matrix of language in which the various activities are situated in which our talk of triangles figures: measurement, geometry, design-creation and so on. The word only makes sense in this skein, in what Humboldt (who followed and developed Herder's thoughts on language) called the web of language. In touching one part of language (a word), the whole is present." Charles Taylor, *Human Agency and Language: Philosophical Papers 1* (Cambridge: Cambridge University Press, 1985), 231.

44. The term "survivals" relates to those ideas, concepts, rules, and words that "had once been at home in terms of which their intelligibility had been spelled out and their rationality justified but which had become detached from that context." Alasdair MacIntyre, *Three Rival Versions of Moral Enquiry: Encyclopaedia, Genealogy and Tradition* (London: Duckworth, 1990), 29.

45. Alasdair MacIntyre, *After Virtue: A Study in Moral Theory* (London: Duckworth, 1981), 4. Also see Alasdair MacIntyre, *A Short History of Ethics* (London: Routledge and Kegan, 1967), 167.

46. Michael Walzer, "Inspectors Yes, War No," in *Arguing About War*, ed. Michael Walzer (New Haven, CT: Yale University Press, 2004), 147. It is not as damaging to Walzer's belief in the possibility of a shared transgenerational morality as one might first imagine. Remember, Walzer asserts that the stability and continuity of moral languages is in some senses contingent; there is always the possibility of change such as this—it is merely the case that it does not happen that often. See Chapter 5 on Walzer.

47. Walzer, "Inspectors Yes, War No," 147. Also see Walzer's contribution to Pew Forum on Religion and Public Life, "Iraq and Just War.'"

48. Byers, "Preemptive Self-Defense."

49. Kaufman, "What's Wrong with Preventive War?" 32.

50. Johnson, *The War to Oust Saddam Hussein*, 18; Michael Glennon, "Why the Security Council Failed," *Foreign Affairs*, May/June 2003.

51. Elshtain, *Just War against Terror*.

52. Kaufman, "What's Wrong with Preventive War?" 38.

53. Nicholas J. Rengger, "The Just War Tradition in the Twenty First Century," *International Affairs* 78, no. 2 (2002): 358–59.

54. Oliver O'Donovan, *The Just War Revisited* (Cambridge: Cambridge University Press, 2003), 57.

55. Joseph Boyle, "Just War Doctrine and the Military Response to Terrorism," *Journal of Political Philosophy* 11, no. 2 (2003): 160–61.

56. Pew Forum on Religion and Public Life, "Iraq and Just War."

57. Robert H. Jackson, *The Global Covenant* (Oxford: Oxford University Press, 2000), 19; Richard B. Miller, *Interpretations of Conflict: Ethics, Pacifism and the Just War Tradition* (Chicago: University of Chicago Press, 1991), 13.

58. Anthony F. Lang, "Punishing States: From Grotius to the ILC" (paper presented at the Third Workshop of the British Academy Network on Ethics, Institutions and International Relations: Responding to Delinquent Institutions: Blame, Punishment and Rehabilitation, Carnegie Council on Ethics and International Affairs, New York, May 12–14, 2004).

59. For example David Cesarani, "Why Tyrants Must Stand Trial," *Observer*, July 11, 2004, 28.

60. Lang, "Punishing States."

61. Examples of some contemporary just war theorists who still speak in terms of good and evil: James Turner Johnson, "The Just War Tradition and the American Military," in *Just War and the Gulf War*, ed. James Turner Johnson and George Weigel (Lanham, MD: Ethics and Public Policy Centre, 1991), 1–61; George Weigel, "Churches and the Gulf Crisis," in *Just War and the Gulf War*, ed. James Turner Johnson and George Weigel (Lanham, MD: Ethics and Public Policy Centre, 1991), 63.

62. Johnson, "The Just War Tradition and the American Military," 21.

63. Walzer, *Arguing About War Interview*.

64. Crawford, "Just War Theory and the US Counterterror War," note 15.

65. Skidelsky, "The Just War," 31.

66. Roy F. Baumeister, *Evil: Inside Human Violence and Cruelty* (New York: W. H. Freeman and Company, 1997), 7.

67. Pew Forum on Religion and Public Life, "Iraq and Just War."

68. Boyle, "Just War Doctrine and the Military Response to Terrorism," 163.

69. Ibid., 162.

70. Ibid., 161.

71. Ibid., 162.

72. Pew Forum on Religion and Public Life, "Iraq and Just War."

73. Jean Bethke Elshtain, "How to Fight a Just War," in *Worlds in Collision: Terror and the Future of Global Order*, ed. Ken Booth and Tim Dunne (Basingstoke and New York: Palgrave Macmillan, 2002), 265–66. Also Elshtain, *Just War against Terror*, 61.

74. Johnson, *The War to Oust Saddam Hussein*, 55.

75. Ibid., 63

76. See James Turner Johnson, "The Broken Tradition," *National Interest* 45 (1996): 30; James Turner Johnson, *Ideology, Reason and the Limitation of War* (Princeton,

NJ: Princeton University Press, 1975), 39–47; Johnson, "Just War Tradition and the American Military," 21–22.

77. O'Donovan, *The Just War Revisited*, 6.
78. Ibid., 25.
79. Ibid., 6–7.
80. After all, O'Donovan argues that to punish is to restore *the right* by correcting the guilt of the actor who disturbs it. O'Donovan, *The Just War Revisited*, 57.
81. Ibid., 131–34.
82. Ibid., 55.
83. Brunnee and Toope, "Slouching Towards New 'Just' Wars."
84. Elshtain, *Just War against Terror*, 1.
85. Michael Novak, "The Return of Good and Evil," *Wall Street Journal*, February 7, 2002, http://www.opinionjournal.com/editorial/feature.html?id=95001831 (accessed August 27, 2007).
86. Novak, "The Return of Good and Evil."
87. Lawrence F. Kaplan and William Kristol, *The War over Iraq: Saddam's Tyranny and America's Mission* (San Francisco: Encounter Books, 2003), 3.
88. It is also important to note that there have always been people advocating this position, even during the cold war. The point, however, is that these people were always very much in the minority.
89. Adam Roberts, "Law and the Use of Force after Iraq," *Survival* 45, no. 2 (2003): 34.
90. Ken Booth, "Ten Flaws of Just Wars," in *The Kosovo Tragedy*, ed. Ken Booth (London: Frank Cass, 2001), 314–24; David Welsh, *Justice and the Genesis of War* (Cambridge: Cambridge University Press, 1995).
91. Gabriella Slomp, "Carl Schmitt and the Just War Tradition," *Cambridge Review of International Affairs* 19, no. 3 (2006): 435–47.
92. Brunnee and Toope, "Slouching Towards New 'Just' Wars."
93. O'Donovan, *The Just War Revisited*, 58.
94. Elshtain, *Just War against Terror*, 25.
95. Ibid., 112.
96. James Turner Johnson, "Threats, Values, and Defence: Does the Defence of Values by Force Remain a Moral Possibility?" in *Just War Theory*, ed. Jean Bethke Elshtain (Oxford: Blackwell, 1992), 55.
97. Michael Walzer, *Just and Unjust Wars: A Moral Argument with Historical Illustrations*, 2nd ed. (New York: Basic Books, 1992), xx. Walzer, *Arguing About War*, ix.
98. Burke, "Against the New Internationalism," 82.
99. O'Donovan, *The Just War Revisited*, 18–19.
100. Ibid., 19.
101. Nicholas J. Rengger, "The Judgement of War," *Review of International Studies* 31 (2005): 153.
102. O'Donovan, *The Just War Revisited*, 14.
103. Burke, "Against the New Internationalism," 83.

104. Elshtain, *Just War against Terror*, 112.

105. Alex J. Bellamy, "Motives, Outcomes, Intent and the Legitimacy of Humanitarian Intervention," *Journal of Military Ethics* 3, no. 3 (2004): 216.

106. Nicholas J. Wheeler, *Saving Strangers: Humanitarian Intervention in International Society* (Oxford: Oxford University Press, 2000), 34. Also see International Commission on Intervention State Sovereignty, *The Responsibility to Protect*, 31–32; Terry Nardin, "The Moral Basis of Humanitarian Intervention," *Ethics & International Affairs* 16 (2002): 66.

107. R. J. Vincent, *Human Rights and International Relations* (Cambridge: Cambridge University Press, 1986), 126–27.

108. Walzer, *Just and Unjust Wars*, 107. See footnote 33 in Chapter 4.

109. Michael Walzer, "The Moral Standing of States: A Response to Four Critics," in *International Ethics*, ed. Charles R. Beitz, et al. (Oxford: Princeton University Press, 1985), 217–38; Michael Walzer, "The Politics of Rescue," in *Arguing about War*, ed. Michael Walzer (New Haven, CT: Yale University Press, 2004), 67–85.

110. Michael Walzer, "The Argument About Humanitarian Intervention," *Dissent* 49, no. 1 (2002).

111. Fernando Teson, "Ending Tyranny in Iraq," *Ethics & International Affairs* 19, no. 2 (2005): 9.

112. Teson, "Ending Tyranny," 11.

113. Ibid., 15.

114. Terry Nardin, "Humanitarian Imperialism: Response to 'Ending Tyranny in Iraq,'" *Ethics & International Affairs* 19, no. 2 (2005): 21.

115. Nardin, "Humanitarian Imperialism," 21; Gareth Evans, "Humanity Did Not Justify This War," *Financial Times*, May 15, 2003.

116. Prime Minister Tony Blair, "The Sedgefield Speech," March 5, 2004, http://politics.guardian.co.uk/iraq/story/0,12956,1162991,00.html (accessed April 12, 2004).

117. Nicholas J. Wheeler and Justin Morris, "Justifying Iraq as a Humanitarian Intervention: The Cure is Worse than the Disease," in *The Iraq Crisis and World Order: Structural and Normative Challenges*, ed. W. P. S. Sidhu and R. Thakur (Tokyo: United Nations University Press, 2006); Nardin, "Humanitarian Imperialism," 22.

118. Nardin, "Humanitarian Imperialism," 22.

119. Teson, "Ending Tyranny in Iraq," 11–12.

120. Ibid., 11.

121. Nardin, "Humanitarian Imperialism," 22.

122. Ibid., 25.

123. Ibid., 21–22.

124. Wheeler and Morris, "Justifying Iraq."

125. Walzer, "Inspectors Yes, War No," 147.

126. Ibid., 149.

127. Evans, "Humanity Did Not Justify This War."

128. Kenneth Roth, "War in Iraq: Not a Humanitarian Intervention," Human Rights Watch Report 2004, http://www.hrw.org/wr2k4/3.htm (accessed August 16, 2006).

129. Roth, *War in Iraq*.

130. Alex J. Bellamy, "Ethics and Intervention: The 'Humanitarian Exception' and the Problem of Abuse in the Case of Iraq," *Journal of Peace Research* 41, no. 2 (2004): 143.

131. Teson, "Ending Tyranny in Iraq," 14.

132. Teson, "Ending Tyranny in Iraq," 3. Also Fernando Teson, "Of Tyrants and Empires: Reply to Terry Nardin," *Ethics & International Affairs* 19, no. 2 (2005): 28.

133. Teson, "Ending Tyranny in Iraq," 15.

134. James Turner Johnson, "Humanitarian Intervention after Iraq: Just War and International Law Perspectives," *Journal of Military Ethics* 5, no. 2 (2006): 115.

135. Johnson, "Humanitarian Intervention," 115. Johnson, *The War to Oust Saddam Hussein*, 122.

136. Jean Bethke Elshtain, "International Justice as Equal Regard and the Use of Force," *Ethics & International Affairs* 17, no. 2 (2003): 68.

137. Elshtain, "International Justice," 67.

138. Elshtain also remarks in the same article, and elsewhere, that she prefers the term "humanitarian war" to "humanitarian intervention." Jean Bethke Elshtain, "Just War and Humanitarian Intervention," *Ideas* 8, no. 2 (2001): 8.

139. R. W. Dyson, *Normative Theories of Society and Government in Five Medieval Thinkers* (Lewisten, NY: Edwin Mellen, 2003), 40.

140. Augustine, *City of God*, 224–25.

141. Ibid.

142. Dyson, *Normative Theories*, 42.

143. Michael Ignatieff, *The Rights Revolution* (Toronto: Anansi, 2000).

144. Elshtain, "International Justice as Equal Regard," 66.

145. See Rengger's critique of Elshtain's reading of Augustine: Nicholas J. Rengger, "Just a War against Terror? Jean Bethke Elshtain's Burden and American Power," *International Affairs* 80, no. 1 (2004): 107–16. Also Rengger, "Judgment of War," 157.

146. Quoted in Peter Stothard, *30 Days: A Month at the Heart of Blair's War* (London: HarperCollins, 2003), 42–43.

147. Elshtain, *Just War against Terror*, 57.

148. Teson, "Of Tyrants and Empires," 30.

149. Elshtain, *Just War against Terror*, 55.

150. Ibid., 50.

151. Prime Minister Tony Blair, "Address to the Labour Party Conference at Brighton," October 2, 2001, http://politics.guardian.co.uk/labour2001/story/0,,562006,00.html (accessed October 29, 2007).

152. Rengger, "Judgment of War"; Boyle, "Just War Doctrine and the Military Response to Terrorism"; Nardin, "The Moral Basis of Humanitarian

Intervention"; George Lopez, "Iraq and Just War Thinking: The Presumption against the Use of Force," *Commonweal*, September 27, 2002.

153. Bellamy, "Ethics and Intervention"; Alex J. Bellamy and Paul D. Williams, "The Responsibility to Protect and the Crisis in Darfur," *Security Dialogue* 36, no. 1 (2005): 27–47; Johnson, "Humanitarian Intervention," 116; Thomas G. Weiss, "The Sunset of Humanitarian Intervention? The Responsibility to Protect in a Unipolar Era," *Security Dialogue* 35, no. 2 (2004): 135.

154. Nicholas Wheeler has demonstrated how the idea of humanitarian intervention did not register in public rhetoric prior to the end of the cold war. See Wheeler, *Saving Strangers*. For a good example of cold war era just war theorizing, see the writings of William V. O'Brien.

Conclusion

1. Michael Walzer, *Interpretation and Social Criticism* (Cambridge and London: Harvard University Press, 1987), 20.

2. Alex Bellamy's latest book stands out as an exception here: Alex Bellamy, *Just Wars: From Cicero to Iraq* (Cambridge and Malden, MA: Polity, 2006).

3. Michael Walzer, "Inspectors Yes, War No," in *Arguing About War*, ed. Michael Walzer (New Haven, CT: Yale University Press, 2004), 147.

4. Jean Bethke Elshtain, *Just War against Terror: The Burden of American Power in a Violent World* (New York: Basic Books, 2004), 184.

5. Richard Tuck, "Why Is Authority Such a Problem?" in *Philosophy, Politics and Society*, ed. Peter Laslett, W. G. Runciman, and Quentin Skinner (London: Blackwell, 1972), 194–95.

6. James Boyd White, *When Words Lose Their Meaning: Constitutions and Reconstitutions of Language, Character, and Community* (Chicago and London: University of Chicago Press, 1984), 8.

7. In this sense, we might note that the image of "America/Gulliver unbound" from the ties that have historically bound it has been a prominent trope on the American right. See Ivo H. Daalder and James M. Lindsay, *America Unbound: The Bush Revolution in Foreign Policy* (Washington, D.C.: Brookings Institute, 2003); Gary Rosen, ed., *The Right War? The Conservative Debate on Iraq* (Cambridge: Cambridge University Press, 2005).

8. On a more specific note, consider the idea of rehabilitation: it provides a clear example of how the notion of punitive war has undergone profound transformation as a reflection of broader changes in the international system. Historical understandings of rehabilitation focused on the state or state leader as the object of reform, whereas contemporary approaches tend to refer to the people of a given state. The goal of rehabilitation in Iraq, for example, was presented as a means of revitalizing the Iraqi people rather than reforming the Iraqi leadership.

9. Philip Wheelwright, *Heraclitus* (Princeton, NJ: Princeton University Press, 1959), 29.

10. Terry Nardin, "Ethical Traditions in International Affairs," in *Traditions of International Ethics*, ed. Terry Nardin and David R. Mapel (Cambridge: Cambridge University Press, 1992), 3.

11. Quentin Skinner, *Visions of Politics, Volume 1: Regarding Method* (Cambridge: Cambridge University Press, 2002), 150.

12. Alasdair MacIntyre, *After Virtue: A Study in Moral Theory* (London: Duckworth, 1981), 206. Quoted in Tim Dunne, "Mythology or Methodology? Traditions in International Relations," *Review of International Studies* 19, no. 3 (1993): 312.

13. White, *When Words Lose Their Meaning*, 35. This passage actually refers not to the just war tradition or the Iraq debate, but to the world of the Ancient Greeks as it is presented by Homer in *The Iliad*.

14. J. G. A. Pocock, *Virtue, Commerce, and History—Essays on Political Thought and History, Chiefly in the 18th Century* (Cambridge: Cambridge University Press, 1985), 6.

15. Jean Bethke Elshtain, "Introduction," in *Just War Theory*, ed. Jean Bethke Elshtain (Oxford: Blackwell Press, 1992), 1.

16. Ian Clark, "Traditions of Thought and Classical Theories of International Relations," in *Classical Theories of International Relations*, ed. Ian Clark and Iver B. Neumann (London and New York: Macmillan and St. Martin's, 1996), 15.

Bibliography

Alexander of Hales, "Summa Theologica, III." In *The Ethics of War: Classic and Contemporary Readings*, edited by Gregory Reichberg, Henrik Syse, and Endre Begby, 156–61. Malden, MA: Blackwell, 2006.

Annan, Kofi. The Secretary-General's Address to the General Assembly, September 23, 2003. Available from http://www.un.org/webcast/ga/58/statements/sg2 eng030923.

Aquinas, Saint Thomas. *Aquinas: Political Writings*. Edited by R. W. Dyson and Jeremy Lawrance. Cambridge: Cambridge University Press, 2002.

Arend, Anthony Clark. "International Law and the Preemptive Use of Military Force." *Washington Quarterly* 26, no. 2 (2003): 89–103.

Arendt, Hannah. *Eichmann in Jerusalem: A Report on the Banality of Evil*. New York: Penguin Books, 1994.

Armstrong, David, and Theo Farrell. "Introduction." *Review of International Studies* 31 (2005): 1–11.

Augustine, Saint. *Augustine: Political Writings*. Edited by E. M. Atkins and R. J. Dodaro. Cambridge: Cambridge University Press, 2001.

———. *The City of God against the Pagans*. Translated by R. W. Dyson. Cambridge: Cambridge University Press, 1998.

———. *The Political Writings of Saint Augustine*. Edited by Henry Paolucci. Chicago: Regnory Gateway, 1962.

———. "Quaestionnes in Heptateuchum." In *The Catholic Tradition of the Law of Nations*, edited by John Eppstein, 74. London: Burns, Oates, and Washburne, 1935.

Austin, J. L. *Philosophical Papers*. 2nd edition. Edited by J. O. Urmson and G. J. Warnock. Oxford: Clarendon, 1970.

Bacon, Francis. "Considerations Touching a Warre with Spain." In *Certaine Miscellany Works*, edited by W. Rawley, 1–76. London: Da Capo, 1629.

———. *The Essays*. Edited by John Pitcher. London: Penguin Books, 1985.

Ball, Terence. *Transforming Political Discourse: Political Theory and Critical Conceptual History*. Oxford: Basil Blackwell, 1988.

Ball, Terence, James Farr, and Russell L. Hanson. "Editors' Introduction." In *Political Innovation and Conceptual Change*, edited by Terence Ball, James Farr, and Russell L. Hanson, 1–6. Cambridge: Cambridge University Press, 1989.

Barnes, Jonathan. "The Just War." In *The Cambridge History of Later Medieval Philosophy*, edited by Norman Kretzman, Anthony Kenny, and Jan Pinborg, 771–84. Cambridge: Cambridge University Press, 1982.

Baumeister, Roy F. *Evil: Inside Human Violence and Cruelty*. New York: W. H. Freeman, 1997.

Beitz, Charles R., Marshall Cohen, Thomas Scanlon, and John A. Simmons, eds. *International Ethics: A Philosophy and Public Affairs Reader*. Oxford: Princeton University Press, 1985.

Bellamy, Alex J. "Ethics and Intervention: The 'Humanitarian Exception' and the Problem of Abuse in the Case of Iraq." *Journal of Peace Research* 41, no. 2 (2004): 131–47.

———. *Just Wars: From Cicero to Iraq*. Cambridge: Polity, 2006.

———. "Motives, Outcomes, Intent and the Legitimacy of Humanitarian Intervention." *Journal of Military Ethics* 3, no. 3 (2004): 216–32.

Bellamy, Alex J., and Paul D. Williams. "The Responsibility to Protect and the Crisis in Darfur." *Security Dialogue* 36, no. 1 (2005): 27–47.

Best, Geoffrey. *Humanity and Warfare*. New York: Columbia University Press, 1980.

———. *War and Law Since 1945*. Oxford: Clarendon, 1994.

Blair, Tony. Address to the Labour Party Conference at Brighton, October 2, 2001. Available from http://politics.guardian.co.uk/labour2001/story/0,,562006,00 .html.

———. Doctrine of the International Community: Remarks at the Economics Club of Chicago, April 22, 1999. Available from http://www.ndol.org/print.cfm ?contentid=829.

———. "Foreword." In Reclaiming the Ground: Christianity and Socialism, edited by Christopher Bryant. London: Spire, 1993.

———. Prime Minister Interviewed on Iraq, WMD, Europe, and the Euro. Available from http://www.number-10.gov.uk/output/page3797.asp.

———. Prime Minister's Address to the Nation, March 20, 2003. Available from http://www.number-10.gov.uk/output/page3327.asp.

———. Prime Minister's Iraq Statement to Parliament, September 24, 2002. Available from http://www.number-10.gov.uk/output/page1727.asp.

———. Prime Minister's Message to Iraqi People, April 8, 2003. Available from http://www.number-10.gov.uk/output/page3449.asp.

———. Prime Minister's Speech Opening Commons Debate on Iraq, March 18, 2003. Available from http://www.politics.guardian.co.uk/iraq/story/0,12956 ,916790,00.html.

———. Prime Minister's Speech to TUC Conference in Blackpool, September 10, 2002. Available from http://www.number-10.gov.uk/output/page1725.asp.

———. Prime Minister's Statement on Iraq, February 25, 2003. Available from http://www.number-10.gov.uk/output/page3088.asp.

———. The Sedgefield Speech, March 5, 2004. Available from http://politics .guardian.co.uk/iraq/story/0,12956,1162991,00.html.

———. Speech to the Labour Party's Glasgow Conference, February 15, 2003. Available from http://www.iraqcrisis.co.uk/resources.php?idtag=R3E50FD20ED CFA.

———. Statement in Response to Terrorist Attacks in the United States, September 11, 2001. Available from http://www.number-10.gov.uk/output/page1596.asp.

Bluth, Christopher. "The British Road to War: Blair, Bush, and the Decision to Invade Iraq." *International Affairs* 80, no. 5 (2004): 871–92.

Booth, Ken. "Ten Flaws of Just Wars." In *The Kosovo Tragedy*, edited by Ken Booth, 314–24. London: Frank Cass, 2001.

———. "The Three Tyrannies." In *Human Rights in Global Politics*, edited by Tim Dunne and Nicholas J. Wheeler, 31–70. Cambridge: Cambridge University Press, 1999.

Boucher, David. *Political Theories of International Relations*. Oxford: Oxford University Press, 1998.

Boyle, Joseph. "Just War Doctrine and the Military Response to Terrorism." *Journal of Political Philosophy* 11, no. 2 (2003): 153–70.

Brown, Chris. "IR Theory in Britain—The New Black?" *Review of International Studies* 32 (2006): 677–87

———. "A Qualified Defence of the Use of Force for Humanitarian Reasons." In *The Kosovo Tragedy*, edited by Ken Booth, 283–88. London: Frank Cass, 2001.

———. "Self-Defense in an Imperfect World." *Ethics & International Affairs* 17 (2003): 2–8.

———. *Sovereignty, Rights and Justice: International Political Theory Today*. Cambridge: Polity, 2002.

Brown, Chris, Terry Nardin, and Nicholas J. Rengger, eds. *International Relations in Political Thought*. Cambridge: Cambridge University Press, 2002.

Brown, Peter. *Augustine of Hippo: A Biography*. London: Faber and Faber, 1967.

Brown, Seyom. *The Illusion of Control: Force and Foreign Policy in the 21st Century*. Washington, DC: Brookings Institution Press, 2003.

Brunnee, Jutta, and Stephen J. Toope. "Slouching Towards New 'Just' Wars: The Hegemon after September 11." *International Relations* 18, no. 4 (2004): 405–23.

Buchanan, Allen, and Robert O. Keohane. "The Preventive Use of Force: A Cosmopolitan Institutional Approach." *Ethics & International Affairs* 17, no. 1 (2004): 1–18.

Bull, Hedley. "The Importance of Hugo Grotius in the Study of International Relations." In *Hugo Grotius and International Relations*, edited by Hedley Bull, Benedict Kingsbury, and Adam Roberts, 65–93. Oxford: Clarendon, 1990.

Burke, Anthony. "Against the New Internationalism." *Ethics & International Affairs* 19, no. (2005): 73–89.

Burke, Edmund. *Reflections on the Revolution in France and on The Proceedings in Certain Societies in London Relative to that Event*. Edited by Conor Cruise O'Brien. Baltimore: Penguin, 1969.

Bush, George W. *A Charge to Keep*. New York: William Morrow, 1999.

————. *The National Security Strategy of the USA*. Washington DC: White House, 2002. Available from http://www.whitehouse.gov/nsc/nss.html.

————. "President Bush Addresses the Nation," March 19, 2003. Available from http://www.whitehouse.gov/news/releases/2003/03/print/20030319–17.html.

————. "President Bush Announces Major Combat Operations in Iraq Have Ended," May 1, 2003. Available from http://www.whitehouse.gov/news/releases/2003/05/iraq/20030501–15.html.

————. "President Bush Delivers Graduation Speech at West Point," June 1, 2002. Available from http://www.whitehouse.gov/news/releases/2002/06/20020601–1.html.

————. "President Bush Delivers State of the Union Address," January 29, 2002. Available from http://www.whitehouse.gov/news/releases/2002/01/20020129–11.html.

————. "President Bush Discusses Iraq with Congressional Leaders," September 26, 2002. Available from http://www.whitehouse.gov/news/releases/2002/09/print/20020926–7.html.

————. "President Bush Meets with Prime Minister Howard of Australia," February 10, 2003. Available from http://www.whitehouse.gov/news/releases/2003/02/print/20030210–10.html.

————. "President Bush Outlines Iraqi Threat," October 7, 2002. Available from http://www.whitehouse.gov/news/releases/2002/10/print/20021007–8.html.

————. "President Calls for Quick Passage of Defense Bill," March 15, 2002. Available from http://www.whitehouse.gov/news/releases/2002/03/print/20020315.html.

————. "President Delivers State of the Union Address," January 28, 2003. Available from http://www.whitehouse.gov/news/releases/2003/01/print/20030128–19.html.

————. "President Discusses the Future of Iraq," February 26, 2003. Available from http://www.whitehouse.gov/news/releases/2003/02/print/20030226–11.html.

————. "President Discusses Growing Danger Posed by Saddam Hussein's Regime," September 14, 2002. Available from http://www.whitehouse.gov/news/releases/2002/09/print/20020914.html.

————. "President, House Leadership Agree on Iraq Resolution," October 2, 2002. Available from http://www.whitehouse.gov/news/releases/2002/10/print/20021002–7.html.

————. "President Rallies Troops at Macdill Airforce Base in Tampa," March 26, 2003. Available from http://www.whitehouse.gov/news/releases/2003/03/print/20030326–4.html.

————. "President Salutes Sailors at Naval Station Mayport in Jacksonville," February 13, 2003. Available from http://www.whitehouse.gov/news/releases/2003/02/print/20030213–3.html.

————. "President Says Saddam Hussein Must Leave Iraq Within 48 Hours," March 17, 2003. Available from http://www.whitehouse.gov/news/releases/2003/03/print/20030317–7.html.

————. "President Signs Iraq Resolution," October 16, 2002. Available from http://www.whitehouse.gov/news/releases/2002/10/print/20021016–1.html.

————. "President's Remarks at National Day of Prayer and Remembrance, the National Cathedral, Washington, DC," September 14, 2001. Available from http://www.whitehouse.gov/news/releases/2001/09/20010914–2.html.

————. "President's Remarks at the United Nations General Assembly," September 12, 2002. Available from http://www.whitehouse.gov/news/releases/2002/09/print/20020912–1.html.

————. "Remarks by the President at Massachusetts Victory 2002 Reception," October 4, 2002. Available from http://www.whitehouse.gov/news/releases/2002/10/print/20021004–3.html.

————. "Statement by the President in his Address to the Nation," September 11, 2001. Available from http://www.whitehouse.gov/news/releases/2001/09/20010911–16.html.

————. "World Can Rise to This Moment," February 6, 2003. Available from http://www.whitehouse.gov/news/releases/2003/02/print/20030206–17.html.

Byers, Michael. "Not Yet Havoc: Geopolitical Change and the International Rules on Military Force." *Review of International Studies* 31 (2005): 51–71.

————. "Preemptive Self-Defense: Hegemony, Equality and Strategies of Legal Change." *Journal of Political Philosophy* 11, no. 2 (2003): 171–90.

————. *War Law: International Law and Armed Conflict.* London: Atlantic Books, 2005.

Cady, Duane L., and Robert L. Phillips. *Humanitarian Intervention: Just War versus Pacifism.* London: Rowman and Littlefield, 1996.

Cahill, Lisa Sowle. "Christian Just War Tradition: Tensions and Development." In *The Return of the Just War*, edited by Maria Pilar Aquino and Dieter Mieth, 74–82. London: SCM, 2001.

Cesarani, David. "Why Tyrants Must Stand Trial." *Observer*, July 11, 2004, p. 28.

Cheney, Dick. "Vice-President Speaks at VFW 103rd National Convention," August 26, 2002. Available from http://www.whitehouse.gov/news/releases/2002/08/print/20020826.html.

Chesterman, Simon. *Just War or Just Peace? Humanitarian Intervention and International Law.* Oxford: Oxford University Press, 2002.

Christopher, Paul. *The Ethics of War and Peace: An Introduction to Legal and Political Issues.* 3rd edition. Englewood Cliffs, NJ: Prentice Hall, 2004.

Cicero. *On Duties.* Cambridge: Cambridge University Press, 1991.

Clark, Ian. *Legitimacy in International Society.* Oxford: Oxford University Press, 2005.

————. *The Post–Cold War Order: The Spoils of Peace.* Oxford: Oxford University Press, 2001.

————. "Traditions of Thought and Classical Theories of International Relations." In *Classical Theories of International Relations*, edited by Ian Clark and Iver B. Neumann, 1–20. London: Macmillan, 1996.

————. *Waging War: A Philosophical Introduction.* Oxford: Clarendon, 1990.

Coates, A. J. *The Ethics of War.* Manchester: Manchester University Press, 1997.

Coates, David, and Joel Krieger. *Blair's War*. Cambridge: Polity, 2004.

Coker, Christopher. *Humane Warfare*. London: Routledge, 2001.

Crawford, Neta C. "The Best Defense." *Boston Review*, February/March 2003. Available from http://www.bostonreview.net.br28.1/crawford.html.

———. "Just War Theory and the U.S. Counterterror War." *Perspectives on Politics* 1, no. 1 (2003): 5–23.

———. "The Slippery Slope to Preventive War." *Ethics & International Affairs* 17 (2003): 30–36.

Crisher, Brian. "Altering the Jus ad Bellum: Just War Theory in the 21st Century and the 2002 National Security Strategy of the United States." *Critique: A Worldwide Journal of Politics* (Spring 2005): 1–29.

Daalder, Ivo, and James M. Lindsay. *America Unbound: The Bush Revolution in Foreign Policy*. Washington, DC: Brookings Institution, 2003.

Damrosch, Lori Fisler, and Bernard H. Oxman. "Editor's Introduction to Agora: Future Implications of the Iraq Conflict." *American Journal of International Law* 97, no. 3 (2003): 553–57.

Deane, Herbert A. *The Political and Social Ideas of Saint Augustine*. New York: Columbia University Press, 1963.

Deane, Herbert A. "The Political and Social Ideas of Saint Augustine." In *Essays in the History of Political Thought*, edited by Isaac Kramnick, 85–96. Englewood Cliffs, NJ: Prentice Hall, 1969.

Dershowitz, Alan M. *Pre-Emption: A Knife That Cuts Both Ways*. New York: W. W. Norton, 2006.

Draper, G. I. A. D. "Grotius's Place in the Development of Legal Ideas about War." In *Hugo Grotius and International Relations*, edited by Hedley Bull, Benedict Kingsbury, and Adam Roberts, 177–207. Oxford: Clarendon, 1992.

Duff, R. A., and David Garland. "Introduction: Thinking about Punishment." In *A Reader on Punishment*, edited by Antony Duff and David Garland. Oxford: Oxford University Press, 1994.

Dula, Peter. "The War in Iraq: How Catholic Conservatives Got it Wrong." *Commonweal* CXXXI, no. 21 (December 2004).

Dumbrowski, Peter, and Rodger A. Payne. "The Emerging Consensus for Preventive War." *Survival* 48, no. 2 (2006): 115–36.

Dunne, Tim. "Mythology or Methodology? Traditions in International Relations." *Review of International Studies* 19, no. 3 (1993): 305–18.

Dworkin, Ronald M. "To Each His Own." *New York Review of Books*, April 1983.

Dyson, R. W. *Normative Theories of Society and Government in Five Medieval Thinkers*. Lewisten, NY: Edwin Mellen, 2003.

Eagleton, Terry. *After Theory*. London: Allen Lane, 2003.

Elshtain, Jean Bethke. "Epilogue: Continuing Implications of the Just War Tradition." In *Just War Theory*, edited by Jean Bethke Elshtain, 323–33. Oxford: Blackwell, 1992.

———. "How to Fight a Just War." In *Worlds in Collision: Terror and the Future of Global Order*, edited by Ken Booth and Tim Dunne, 263–70. Basingstoke: Palgrave Macmillan, 2002.

———. "International Justice as Equal Regard and the Use of Force." *Ethics & International Affairs* 17, no. 2 (2003): 63–75.

———. "Introduction." In *Just War Theory*, edited by Jean Bethke Elshtain, 1–7. Oxford: Blackwell, 1992.

———. "Just War and Humanitarian Intervention." *Ideas* 8, no. 2 (2001): 1–21.

———. *Just War against Terror: The Burden of American Power in a Violent World*. New York: Basic Books, 2004.

———. "Reflections on War and Political Discourse: Realism, Just War, and Feminism in a Nuclear Age." In *Just War Theory*, edited by Jean Bethke Elshtain, 260–79. Oxford: Blackwell, 1992.

———. "Response." *International Relations* 21, no. 4 (2007).

Erskine, Toni. *Embedded Cosmopolitanism*. Oxford: Oxford University Press, 2007.

———. "Qualifying Cosmopolitanism? Solidarity, Criticism, and Michael Walzer's 'View from the Cave.'" *International Politics* 44, no. 1 (2007): 125–49.

———. "'As Rays of Light to the Human Soul'? Moral Agents and Intelligence Gathering." *Intelligence and National Security* 19, no. 2 (2004): 359–81.

Evans, Gareth. "Humanity Did Not Justify This War." *Financial Times*, May 15, 2003.

———. "When Is It Right to Fight?" *Survival* 46, no. 3 (2004): 59–82.

Falk, Richard. *Law, Morality and War in the Contemporary World*. New York: Praeger, 1963.

———. "What Future for the UN Charter System of War Prevention?" *American Journal of International Law* 97, no. 3 (2003): 590–98.

Feinberg, Joel. *Doing and Deserving: Essays in the Theory of Responsibility*. Princeton, NJ: Princeton University Press, 1970.

Feinstein, Lee, and Anne-Marie Slaughter. "A Duty to Prevent." *Foreign Affairs* 83, no. 1 (2004): 136–50.

Finnis, John. *Aquinas: Moral, Political, and Legal Theory*. Oxford: Oxford University Press, 1998.

Fixdal, Mona, and Dan Smith. "Humanitarian Intervention and Just War." *Mershon International Studies Review* 42 (1998): 283–312.

Foucault, Michel. *Discipline and Punish: The Birth of the Prison*. London: Penguin Books, 1977.

Franck, Thomas M. *Recourse to Force: State Action Against Threats and Armed Attacks*. Cambridge: Cambridge University Press, 2002.

Freedman, Lawrence. "Prevention, Not Preemption." *Washington Quarterly* 26, no. 2 (2003): 105–14.

———. "War in Iraq: Selling the Threat." *Survival* 46, no. 2 (2004): 7–50.

Frum, David, and Richard Perle. *An End to Evil*. New York: Random House, 2004.

Gadamer, Hans-Georg. *Truth and Method*. 2nd revised edition. Translated by Joel Weinsheimer and Donald Marshall. New York: Continuum, 1994.

Gentili, Alberico. *De Iure Belli Libri Tres*. Translated by John C. Rolfe. Oxford: Clarendon, 1933.

Glennon, Michael. "Why the Security Council Failed?" *Foreign Affairs* 82, no. 3 (2003): 16–36.

Gordon, Philip H. "Bush's Middle East Vision." *Survival* 45, no. 1 (2003): 155–65.

Gross, Hyman. *A Theory of Criminal Justice*. New York: Oxford University Press, 1979.

Grotius, Hugo. *The Rights of War and Peace*. Edited by Richard Tuck. Indianapolis: Liberty Fund, 2005.

Gunnell, John G. "The Myth of the Tradition." *American Political Science Review* 72 (1978): 122–34.

Haass, Richard. "Sovereignty: Existing Rights, Evolving Responsibilities—Remarks to the Mortara Center for International Studies at Georgetown." Available from http://usinfo.state.gov/topical/pol/terror/03011501.htm.

Hall, W. E. *International Law*. 8th edition. Oxford: Clarendon, 1924.

Halper, Stefan, and Jonathan Clarke. *America Alone: The Neo-Conservatives and the Global Order*. Cambridge: Cambridge University Press, 2004.

Hamilton, Bernice. *Political Thought in Sixteenth Spain: A Study of the Political Ideas of Vitoria, de Soto, Suarez, and Molina*. Oxford: Clarendon, 1963.

Hampsher-Monk, Iain. *The Political Philosophy of Edmund Burke*. London: Longman, 1987.

Hart, H. L. A. *Punishment and Responsibility—Essays in the Philosophy of Law*. Oxford: Clarendon, 1968.

Hehir, J. Bryan. "In Defense of Justice." *Commonweal* 127, no. 5 (2000): 32–33.

———. "Intervention: From Theories to Cases." *Ethics & International Affairs* 9 (1995): 1–13.

Heisbourg, Francois. "A Work in Progress: The Bush Doctrine and Its Consequences." *Washington Quarterly* 26, no. 2 (2003): 75–88.

Higgins, Rosalyn. "Grotius and the Development of International Law in the UN Period." In *Hugo Grotius and International Relations*, edited by Hedley Bull, Benedict Kingsbury, and Adam Roberts. Oxford: Clarendon, 1992.

Hirst, P. "The Concept of Punishment." In *A Reader on Punishment*, edited by Antony Duff and David Garland. Oxford: Oxford University Press, 1994.

Hobbes, Thomas. *De Cive*. Edited by Richard Tuck and Michael Silverthorne. Cambridge: Cambridge University Press, 1998.

———. *Leviathan*. Cambridge: Cambridge University Press, 1996.

Hobsbawm, Eric. *The New Century*. London: Abbacus, 2000.

Hoffmann, Stanley. "Intervention: Should it Go On, Can it Go On?" In *Ethics and Foreign Intervention*, edited by Dean K. Chatterjee and Don E. Scheid, 21–31. Cambridge: Cambridge University Press, 2003.

Hoggett, Paul. "Iraq: Blair's Mission Impossible." *British Journal of Politics and International Relations* 7, no. 3 (2005): 418–29.

Hunt, Michael. *Ideology and U.S. Foreign Policy*. New Haven, CT: Yale University Press, 1987.

Hurrell, Andrew. "'There are no Rules': International Order after September the 11th." *International Relations* 16, no. 2 (2002): 185–204.

Ignatieff, Michael. *The Lesser Evil–Political Ethics in an Age of Terror*. Edinburgh, UK: Edinburgh University Press, 2004.

———. *The Rights Revolution*. Toronto: Anansi, 2000.

———. *Virtual War*. Toronto: Viking Books, 2000.

———. *The Warrior's Honour*. New York: Metropolitan Books, 1997.

International Commission on Intervention and State Sovereignty. The Responsibility to Protect: The Report of the ICISS. Toronto: International Commission on Intervention and State Sovereignty, 2001.

Jackson, Robert H. *The Global Covenant*. Oxford: Oxford University Press, 2000.

Janssen, Dieter. "Preventive Defense and Forcible Regime Change: A 'Normative Assessment." *Journal of Military Ethics* 3, no. 2 (2004): 105–28.

Jeffery, Renee. "Tradition as Invention: The 'Traditions Tradition' and the History of Ideas in International Relations." *Millennium: Journal of International Studies* 34, no. 1 (2005): 57–84.

Johnson, James Turner. "The Broken Tradition." *National Interest* 45 (1996): 27–37.

———. *Can Modern War Be Just?* New Haven, CT: Yale University Press, 1984.

———. "Humanitarian Intervention after Iraq: Just War and International Law Perspectives." *Journal of Military Ethics* 5, no. 2 (2006): 114–27.

———. *Ideology, Reason and the Limitation of War*. Princeton, NJ: Princeton University Press, 1975.

———. "The Just War Idea: The State of the Question." *Social Philosophy and Policy* 23, no. 1 (2006): 167–95.

———. "The Just War Tradition and the American Military." In *Just War and the Gulf War*, edited by James Turner Johnson and George Weigel, 6–60. Lanham, MD: Ethics and Public Policy Centre, 1991.

———. *Just War Tradition and the Restraint of War*. Princeton, NJ: Princeton University Press, 1981.

———. "From Moral Norm to Criminal Code: The Law of Armed Conflict and the Restraint of Contemporary Warfare." In *Ethics and the Future of Conflict*, edited by Anthony F. Lang, 68–90. New Jersey: Pearson Education, 2004.

———. *Morality and Contemporary Warfare*. New Haven, CT: Yale University Press, 1999.

———. "Threats, Values, and Defense: Does the Defense of Values by Force Remain a Moral Possibility?" In *Just War Theory*, edited by Jean Bethke Elshtain, 55–76. Oxford: Blackwell, 1992.

———. *The War to Oust Saddam Hussein: Just War and the New Face of Conflict*. Lanham, MD: Rowman and Littlefield, 2005.

Johnson, James Turner, and John Kelsay, eds. *Cross, Crescent, and Sword*. Westport, CT: Greenwood, 1990.

Jones, Dorothy V. *Code of Peace: Ethics and Security in the World of States*. London: University of Chicago Press, 1991.

Kaldor, Mary. *New and Old Wars: Organized Violence in a Global Era*. Cambridge: Polity, 2001.

Kaplan, Lawrence F., and William Kristol. *The War over Iraq: Saddam's Tyranny and America's Mission*. San Francisco: Encounter Books, 2003.

Karoubi, Mohammad Taghi. *Just or Unjust War: International Law and the Unilateral Use of Force at the Turn of the Twentieth Century*. Dartmouth, NH: Ashgate, 2004.

Kaufman, Whitley. "What's Wrong with Preventive War? The Moral and Legal Basis for the Preventive Use of Force." *Ethics & International Affairs* 19, no. 3 (2005): 23–38.

Lackey, Douglas P. *The Ethics of War and Peace*. Englewood Cliffs, NJ: Prentice Hall, 1989.

Lacroix, W. L. *War and International Ethics: Tradition and Today*. Lanham, MD: University Press of America, 1988.

Lammers, Stephen E. "Approaches to Limits on War in Western Just War Discourse." In *Cross, Crescent, and Sword*, edited by James Turner Johnson and John Kelsay, 51–78. Westport, CT: Greenwood, 1990.

Lang, Anthony F., ed. *Just Intervention*. Washington, DC: Georgetown University Press, 2003.

———. "Punishing States: From Grotius to the ILC." Paper presented at the 3rd Workshop of the British Academy Network on Ethics, Institutions and International Relations: Responding to Delinquent Institutions: Blame, Punishment and Rehabilitation, Carnegie Council on Ethics and International Affairs, New York, May 12–14, 2004.

———. "Punitive Intervention: Enforcing Justice or Generating Conflict?" In *Just War Theory: A Reappraisal*, edited by Mark Evans, 50–70. New York: Palgrave Macmillan, 2005.

Leffler, Melvyn P. "9/11 and the Past and Future of American Foreign Policy." *International Affairs* 79, no. 5 (2003): 1045–63.

Lieber, Francis. "Instructions for the Government of Armies of the United States in the Field, General Orders No. 100." In *The Ethics of War: Classic and Contemporary Readings*, edited by Gregory M. Reichberg, Henrik Syse, and Endre Begby, 566–72. Malden, MA: Blackwell, 2006.

Litwak, Robert S. "The New Calculus of Preemption." *Survival* 44, no. 4 (2002–3): 53–80.

Lopez, George. "Iraq and Just War Thinking: The Presumption against the Use of Force." *Commonweal*, CXXIX, no. 16 (September 2002).

Lucas, George R. "From Jus ad Bellum to Jus ad Pacem: Re-thinking Just War Criteria for the Use of Military Force for Humanitarian Ends." In *Ethics and Foreign Intervention*, edited by Dean K. Chatterjee and Don E. Scheid, 72–96. Cambridge: Cambridge University Press, 2003.

———. "The Role of the International Community in Just War Tradition—Confronting the Challenges of Humanitarian Intervention and Preemptive War." *Journal of Military Ethics* 2, no. 2 (2003): 122–44.

Machiavelli, Niccollo. *The Prince*. Edited and translated by David Wootton. Cambridge: Hackett, 1995.

MacIntyre, Alasdair. *A Short History of Ethics*. London: Routledge and Kegan, 1967.

———. *After Virtue: A Study in Moral Theory*. London: Duckworth, 1981.

———. *Three Rival Versions of Moral Enquiry: Encyclopaedia, Genealogy and Tradition*. London: Duckworth, 1990.

Malcolm, Noel. *Aspects of Hobbes*. Oxford and New York: Oxford University Press, 2002.

Marqusee, Mike. "A Name That Lives in Infamy." *Guardian*, November 10, 2005, p. 32.

Martinich, A. P. *A Hobbes Dictionary*. Oxford: Blackwell, 1995.

Mazarr, Michael J. "George W. Bush, Idealist." *International Affairs* 79, no. 3 (2003): 503–22.

McDonagh, Melanie. "Can There Be Such a Thing as a Just War?" In *The Kosovo Tragedy*, edited by Ken Booth, 289–94. London: Frank Cass, 2001.

McMahan, Jeff. "Just Cause for War." *Ethics & International Affairs* 19, no. 3 (2005): 1–23.

———. "Preventive War and the Killing of the Innocent." In *The Ethics of War: Shared Problems in Different Traditions*, edited by David Rodin and Richard Sorabji, 169–91. Aldershot: Ashgate, 2006.

Miller, Richard B. *Interpretations of Conflict: Ethics, Pacifism and the Just War Tradition*. Chicago: University of Chicago Press, 1991.

Minogue, K. R. "Revolution, Tradition and Political Continuity." In *Politics and Experience: Essays Presented to Professor Michael Oakeshott on the Occasion of his Retirement*, edited by Preston King and B. C. Parekh, 283–309. Cambridge: Cambridge University Press, 1968.

Nardin, Terry. "Ethical Traditions in International Affairs." In *Traditions of International Ethics*, edited by Terry Nardin and David R. Mapel, 1–23. Cambridge: Cambridge University Press.

———. "Humanitarian Imperialism: Response to 'Ending Tyranny in Iraq.'" *Ethics & International Affairs* 19, no. 2 (2005): 21–27.

———. "The Moral Basis of Humanitarian Intervention." *Ethics & International Affairs* 16 (2002): 57–70.

National Conference of Catholic Bishops (NCCB). "The Challenge of Peace: God's Promise and our Response—the Pastoral Letter on War and Peace." In *Just War Theory*, edited by Jean Bethke Elshtain, 77–168. Oxford: Blackwell, 1992.

Neiman, Susan. *Evil in Modern Thought*. Princeton, NJ: Princeton University Press, 2002.

Novak, Michael. "The Return of Good and Evil." *Wall Street Journal*, February 7, 2002.

Nussbaum, Arthur. *A Concise History of the Law of Nations*. New York: Macmillan, 1954.

Oakeshott, Michael. *On Human Conduct*. Oxford: Oxford University Press, 1975.

———. *Rationalism in Politics and other Essays*. Indianapolis: Liberty Fund, 1991.

O'Brien, William V. "The Challenge of War: A Christian Realist Perspective." In *Just War Theory*, edited by Jean Bethke Elshtain, 169–96. Oxford: Blackwell, 1992.

———. *The Conduct of Just and Limited Wars*. New York: Praeger, 1981.

———. *War and/or Survival*. New York: Doubleday, 1969.

O'Brien, William V., and John D. Langan, eds. *The Nuclear Dilemma and the Just War*. Lexington, MA: Lexington Books, 1986.

O'Donovan, Oliver. *The Just War Revisited*. Cambridge: Cambridge University Press, 2003.

O'Driscoll, Cian. "Jean Bethke Elshtain's Just War Against Terror: A Tale of Two Cities?" *International Relations* 21, no. 4 (forthcoming, 2007).

———. "Learning the Language of Just War Theory: The Value of Engagement." *Journal of Military Ethics* 6, no. 2 (2007): 107–16.

———. "New Thinking in the Just War Tradition: Theorizing the War on Terror." In *Security and the War on Terror*, edited by Alex J. Bellamy, Sara Davies, and Richard Devetak. London: Routledge, 2007.

———. "Re-negotiating the Just War: The Invasion of Iraq and Punitive War." *Cambridge Review of International Affairs* 19, no. 3 (2006): 405–20.

O'Hanlon, Michael E. "Saddam's Bomb: How Close is Iraq to Having a Nuclear Weapon?" Available from http://www.brookings.edu/views/op-ed/ohanlon/2002 0918.htm.

Orend, Brian. *Michael Walzer on War and Justice*. Swansea: University of Wales Press, 2000.

———. *The Morality of War*. Toronto: Broadview, 2006.

Paul VI, Pope. "Gaudiem et Spes: The Pastoral Constitution: On the Church in the Modern World, 1965." Available from http://www.rc.net/rcchurch/vatican2/gaudium.ets.

Pew Forum on Religion and Public Life. Iraq and Just War: A Symposium. September 30, 2002. Available from http://pewforum.org/events/?EventID=36.

———. Just War Tradition and the New War on Terrorism. October 5, 2001. Available from http://pewforum.org/events/?EventID=15.

Pocock, J. G. A. *Politics, Language, and Time: Essays on Political Thought and History*. London: Methuen, 1972.

———. *Virtue, Commerce, and History—Essays on Political Thought and History, Chiefly in the 18th Century*. Cambridge: Cambridge University Press, 1985.

Politis, Nicholas. *Neutrality and Peace*. New York: Carnegie Endowment for International Peace, 1935.

Powell, Colin. "U.S. Secretary of State Colin Powell Addresses the UN Security Council," February 5, 2003. Available from http://www.whitehouse.gov/news/releases/2003/02/print/20030205–1.html.

Project for a New American Century. Statement of Principles. Available from http://www.newamericancentury.org/statementofprinciples.htm.

Pufendorf, Samuel. *The Political Writings of Samuel Pufendorf*. Edited by Craig Carr and Michael Seidler. Oxford: Oxford University Press, 1994.

Ramsey, Paul. *The Just War: Force and Political Responsibility*. Maryland: Catholic University Press of America, 1986.

———. *War and the Christian Conscience*. Durham, NC: Duke University Press, 1961.

Raphael, D. D. *Hobbes: Morals and Politics*. London: Routledge, 1996.

Reichberg, Gregory. "Pre-Emptive War: What Would Aquinas Say? *Commonweal* CXXI, no. 2 (January 2004).

Reichberg, Gregory, and Henrik Syse. "Humanitarian Intervention: A Case of Offensive Force?" *Security Dialogue* 33, no. 3 (2003): 309–22.

Reichberg, Gregory, Henrik Syse, and Endre Begby, eds. *The Ethics of War: Classic and Contemporary Readings*. Oxford: Blackwell, 2006.

Rengger, Nicholas J. "The Judgement of War." *Review of International Studies* 31 (2005): 143–63.

———. "Just a War against Terror? Jean Bethke Elshtain's Burden and American Power." *International Affairs* 80, no. 1 (2004): 107–16.

———. "The Just War Tradition in the Twenty First Century." *International Affairs* 78, no. 2 (2002): 353–63.

Rentoul, John. *Tony Blair: Prime Minister*. London: Little Brown, 2001.

Reus-Smit, Christian. "Liberal Hierarchy and the Liberal Licence to Use Force." *Review of International Studies* 31 (2005): 71–93.

Rice, Condoleezza. "Dr. Condoleezza Rice Discusses President's National Security Strategy," October 1, 2002. Available from http://www.whitehouse.gov/news/releases/2002/10/print/20021001-6.html.

Roberts, Adam. "Humanitarian War: Military Intervention and Human Rights." *International Affairs* 69, no. 3 (1993): 429–49.

———. "Law and the Use of Force after Iraq." *Survival* 45, no. 2 (2003): 31–56.

Robertson, George. "This is a Just War." *Sunday Business Newspaper*, April 11, 1999. Available from http://www.fco.gov.uk/news/speechtext.asp?2316.

Roelofsen, C. G. "Grotius and the International Politics of the Seventeenth Century." In *Hugo Grotius and International Relations*, edited by Hedley Bull, Benedict Kingsbury, and Adam Roberts, 93–131. Oxford: Clarendon, 1990.

Rosen, Gary, ed. *The Right War? The Conservative Debate on Iraq*. Cambridge: Cambridge University Press, 2005.

Roth, Kenneth. "War in Iraq: Not a Humanitarian Intervention." Human Rights Watch Report, 2004. Available from www.hrw.org/wr2k4/3.htm.

Rousseau, Jean-Jacques. *The Social Contract*. Translated by H. J. Tozer. Ware, Hertfordshire: Wordsworth, 1998.

Rubin, James P. "Stumbling into War." *Foreign Affairs* 82, no. 5 (2003): 46–65.

Rumsfeld, Donald H. Secretary Rumsfeld Press Conference at NATO Headquarters, Brussels, June 6, 2002. Available from http://www.defenselink.mil/transcripts/2002/t06062002_t0606sd.html.

Russell, F. H. *The Just War in the Middle Ages*. Cambridge: Cambridge University Press, 1975.

Sapiro, Miriam. "Iraq: The Shifting Sands of Pre-Emptive Self-Defense." *American Journal of International Law* 97, no. 3 (2003): 599–607.

Schmitt, Michael N. "The Legality of Operation Iraqi Freedom under International Law." *Journal of Military Ethics* 3, no. 2 (2004): 82–104.

Scott, James Brown. *The Spanish Origins of International Law: Francisco de Victoria and his Law of Nations.* Oxford: Clarendon, 1934.

Searle, J. R. *Speech Acts.* Cambridge: Cambridge University Press, 1969.

Shapcott, Richard. *Justice, Community, and Dialogue in International Relations.* Cambridge: Cambridge University Press, 2001.

Shawcross, William. *Deliver Us From Evil: Warlords and Peacekeepers in a World of Endless Conflict.* London: Bloomsbury, 2000.

Sherry, Michael. "Dead or Alive: American Vengeance Goes Global." *Review of International Studies* 31 (2005): 245–65.

Simons, Penelope C. "Humanitarian Intervention: A Review of Literature." Project Ploughshares Working Papers. Available from http://www.ploughshares.ca/content/working%20papers/wp012.html.

Singer, Peter. *The President of Good and Evil.* London: Granta Books, 2004.

Skidelsky, Robert. "The Just War Tradition." *Prospect*, December 2004, pp. 28–33.

Skinner, Quentin. *The Foundations of Modern Political Thought, Volume I: The Renaissance.* Cambridge: Cambridge University Press, 1978.

———. "Language and Political Change." In *Political Innovation and Conceptual Change*, edited by Terence Ball, James Farr, and Russell Hanson, 6–23. Cambridge: Cambridge University Press, 1989.

———. *Visions of Politics, Volume I: Regarding Method.* Cambridge: Cambridge University Press, 2002.

Slocombe, Walter B. "Force, Preemption and Legitimacy." *Survival* 45, no. 1 (2003): 117–30.

Slomp, Gabriella. "Carl Schmitt and the Just War Tradition." *Cambridge Review of International Affairs* 19, no. 3 (2006): 435–47.

Smith, Michael J. "Growing Up With Just and Unjust Wars: An Appreciation." *Ethics & International Affairs* 11 (1997): 1–18.

———. "Humanitarian Intervention: An Overview of the Issues." *Ethics & International Affairs* 12 (1998): 63–81.

Steinberg, James. "Preventive Force in U.S. National Security Strategy." *Survival* 47, no. 4 (2005): 55–72.

Stephens, Philip. *Tony Blair: The Price of Leadership.* London: Politico's, 2004.

Stothard, Peter. *30 Days: A Month at the Heart of Blair's War.* London: Harper-Collins, 2003.

Suarez, Francisco. *Selections from Three Works.* Edited by Gwlady's Williams. Oxford: Oxford University Press, 1994.

Suskind, Ron. "Without a Doubt." *New York Times*, October 17, 2004.

Tanter, Raymond. *Classifying Evil: Bush Administration Rhetoric and Policy toward Rogue Regimes: Research Memorandum 44.* Washington, DC: Washington Institute for Near East Policy, 2003.

Taylor, Charles. *Human Agency and Language: Philosophical Papers 1*. Cambidge: Cambridge University Press, 1985.

Taylor, Terence. "The End of Imminence?" *Washington Quarterly* 27, no. 4 (2004): 57–72.

Ten, C. L. *Crime, Guilt, and Punishment: A Philosophical Introduction*. Oxford: Clarendon, 1987.

Teson, Fernando. "Ending Tyranny in Iraq." *Ethics & International Affairs* 19, no. 2 (2005): 1–21.

———. "Of Tyrants and Empires: Reply to Terry Nardin." *Ethics & International Affairs* 19, no. 2 (2005): 27–31.

Thucydides. *History of the Peloponnesian War*. Translated by Rex Warner. Harmondsworth: Penguin, 1972.

Tuck, Richard. *Hobbes*. Oxford: Oxford University Press, 1989.

———. *The Rights of War and Peace: Political Thought and the International Order from Grotius to Kant*. Oxford: Oxford University Press, 1999.

———. "Why is Authority Such a Problem?" In *Philosophy, Politics, and Society*, edited by Peter Laslett, W. G. Runciman, and Quentin Skinner, 194–207. London: Blackwell, 1972.

Tucker, Robert W. *The Just War*. Baltimore: Johns Hopkins University Press, 1963.

Tulley, James. "The Pen is a Mighty Sword: Quentin Skinner's Analysis of Politics." In *Meaning and Context: Quentin Skinner and his Critics*, edited by James Tulley, 7–29. Cambridge: Polity, 1988.

United Nations. *A More Secure World: Our Shared Responsibility*. Report of the High-Level Panel on Threats, Challenges and Change. United Nations, 2004.

U.S. Conference of Catholic Bishops (USCCB). Statement on Iraq, February 26, 2003. Available from http://www.usccb.org/sdwp/international/iraqstatement 0203.shtml.

Varouxakis, Georgios. "John Stuart Mill on Intervention and Non-Intervention." *Millennium: Journal of International Studies* 26, no. 1 (1997): 57–76.

Vattel, Emmerich de. *The Law of Nations or the Principles of Natural Law*. Translated by Charles G. Fenwick, edited by James Brown Scott. London: Wildy and Sons, 1902.

Vincent, R. J. *Human Rights and International Relations*. Cambridge: Cambridge University Press, 1986.

Vitoria, Francisco de. *Vitoria: Political Writings*. Edited by Anthony Pagden and Jeremy Lawrance. Cambridge: Cambridge University Press, 1991.

Walker, Nigel. *Why Punish?* Oxford: Oxford University Press, 1991.

Walker, R. B. J. "History and Structure in the Theory of International Relations." In *International Theory: Critical Investigations*, edited by James Der Derian, 308–40. London: MacMillan, 1995.

———. *Inside/Outside: International Relations as Political Theory*. Cambridge: Cambridge University Press, 1993.

Walzer, Michael. Arguing About War: Interview at the Carnegie Council on Ethics & International Affairs, 2004. Available from http://www.carnegiecouncil.org/printerfriendlymedia.php/prmID/5024?PHPSESSID.

———. *Arguing About War*. London: Yale University Press, 2004.

———. "The Argument about Humanitarian Intervention." *Dissent* 49, no. 1 (2002). Available from http://www.dissentmagazine.org/menutest/archives/2002/wi02/walzer_hum.shtml.

———. *Interpretation and Social Criticism*. London: Harvard University Press, 1987.

———. *Just and Unjust Wars: A Moral Argument with Historical Illustrations*. 2nd edition. New Jersey: Basic Books, 1992.

———. "The Moral Standing of States: A Response to Four Critics." In *International Ethics*, edited by Charles R. Beitz, Marshall Cohen, Thomas Scanlon, and John A. Simmons, 217–38. Oxford: Princeton University Press, 1985.

———. "Spheres of Justice: An Exchange." New York, *New York Review of Books*, July 21, 1983.

———. "Universalism, Equality, and Immigration." In *Constructions of Practical Reason: Interviews on Moral and Political Philosophy*, edited by Herlinde Pauer-Studer, 194–213. Stanford, CA: Stanford University Press, 2003.

Warnke, Georgia. "Walzer, Rawls, and Gadamer: Hermeneutics and Political Theory." In *Festivals of Interpretation: Essays on Hans-Georg Gadamer*, edited by Kathleen Wright, 136–61. Albany, NY: SUNY Press, 1990.

Webster, Daniel. "Letter to British Ambassador Henry Fox, 24 April 1841." In *The Ethics of War: Classic and Contemporary Readings*, edited by Gregory Reichberg, Henrik Syse, and Endre Begby, 563–64. Oxford: Blackwell, 2006.

Wedgwood, Ruth. "The Fall of Saddam Hussein: Security Council Mandates and Preemptive Self-Defense." *American Journal of International Law* 97, no. 3 (2003): 576–85.

Weigel, George. "Churches and the Gulf Crisis." In *Just War and the Gulf War*, edited by James Turner Johnson and George Weigel. Lanham, MD: Ethics and Public Policy Centre, 1991.

———. *Tranquillitas Ordinas: The Present Failure and Future Promise of American Catholic Thought on War and Peace*. Oxford: Oxford University Press, 1987.

Weiss, Thomas G. "The Sunset of Humanitarian Intervention? The Responsibility to Protect in a Unipolar Era." *Security Dialogue* 35, no. 2 (2004): 135–53.

Welsh, David. *Justice and the Genesis of War*. Cambridge: Cambridge University Press, 1995.

Wheeler, Nicholas J. *Saving Strangers: Humanitarian Intervention in International Society*. Oxford: Oxford University Press, 2000.

Wheeler, Nicholas J., and Justin Morris. "Justifying Iraq as a Humanitarian Intervention: The Cure is Worse Than the Disease." In *The Iraq Crisis and World Order: Structural and Normative Challenges*, edited by W. P. S. Sidhu and Ramesh Thakur. Tokyo: United Nations University Press, 2006.

Wheelwright, Philip. *Heraclitus*. Princeton, NJ: Princeton University Press, 1959.

White, James Boyd. *When Words Lose Their Meaning: Constitutions and Reconstitutions of Language, Character, and Community*. Chicago: University of Chicago Press, 1984.

Williams, Michael C. *The Realist Tradition and the Limits of International Relations*. Cambridge: Cambridge University Press, 2005.

Woodward, Bob. *Plan of Attack*. London: Simon and Schuster, 2004.

Yoo, John. "International Law and the War in Iraq." *American Journal of International Law* 97, no. 3 (2003): 563–76.

Index